Dear People,

with Love and Care, Your Doctors

Dear People,

with Love and Care, Your Doctors

Heartfelt Stories about Doctor-Patient Relationship

Debraj Shome
Aparna Govil Bhasker

BLOOMSBURY
NEW DELHI • LONDON • OXFORD • NEW YORK • SYDNEY

BLOOMSBURY INDIA
Bloomsbury Publishing India Pvt. Ltd
Second Floor, LSC Building No. 4, DDA Complex, Pocket C – 6 & 7,
Vasant Kunj New Delhi 110070

BLOOMSBURY, BLOOMSBURY INDIA and the Diana logo are trademarks of Bloomsbury Publishing Plc

First published in India 2019
This edition published in 2019

ISBN: PB: 978-9-3871-4694-5; eBook: 978-9-3871-4695-2

2 4 6 8 10 9 7 5 3 1

Typeset by Manipal Digital
Printed and bound in India by Thomson Press

The opinions expressed in the ensuing chapters and stories are the personal opinions of individual authors of those chapters. The facts and opinions appearing in the chapters do not reflect the views of Dr Debraj Shome, Dr Aparna Govil Bhasker and Bloomsbury Publishing. We do not assume any responsibility or liability for the same.

Names of patients have been changed in all the chapters in view of patient confidentiality.

To my five-year-old son, Arvin, for being ever accommodating and understanding that his mother may sometimes need to care more for other people

—Aparna Govil Bhasker

To every patient, in the hope of beginning a new chapter in the doctor-patient relationship

—Debraj Shome

Debabrata-Auro Foundation

The authors pledge to perform 101 subsidised surgeries for needy patients, from the proceeds of this book, through the Debabrata Auro Foundation.

CONTENTS

THE DALAI LAMA

FOREWORD

Doctors play an essential role in our society as they devote themselves to caring for their patients. The treatment of an ailment does not depend only on the medical expertise of a doctor; his or her warm heartedness, care and concern for a patient are essential for the treatment to be effective. I truly believe that when my gallstones were removed a few years ago, the affectionate care of doctors, nurses and other hospital staff were essential to my speedy recovery.

While doctors and medical staff do their best to save lives, it is important to accept that a successful outcome is sometimes beyond their control. As in all situations in life, it is important that we do our best while understanding that we won't always be successful.

I commend Dr. Debraj Shome and Dr. Aparna Govil Bhasker for presenting the thoughts of many of their fellow physicians in their book, *Dear People, with Love, and Care, Your Doctors*.

4 February 2019

INDIAN MEDICAL ASSOCIATION (HQs.)

(Registered under the Societies Act XXI of 1860)
Mutually Affiliated with the British & Nepal Medical Associations
I.M.A. House, Indraprastha Marg, New Delhi-110 002
Telephones : +91-11-2337 0009 (10 lines), 23378680, 23378053, 23370352 / +91-9999116375, 9999116376, Fax: +91-11-23379470, 23370375
Website: www.ima-india.org ; Email: hsg@ima-india.org

National President
Dr. Santanu Sen
Email: shantanu_sen2007@yahoo.com
Skype: drsantanu.mp

Honorary Secretary General
Dr. R. V. Asokan
Email: rvasokan@gmail.com

09.05.2019

HSG/Camp office /75/2019

Message

The book *Dear People, with Love and Care, Your Doctors* is a very relevant treatise for all doctors and patients alike. The doctor-patient trust is one of the most important relationships for better patient care and outcome and a healthy society. In the present era, there is a declining trust in the patient-doctor relationship and efforts from medical leaders and societies are needed to regain and re-strengthen doctor-patient trust.

Health and healing need faith. And, when societies lose faith in their healers, entire societies suffer.

I congratulate Dr Debraj Shome and Dr Aparna Govil Bhasker for doing excellent work by getting together some of the most renowned doctors globally and compiling several interesting stories that will be helpful to strengthen the doctor-patient bonding. The authors are all very respected doctors globally and have commendably put together stories which bring together the empathetic nature of the relationship. Patients have also contributed to this book and this brings a balanced perspective to the book.

I also specially congratulate Dr Shome and Dr Bhasker for putting together a manifesto of patient and doctor,s rights and responsibilities. A document of this kind is the need of the hour, to allow both parties to introspect and treat each other with respect, love and care.

I strongly recommend this book for all doctors (especially IMA members) and patients as well as society at large. I hope that this outstanding book will benefit all of us.

Thanking you,
Yours sincerely

Dr R V Asokan
Hony Secretary General
Indian Medical Association

PREFACE

Dear People,

Once upon a time, doctors were considered akin to God. The stethoscope was revered and their healing touch was discussed far and wide. The doctor-patient relationship was a pure bond, unaltered by technological interference. Don't get us wrong; there's much to cheer in the way we live today, but a lot is still elusive. Times have changed and from being thought of as divine, doctors are now routinely assaulted and hospitals vandalised. There are many discouraging stories of the strained doctor-patient relationship in the media on a daily basis. Widespread distrust exists between both, patients and doctors, such that it almost feels like people are at war with their healthcare providers. The reasons are plenty and maybe they can be best addressed by a deep introspection by both doctors and patients.

Let us begin by telling you our side of the story, the doctors' perspective.

Millions dream of becoming a doctor one day. As did we. It remains one of the most coveted career options for young people globally. The journey is not easy, and only a select few are able to fulfil this aspiration. It takes more than a decade to become a super-specialist and a lifetime to understand and master the art of healing. This is probably the longest that any professional needs to train. But, learning about the human body and mind is merely one of its many facets. Medicine is also about connecting with people, getting them to trust you, reassuring them of recovery, and being with them in their most difficult times. In that respect, medicine isn't an absolute science and at the end of the day, doctors too, are only *human*.

When we graduated from medical school, we believed that we would diagnose with honesty and treat with compassion and kindness. We thought that we would have the knowledge and power to be able to cure each and every patient of their illness. What we didn't know was that the idealism developed in medical school would not teach us the frailty of medicine and the challenges staring at us in the form of real-life patients. Unlike machines that are standardised, human beings do not come with a user manual. Each person is different from another. Despite the technological advances, our predictions of a response to a certain therapy are still not, and can never be, absolute. The complexities of medicine are not easy to decipher and, thus, despite best efforts, no doctor can promise a foolproof final solution. Doctors often fail, and that's a burden we learn to live with. Does that mean we wish ill for our patients? No. None of us would intentionally harm them. Of course, like any other profession, there are some black sheep in medicine too. But it may be myopic and self-destructive to paint the whole profession in the same colour.

While we lament that doctors who used to be treated like gods are now mercilessly assaulted, we don't wish for doctors to be accorded the status of a deity at all. No doctor is or can ever be God! Still, even today, a lot of doctors are revered. However, they lead a life of veneration and often are expected to be all things at once: empathetic listeners, clear thinkers, skilled practitioners, conscientious individuals and altruistic healers. The expectations that society has from its doctors require them to be almost superhuman. As doctors, we fight two of the fiercest enemies of mankind—disease and death, and while we may succeed in defeating disease, death is inevitable. Impossible expectations may thus weigh us down and even though we strive to do our best, we might often fail to meet expectations. It's at times like these we must make an attempt to remember that *doctors are humans too*!

The altruistic idea of healthcare which places a doctor above all others in society also interferes with the doctor's ability to make a good living. People might believe that medicine is not just a profession but a calling. Sadly, many a times, money is the root cause for discord between patients and doctors. While quality healthcare is expensive, doctors often complain of a general unwillingness of the people to pay, even those who can afford it. Many people do not think twice about spending money on recreational activities, but they resent spending money on medical treatment. Even if healthcare is considered an essential service, there is an unreasonable expectation of philanthropy from medical practitioners. The truth remains that even if medicine is a doctor's calling, it is also their livelihood. Doctors pay commercial rates for rent, electricity, water and staff salaries. They pay as much income tax as other professionals and private medical practitioners do not receive any sops from the government. At the end of the day, doctors, too, need to support their families, educate their children, and fulfil their basic desires and wants. Even if human life can never be valued in money, there's a fee for every service. Or, just as money can never make up for the loss of a loved one, the service of a doctor who saves a loved one is also priceless.

While one of the biggest allegations against good doctors globally is their high fees, the truth is that most doctors are empathetic towards patients who find healthcare unaffordable. However, the problem is much deeper than the way it is understood. India, for instance, has one of the lowest per-capita expenditures on public healthcare in the world. Blaming doctors for the high price of healthcare is like blaming a pilot for the high cost of air travel. Clearly, it is not something that is completely under a doctor's control. The problem is systemic and being the face of medicine, doctors often bear the ire of the disgruntled public.

It also goes back to how students become doctors in India. Today, many privately-run medical colleges often operate under political patronage. These institutions are prohibitively expensive. Hence a discussion on the cost of healthcare must also delve into the cost that individuals are paying to become doctors, without which, an economic discussion is non-tenable and indeed non-sustainable. In the 1980s, healthcare in India was mainly run by the state. Once the Indian economy liberalised in the 1990s, the market trends changed. Yet, healthcare in India has been forced to retain a quasi-socialistic structure. It appears at times that India is confused. On the one hand, healthcare is expected to be a basic, fundamental human right while on the other hand, India has one of the lowest allocations of funds for healthcare in the world. While more and more rules are being pushed on to govern private healthcare, which caters to almost 80% of the patients in India, government hospitals and medical colleges lie in a seemingly perpetual state of decay. Healthcare is a complex subject and no healthcare system in the world is perfect. Regardless of whether people are under state-administered healthcare systems like the National Health System (NHS) in the UK where the waiting time to see a specialist may range from weeks to months, or the insurance-run private healthcare system of the US, people, everywhere, are unhappy and want more.

Today, statistically, people are living longer and better lives than any other time in history. Modern science has proved its capability of altering the course of life. However, a little more than a cursory glance can take us closer to the truths lived and experienced by doctors. In the 1980s, for instance, in India, healthcare was brought under the purview of the Consumer Protection Act (CPA). This by default rendered patients as consumers and doctors as traders. Even though the intention was to hear cases of medical negligence, such as when doctors operated on the wrong limb or inadvertently left a mop in the abdominal cavity during surgery, there is a deluge of consumer cases in the tribunal today. Yes, defaulters should be punished, but the scope of it being misused because of the vagaries of medicine cannot be denied. The status quo has led doctors to become defensive. This often poses the Hobson's choice for doctors—Do you order tests and risk being called corrupt, or do you not order tests and risk being called negligent?

If we are prepared to know what lies beneath the surface of a doctor's life, we will uncover how alarmingly unprepared we are to deal with the complexities of this profession. Medicine cannot be compared to any other profession because here, lives are at stake. We face unparalleled expectations while helping people live a life as far away from health complications as modern medicine would allow. This means mastering vast medical knowledge that in itself may be incomplete. It also means acting with speed and swiftness, bringing to the fore other doctors, nurses, and laboratory technicians, in situations that might need hours of thinking. In doing so, doctors must also show patience, empathy and genuine concern. A doctor's job encapsulates all of the above, but certain incidents have made us evaluate the patients' responsibility towards their own health.

Sometimes, patients fail to realise that along with rights, they have as much (if not more) responsibility towards their own health. Without that, the doctor cannot even begin to do his/her job. This responsibility towards our health may mean taking care of our diet and exercising regularly but it also means making full and fair disclosures to the doctors, which would allow them to decide further course of treatment. Dr Shome once had a patient who met with an accident and suffered multiple facial fractures. The patient had already been operated on multiple times and had come in for another facial surgery. Surgery under general anaesthesia means that the patient must be 'nil by mouth' for at least 8 to 10 hours prior.

Despite receiving clear instructions, the patient had a glass of milk an hour before the surgery. As the surgical team wasn't informed, it led to aspiration of fluid into the lungs during the surgery. Within 30 minutes, the patient's vital parameters started dropping. An emergency chest X-ray was performed in the operation room, and it showed that the patient had aspirated the milk into the lungs, leading to a complete shutdown of the lungs. When we informed the parents, the first reaction of the patient's mother was to blame the medical team! The patient had to be kept in the ICU and eventually recovered completely, without any sequelae. But we kept thinking to ourselves—shouldn't responsibility be a two-way street? Shouldn't patients take some ownership of their own health?

Similarly, we have patients whose post-surgery recovery doesn't go as planned. Multiple factors can contribute to this, but sometimes, patients do not find it important to disclose crucial details, like addictions, to the medical team. For instance, if there is smoking, drinking and drug abuse post-surgery, how can the surgical team ensure uneventful healing of the wounds? We have had numerous experiences when patients complain that post-surgical wounds aren't healing and disclose their addictions to tobacco, alcohol and drugs, only after repeated and persistent questioning. Healthcare is a complex web of choices with uncontrollable outcomes. And when things go wrong, we as humans tend to look for easy targets. In the age of social media, it is very easy to point fingers at someone without any evidence. This leads to increased disappointment and discontentment in the medical and patient fraternity. Thus, the doctor-patient relationship is becoming ever more disillusioned and disheartened.

Trust, of course, is also a two-way street. Like patients and their families look for doctors who they can trust, doctors also want to treat patients who can be trusted. Breach of trust can be from either side and the repercussions are equally strong. More than anything else, today, the relationship between doctors and patients seems to have been pushed into being defensive and it has almost become, a 'Us vs Them' situation.

Take a moment to think: Aren't doctors today, too, a part and product of the system? How can subjecting them to a different ideal be fair? Unfortunately, from trust, we seem to have moved to disbelief, doubt, and plain rejection of what the doctor is saying. Doctors are fallible like all human beings, and they should not be subjected to an ideal they cannot necessarily live up to. Doing so has resulted in an unprecedented change in the doctor-patient relationship globally and it's upon us now to think of a way forward. A new world order that takes into cognisance the needs and demands of both doctors and patients.

Three years ago, we started thinking about this. Must it really be, 'Us vs Them'?

We began to talk to doctors from multiple specialities and patients from across India and the world. The issues, we realised, are complicated with no easy answers. The problems are systemic with solutions a few years ahead of us. However, we realised that as doctors and patients, we all do have stories to tell. Stories of triumph, stories of success, stories of humility, stories of concern, stories of love and sometimes even stories of failures. We both strongly felt that these stories needed to be told. That is how the idea of putting this book together came to be. This book is a collection of heartfelt stories by doctors and patients across the globe. It is a peek into our lives which are closely intertwined together, the predicaments and ethical dilemmas both doctors and patients face, and most importantly it is about the changing metrics of the doctor-patient relationship. We believe that the time has come to initiate a conversation, as there is an ocean of positivity waiting to be discovered.

We feel this book needs to be read by doctors and patients alike and the masses as well. We hope that instead of just pinning the blame on someone, both parties will start donning our thinking caps. It doesn't have to be, 'Us vs Them'. Both doctors and patients need to realise that they cannot survive without each other.

This book is also about the modern experiences of doctors and patients—about what has changed and hasn't, about recording that change and reflecting upon a way forward. Immediate solutions and answers might elude us but we aim to launch a conversation on what it means to be a doctor in today's world and what a doctor-patient relationship must be. And that is why we wanted to conclude this book with a manifesto—a statement of rights of both doctors and patients that must be followed to build a society that's far more tolerable and less treacherous than it currently seems to be.

We are immensely grateful to His Holiness, the Dalai Lama for blessing this book with the foreword. At the end of the day, medicine is about love, kindness and compassion, and there can be no one better than His Holiness to talk about the crucial need of reviving these values for doctors and patients.

While we are the editors of this book, it would have been impossible to come this far without the contributions of our authors. We are deeply indebted to all contributing authors for making this possible. This has been a beautiful journey and a great learning experience for both of us. We sincerely hope that this book does justice to what we set out to do. We would also like to thank the patients who have contributed their stories and brought in balance. We are extremely grateful to Bloomsbury for seeing merit in publishing this book and thank them for their support.

Last but not the least, we dedicate this book to all our patients. Together, let us try and turn a new leaf.

With love,

Dr Debraj Shome and Dr Aparna Govil Bhasker

Dear People,

'I learnt the hard way that one might obtain a medical degree in a short time, but becoming a great doctor is a lifelong commitment and endeavour.'

Dr Altaf Patel

The Evolving Doctor-Patient Relationship in the New Millennium

When I started my career as a young physician, I had an incomplete and incorrect impression that saving lives was my calling and passion. If I were unable to save a patient, I would drive home wondering what else I could have done. Often, there was no answer. If ever there was an answer, I would chide myself for not thinking about it sooner and be overcome with a horrible feeling of guilt. After a four-decade-long tug-of-war, where the Almighty kept pulling my patients from above and I from below, I am wiser and understand that death is a natural sequel to life, and doctors are only humans at the end of the day.

Nowadays, success is measured in strange ways. We tend to measure the success of a person according to his/her wealth, not intellect, charity or empathy. As for me, I used to measure my success as a doctor by the number of patients I saved and failure as the number of my patients who died in a month. This was probably my biggest mistake.

Medicine is not an exact science. In this field, a doctor's success must be measured by his/her ability to tread in troubled waters. Medicine was and will always be an art, and the doctor should know when to wait, and when not to. His/her clinical decision-making must be astute. Addressing therapeutic options and adding, subtracting or changing doses of drugs cannot be learnt from a textbook. I learnt the hard way that one might obtain a medical degree in a short time, but becoming a great doctor is a lifelong commitment and endeavour.

About 35 years ago, when I had just started off my career, I was treating a cancer patient when I discovered that the disease had already spread to his lungs. It was confirmed in the chest X-ray but when I examined him, the site of the primary cancer eluded me. My colleague was equally confused. This was before the advent of sophisticated imaging techniques like ultrasound and computed tomography (CT) scan. In the morning, the attendant senior physician arrived and I gave him the patient's history. It took him just about a second to ask the patient to pull down his trousers and I was stunned to see a testicular tumour glaring at us. After the rounds, I casually asked him how he was so quick to arrive at a diagnosis and he told me that two decades ago when he was a resident, he had faced a similar situation. It was then, that I realised that physicians in India rarely look at testicles.

Ten years later, I went for a home visit to examine another patient for lung cancer. This too was before the advent of CT scan and we had scheduled a bronchoscopy. When I examined him and looked at the chest X-ray, it seemed to me that this was not a primary but a metastatic tumour. In a moment of déjà vu, I asked him to pull his pyjamas down and lo and behold—there it was: a testicular tumour. I asked him why he did not bring this to the notice of the cancer surgeon at the premier cancer institute where he was being treated. He told me that he felt shy; so I wrote a note to the doctor. I heard from the patient two days later that the cancer surgeon looked at the note and examined the testicles, after which he lost his temper and asked him to never to come back. Some doctors believe that they are God and often behave arrogantly. The patient then insisted that I treat him. In those days, chemotherapy was in its infancy; I read about the treatment and proceeded to treat him. He made a surprisingly good recovery and was so happy that over the next six months he brought every conceivable cancer patient to see me professionally, though I insisted that this was not my domain or speciality.

Today, however, medical science has advanced. We have newer drugs, imaging techniques and life-support systems such as ventilators and dialysis machines in our armamentarium. These were not available a few decades ago. Today, both patients and doctors don't want to let go and the patient is kept alive with the fervent hope that things will get better. Prolonging lives is a costly affair and makes it terribly expensive for the patient and the relatives at times. When things do not go our way, families of patients often express annoyance and dissatisfaction at the mind-boggling expenses coupled with the loss of a loved one. No wonder such stories make it to the media, with news of a deceased patient's relatives occasionally assaulting doctors. Hence, it is always prudent to discuss the cost of treatment at each step on the road of therapeutics. This, I think, is one of the biggest hurdles in the doctor-patient relationship.

The problem runs deeper as a lot has changed over the last few decades. There is a dearth of government-run medical institutes and existing medical colleges are not able to cater to the thousands of youngsters who aspire to take up medicine as a profession. It is only once you start studying do you see that it's impossible to get through the voluminous study literature and it takes a while to realise that no one can really master medicine. By then, the fees are already paid and it is too late to have second thoughts. It's also disconcerting that medical education has become superlatively expensive and many private medical colleges charge exorbitant sums of money as tuition fees—far beyond the reach of an average Indian family.

Many students opt for private medical colleges and pay a huge amount of money on their medical education. These so-called capitation fee colleges are the scourge in India and deny a poor person an equal opportunity for education. On the other hand, a student who has spent large sums of money for his/her education will obviously try to recover it as soon as possible. This commercialisation is the biggest blow to the doctor-patient relationship.

I remember the late 1990s when medicine had fallen under the purview of the consumer courts. To be treated as a trader, I thought, was demeaning to the profession. Even more problematic was the fact that the doctor would have to face a judge who had little knowledge of medicine. In response to this, there gradually emerged the concept of defensive medicine. This literally means doing every single test in the book to show that one is not negligent and, unsurprisingly, the repercussions are ultimately faced by the patients as this eventually bleeds the patient's pocket profusely.

Medicine is complex! I remember a young nurse who underwent surgery under spinal anaesthesia. A common complication of this was a persistent post-procedure headache. This is often addressed by hydrating the patient, making postural changes and administering analgesics—all of which were done. In two days, she was no better and a blood test and a CT scan of the brain were finally ordered. To my surprise, she turned out to have a brain haemorrhage! Which judge in this situation would condone a 48-hour wait-and-watch policy if the patient went to court? If we are extra-cautious we are blamed for over-investigating and if we avoid getting tests done, we may sometimes be termed negligent. As doctors, we battle this dilemma on a daily basis.

While discussing the commercial nature of medicine, it is also important to understand young doctors' perspectives. Once a student graduates, he/she either goes in for general practice or may choose to specialise. Specialisation and the subsequent super-specialisation take away another five or six years of the prime years of a medical student's life. One is already in their mid-30s by the time they are done with their studies. Then comes the responsibility of marriage and children. During the initial years of private practice, the most distressing feeling is going to work every day without knowing what one is going to earn. Patients who take appointments may not appear. Many who come for consultation may not be able to afford the fee and, finally, everyone expects a discount when it comes to their health. Then there is the great balancing act between income and expenses; every doctor in this country has to face this at some point of time in their career, except those few who are inherently wealthy.

> *This brings us back to the question: What ails the doctor-patient relationship today? From a time and age when the family doctor was involved in every big and small decision of the family—right from marriage to other non-medical problems—what has happened today? There is a lack of trust between doctors and patients. Patients who enter the hospital today are more worried about the cost of treatment.*

The lack of desire to develop proper clinical skills because of the accessibility to sophisticated investigations may often be the order of the day, and too much emphasis may be placed on reports instead of applying proper diagnostic logic. Not that the current doctors can be blamed for this—after all, we only reap what we sow. The fear of courts, the advent of litigation and the practice of defensive medicine have increased the reliance on diagnostic tests, at the sad expense of clinical skills. After all, a judge may want evidence and a CT scan is far better evidence than a doctor's clinical judgement and gut feeling, which are abstract tools to a judge at best.

I often wonder what the science of medicine is all about. Is it about brilliant innovations, is it just about prolonging life or is it about making life more comfortable? The day is not far when research in genetic engineering may enable us to order customised children on the internet, much like online food delivery today.

I guess it is all of the above, but most importantly, it is about empathy. Empathy is the crux of medicine and that is probably why the curriculum of the Royal College of Physicians lays great emphasis on empathy in their qualifying exam. During this examination, one whole practical station deals only with how the student conveys bad news to the patient's family and how he/she explains the various possibilities gently, but truthfully. Medicine is about understanding and trying to walk with the patient through various choices and therapeutic options in what is probably the most difficult time of their life. The art of medicine is all about love for our fellow human beings and that is one of the main reasons why the doctor-patient relationship has survived for thousands of years and will remain strong in the future as well.

Dr Altaf Patel is currently the Director of Medicine at Jaslok Hospital, Mumbai. He was an honorary professor of medicine from 1977 to 2007. He is a medical columnist for many mainstream newspapers like The Times of India *and* Mumbai Mirror *and has many research publications in national and international journals. In his free time, he enjoys reading, travelling and swimming.*

Did You Know?

The cost of medical malpractice lawsuits in the US has risen more than 2,000%, since 1975, to $26.5 billion in 2003, according to Tillinghast, an actuarial consultancy. And to what end? A study of malpractice suits in New York by the Harvard Medical Practice Group found that plaintiffs had actually been injured by doctors' negligence in only 17% of cases. Those patients with small claims often cannot find a lawyer to represent them while those who win find their lawyers have swallowed half the payout from the doctors.

Source: https://www.economist.com/united-states/2005/12/14/scalpel-scissors-lawyer

Dear People,

'Not only is it important for doctors to never give up on patients, it's equally important for patients to never give up hope.'

Dr Anil N. Suchak and Dimple Mishra

Never Give Up

When I was 17 years old, I accompanied my father for his talk on the Bhagavad Gita, *swadharmai*, work ethics and how to conduct a good life. He made two points that made a deep impact on my impressionable mind and have stayed with me since then. First, 'Few people are fortunate to become doctors. It is the noblest of all professions where we get the chance to help people in pain and relieve their suffering'. Second, 'We should treat every patient in the same manner as we would treat a member of our own family.' I grew up to become an anaesthetist and critical care specialist and in a career spanning 37 years, my professional life is rich with countless memories—some outright hilarious and some heart-breaking.

Of course, like any other profession, in medicine too, one must take cognisance of the financial aspect, career goals and job satisfaction but being able to alleviate pain is unlike any other happiness. When we see our patients do well, all the years of study, hard work and sleepless nights melt away.

An elderly lady was admitted to the ICU with heart failure and was put on the ventilator. As her doctor, I apprised her relatives that her condition was critical and unstable. They were initially saddened but seemed to accept the situation a bit too hastily. They asked me if the end was near as they would need to inform their near and dear ones accordingly. Since I do not believe in ever giving up on a patient (like most doctors), I said that was not something I can assert and that we should pray for her to get better.

The next morning as I walked to the ICU, I saw about 30 to 40 people dressed in white, waiting outside. My heart sank and I went inside thinking that the inevitable had transpired.

A visibly shaken resident medical doctor ran to me as I entered and begged me to give him the day off. I reassured him that I would take care of the relatives and gently break the sad news to them.

What he said baffled me and relief washed over my face. He nervously stuttered, 'Sir, the patient is actually improving and I have no idea what to tell these premature "mourners" who've gathered outside. Please let me go home.' I looked at him and had a really difficult time maintaining a straight face. I asked him to leave and told him I would deliver the good news to the family. I went outside and explained to the relatives that their prayers had been answered and good medical treatment had worked wonders. The patient was now much better and out of danger. After hearing this, all the people clad in white miraculously disappeared.

In a few days, the patient got better and went home hale and hearty. Even today when I think of this episode, it brings a smile to my face and I am thankful for the occasional lighter moments in our stressful profession.

However, a doctor's life is rarely a collection of amusing anecdotes. In 2001, an earthquake devastated Kutch in Gujarat and within minutes, the misery was broadcasted on national television. I decided to garner help and quickly put together a team of doctors. We packed our ambulances with whatever medical supplies we could manage and left for Kutch. Ten doctors and a medical staff of eight people accompanied me at literally a moment's notice.

We stopped at a petrol pump at Dahisar in Mumbai and bought whatever supplies—packaged food and water—the adjoining shop had. The owner was, therefore, curious to know where we were going. As soon as we told him the purpose of our journey, he refused to accept any payment from us. His kindness was heart-warming.

The next day, we reached the village of Bidada in Kutch and after acquiring permission from the collector, we began to render our voluntary services. There were hundreds of injured people, critical patients and dead bodies all around us. It was inexplicably miserable to see the suffering the people had to go through.

The casualties were coming in at such a breakneck speed that the doctors, interns, and volunteers worked around the clock. No one slept for more than three to four hours, that too in tents and in parked vehicles.

As there was no electricity, generators were procured and whatever petrol and diesel was available was being brought to us by volunteers. Various organisations, NGOs and hospitals were sending medicines and supplies from different cities to cope with the huge number of patients. Like a factory assembly line, the OT was working relentlessly. But nothing could stop the mass cremation of those who had succumbed to nature's fury.

We worked non-stop, day and night, for 15 days. After that, we decided to shift around 40–50 critical patients to our hospital in Mumbai and flew them to the city along with their surviving family members. Airlines provided their service free of cost. After removing the aircraft seats, almost 15 patients could be accommodated in each carrier. Following the principle of 'triage', we decided to focus our attention on the few patients who needed multiple surgeries and further rehabilitation.

For the next three months, we housed these patients and their families with us, provided them with all medical help, food, clothing, boarding and eventually arranged their transport back to Kutch.

The reason I share this particular story is with the hope that the next time you hear of some unsavoury incidence of malpractice by a doctor, you would take it with a pinch of salt and understand that it is probably a one-off occurrence, as unfortunate as it may be. There are all sorts of individuals in every profession, including medicine. We are all humans.

I have learnt my life's biggest lessons both as a doctor and a patient. I've realised that not only is it important for doctors to never give up on patients, it's equally important for patients to never give up hope. Doctors, after all, want their patients to recover and live healthy lives.

In 1987, I was diagnosed with chronic hepatitis C, which progressed to cirrhosis of the liver by the turn of the century. By 2006, the cirrhosis of the liver had advanced to end-stage liver disease and my general condition had started worsening. I was advised to undergo a liver transplant at the earliest.

A year later, I decided to undergo a liver transplant and my surgeon, Dr Subhash Gupta, was optimistic about the outcome. In a 23-hour complicated surgery, 850 grams of the donor's right lobe of the liver was resected and transplanted into my abdomen. The diseased liver from my body was removed and explanted. My surgery was extremely difficult as there were multiple adhesions in my abdomen. It took Dr Gupta and his team almost nine hours just to be able to get to the liver. This is a classic example of a doctor with the 'never-give-up' approach. Dr Gupta was persistent and did not think of abandoning the surgery at any point in time. It is due to his optimism and confidence in being able to see my surgery through that I am here today, recounting the story of my life. Later, once I recovered, I came to know that during surgery I was bleeding profusely from all organs and more than 60 bottles of blood were transfused in those 23 hours.

The histopathology report of my liver also showed two tumours in addition to the cirrhosis of the liver. Both tumours were cancerous. I feel fortunate that the surgery happened at the right time before these tumours could spread to other organs.

As I regained consciousness, I became aware of the multiple sounds of the various machines I was hooked on to. Post-operatively I was put on a ventilator. I could feel the various tubes inside me—the urinary catheter, nasogastric tube, multiple IV lines, central line and arterial line, among others. As I had an endotracheal tube in my throat that was connected to the ventilator, I could not make any conversation. I was closely watched and monitored by the team of doctors and nurses in the transplant ICU. I underwent frequent blood tests, ultrasounds and doppler tests as and when required. It was important to assess the functionality of the new liver at every step.

Since I could not speak, I learnt to communicate with the doctors and my family members by blinking my eyes once for 'yes' and twice for 'no'. However, I eventually realised that I needed to relax and allow the ventilator to work in order to conserve my energy and recover. There was no point in fighting the life support systems. When my endotracheal tube was removed in a couple of days, I knew, that I was going to survive this.

Subsequently, I was put on immunosuppressant medications so that the new liver was not rejected by my body. Three days after the surgery, I started experiencing hunger pangs. I was started on a liquid diet, followed by semisolids and then a normal high protein diet.

While I thought everything was going smoothly, a complication occurred. There was a biliary leak from the transplanted liver. Bile started collecting in my abdomen and almost 1.5 to 2 litres of bile had to be drained on a daily basis. This went on for three days and finally on post-operative day nine, I was taken up for a re-surgery. A hepaticojejunostomy was performed. This surgery took six hours. I went through tremendous pain, sleepless nights and emotional trauma. Finally, I recovered, but for weeks after that, blood tests were conducted to monitor the levels of immunosuppressant medications and I was kept under a close watch. I visited the hospital every other day and waited my turn like any other patient. Here, I was not the medical director of a well-known hospital or the practising anaesthetist and intensivist. I was not the man in control. I personally experienced the travails, difficulties and challenges that are faced by patients and their families in a hospital.

Liver transplant gave me a new life. After my surgery, my mission has been to spread as much awareness as possible on the subject of organ donation and transplantation. This is a novel science developed over the last couple of decades and even now the awareness about transplantation is very low as was evident when a gentleman dropped into my office five years later. He was visibly upset. His wife had slipped into a coma due to liver failure. I told them that a liver transplant was her only hope. I explained to them about the importance of finding a donor as soon as possible and counselled them about the expenditure involved in undergoing the transplant. They asked numerous questions and understood everything. Once they understood that the liver regenerates, both the husband and his brother were willing to become the donors. I guided them regarding all the necessary arrangements and connected them to the doctor who had treated me, Dr Subhash Gupta, Unfortunately, the patient had a unique condition called the 'situs inversus', that is, all the organs in the body were situated in the opposite location like a mirror image. But Dr Gupta's persistent efforts meant that the transplant surgery went well.

About a month later, a young woman in her early 20s walked into my office. After introducing herself, she bent down to touch my feet. I was really surprised and extremely moved when she thanked me for saving her mother's life. It was then that I found out what had happened: I had assumed that the donor was the husband or my young visitor 's father when, in fact, her father and uncle were both rejected as donors and she was the one who donated a part of her liver to her mother.

She was a young business management student and I couldn't help asking her if she had any concerns about having a large scar on her abdomen. 'Sir, my mother gave birth to me; she brought me into this world and is my life-giver,' she said. 'I have just given her a small part of my liver.' I was overcome with fatherly pride and happiness when I heard her answer.

Such cases are reminiscent of the principles that I have followed in the 39 years of my medical practice. Never refuse a call from a patient. In fact, I spend time taking down a patient's history and educating them on keeping records of their previous illnesses. I not only try to regularly update my medical knowledge, I always give an accurate and honest picture to the family, no matter how critical the situation is. Over and above all, my biggest learning has remained what I heard from my mother as a 17-year-old: Few people get the opportunity to alleviate pain and when you do, never give up and treat your patients like you'd treat a family member. Never stop learning, never stop believing and never give up!

Dr Anil N. Suchak is an anaesthesiologist and an intensivist. He is the medical director of Suchak Hospital, Malad. He has been a member of IMA for the past 37 years, performing various roles from being a member of the managing committee to Vice President of Mumbai (West) to being the joint secretary. He heads the Mumbai branch of The Divine Life Society and is the trustee of a school. He formed

the Indian Liver Foundation to increase awareness about liver transplantation and organ donation. Through this foundation, he has advised hundreds of patients. Being a cancer survivor and having undergone a liver transplant himself this is his way to express his gratitude and giving back to society. He has also been the recipient of the Lifetime Achievement Award given by the Association of Medical Consultant.

Dimple Mishra is a professional Interior Designer and Interior stylist since 1986. An active member and functionary on the managing committee of the Indian Liver Foundation; in her spare time, Dimple contributes towards the written word, she is a published writer and loves to blog about her tryst with the subtle during her fascinating travels.

Did You Know?

A doctor juggles between lots of roles—from being a physician to a provider at home and finally being a member of a family. It's tough to be at all the places and be everything at the same time. For some doctors, patients are the first priority. They love to serve humanity and this is the reason why they chose medicine as their career. In a poll conducted by Curofy, asking doctors what their first priority is, patient's, family or economic independence, out of 1,820 doctors who responded, 60.4% said that they prioritise their patients over everything else.

Source: http://health.cxotv.news/2016/07/01/selfless-service-2-out-of-3-doctors-prioritize-patients-over-family/

Dear People,

'While doctors must adhere to their duty of caring for patients, we must not forget that doctors, no matter how skilled or competent, need care too.'

Dr Aniruddha Malpani

The Night I Nearly Killed My Patient

Many years ago, I was a junior resident in the obstetrics and gynaecology department at a very busy public hospital in Mumbai. As it is one of the most renowned teaching hospitals in the country, many patients with serious and complicated illnesses were referred to us for emergency management and complicated cases which meant conducting over 7,000 deliveries every year. As junior residents, work was never-ending and we were perpetually sleep-deprived. Of course, sleep deprivation was a part of a resident's life as our seniors strongly believed that we had to be trained in keeping midnight vigils—a traditional occupational hazard for obstetricians.

Like most Indian medical institutes, the teaching programme was fairly unstructured, and we followed the traditional 'see one, do one, teach one' approach. During night hours, the unit was managed by the senior registrar and the two of us, along with a senior house surgeon, were responsible for overseeing all obstetric patients who were admitted from 4 pm until 8 am the next day.

I would often be on duty for three or more continuous nights as numerous critical patients would be admitted under our care. As the junior-most doctor on the team, I was responsible for all the drudge work and monitoring the patients. On one such night, a 28-year-old woman, pregnant with her first baby, was referred to us from a private hospital. She was in advanced labour and had severe pre-eclampsia. Pre-eclampsia is a potentially dangerous pregnancy-related complication, which is characterised by high blood pressure, discharge of protein in the urine and severe swelling over of the feet.

The registrar and the senior house surgeon did an emergency caesarean section. Once the baby was safely delivered and the patient stabilised, they went to bed, leaving me to monitor her in the ward with the instructions that I was supposed to give her enough intravenous (IV) fluids to ensure that her blood pressure was maintained.

The patient was tired and drowsy after her surgery, and so was I. Throughout the night, I would meticulously check her vital signs, and every time her blood pressure was low, I would pump in IV fluids, to keep the blood pressure (BP) within the normal range. Unfortunately, her pressure kept dropping and according to the instructions that I had been given, I ordered the nurse on duty to pour in large quantities of IV fluids to maintain her BP level. I was so focused on making sure her pressure level was normal, that I failed to realise that I was making a cardinal mistake. All the extra fluid we were pumping into her was getting trapped in her subcutaneous tissues, causing her to develop systemic swelling.

I was following the orders at a spinal level and was not experienced enough to be aware of the risks of overloading a pre-eclampsia patient with so much fluid. In the morning, the senior houseman came to check the patient and was aghast to find that in my attempt to keep her BP in the normal range, she had received over 12 litres of IV fluids—in less than six hours.

Her entire body had become grotesquely swollen because of the fluid overload, and she was having immense difficulty in breathing. Due to the severe swelling in her throat, it was impossible to intubate her and we had to perform an emergency tracheostomy (a procedure conducted to allow air to enter the lungs) and transfer her to the intensive cardiac care unit (ICCU). She was put on a ventilator to aid her breathing. She had a stormy course but, finally, recovered and was discharged in a couple of weeks. I still have nightmares when I think about her. It was only later that I found out that patients with pre-eclampsia and pregnancy-induced hypertension are known to have leaky blood vessels. Because of this, all the fluid that I was giving her was leaving her blood vessels and getting trapped in her tissues.

I was mercilessly and publicly berated for my incompetence by the senior house surgeon, registrar and professors. The punishment for my indiscretion was being forced to monitor patients every night for the remaining three months of my residency. At that time, I felt guilty and accepted that I deserved the punishment meted out to me and accepted it quietly. I kicked myself many times for not knowing more about how to manage a patient with severe pregnancy-induced hypertension and was extremely grateful to God that the patient had survived despite my ignorance.

Residency can be cruel and, for a long time, I was ostracised by my colleagues and treated like a pariah for having nearly caused a patient's death since this would have been a blot on the hospital's reputation. There was no one I could talk to about what had happened and why, and I had to bottle up my mixed emotions—of fear, guilt, shame, anger, embarrassment and humiliation—through the remainder of my residency.

At that time, I needed emotional support and professional reaffirmation from my seniors and teachers. I needed to be told that, regardless of my mistake, I could be a good doctor.

But I was abandoned and left to fend for myself. The moment my residency was over, I moved to another hospital, to try to erase these unhappy memories.

Most doctors have had similar experiences, where they have unknowingly made a mistake that may have caused harm to their patient. A lot could have been done to protect this patient at many different levels, and this is what we need to focus on. The reason for the error was not just my ignorance; it was also the fact that what I was doing was not supervised and there was a lack of proper infrastructure. Things would never have come to this if there were protocols for the management of pregnancy-induced hypertension in the hospital.

The patients who would come to us were severely ill and should have ideally been in an intensive care unit (ICU), where an experienced clinician would provide 24-hour supervision. The woman should never have been left on a bed in the ward, under the care of an inexperienced house surgeon like me, no matter how well-meaning or sincere I may have been.

Unfortunately, most teaching hospitals are run by junior, inexperienced and unsupervised residents and this is one of medicine's dirty dark secrets. A secret that doctors never discuss in public. I was never given an opportunity to discuss this case, and the other residents were not given a chance to learn from my mistakes either. Even worse, no changes were made to prevent this episode from recurring.

The harsh truth is that all doctors make mistakes, and this is a part of their learning process to become a doctor. Medical errors will continue to happen until we bring them out in the open, talk about them and learn from them. However, most doctors often suffer from a 'God complex' and making an error is extremely shameful for them. This shame is sometimes so powerful that most doctors never come forward to talk about any error that they have made. It is impossible for us to admit to a mistake.

We tend to pick the best of the best as medical students, knowing that the medical system is not for the faint-hearted. There is no place for a 'good enough' doctor—you must be excellent, which means there is absolutely no margin for error. Being perfect is not easy and, sadly, sometimes it may mean hiding your errors from the fraternity to maintain your flawless image in their eyes.

Doctors are not alone in harbouring these expectations of perfection from themselves. Patients too envisage their doctors to be perfect. As doctors, we are trained to take charge—to be the captain of the ship. And we must take personal responsibility for everything that happens to a patient in our care, whether or not it was our fault. We are responsible, and the buck stops with us.

When a complication occurs, the first feeling that envelops us is one of sadness that someone is suffering. Then emerges a feeling of shame that we may have actually caused that suffering, followed by the fear that somehow this will lead to us being ostracised, sued and humiliated publicly. Next comes the anger, because you feel lonely and wonder why the system is not supporting you in this really difficult time. A combination of all these emotions eventually leads to panic.

It's important to remember that medicine is an ambiguous science and as doctors, our knowledge and experience is never enough. We face uncertainties every day and, at times, despite our best intentions, errors may happen. Patients are undoubtedly the victims of these unforeseen 'errors' but after an error, we also need to take care of the doctors and nurses involved. They, too, as my experience has shown, can be the 'victims' of these unexpected and unanticipated medical errors.

Any doctor will tell you that a precise diagnosis is the first step to resolution for a patient but what they won't admit is how important a supportive and nourishing environment is for a doctor to work well. While doctors must adhere to their duty of caring for patients, we mustn't forget that doctors, no matter how skilled or competent, need care too.

Dr Aniruddha Malpani is an IVF specialist. He founded the world's largest free patient education library, HELP at healthlibrary.com, and has authored numerous books. He pioneered the use of innovative technology to educate infertile couples using cartoon films, comic books and e-learning. An active angel investor, Dr Malpani invests across all domains and admires entrepreneurs because they have the potential to change the world.

Did You Know?

As per the Indian Medical Association (IMA), physicians' suicide is almost a public health crisis in India. According to a report published in the Indian journal of psychiatry, 30% of Indian resident doctors suffer from depression and 17% have contemplated suicide. Long working hours, taxing medical training, violence against doctors and the stress of saving lives are some major factors that push doctors to the breaking point of burnout.

Source: Grover, S., Sahoo, S., Bhalla, A., and Avasthi, A. (2018). 'Psychological problems and burnout among medical professionals of a tertiary care hospital of North India: A cross-sectional study'. Indian Journal of Psychiatry, *60(2): 175–188.*

Dear People,

'Grief is not a luxury that we are granted as many more lives await our care and we have no choice but to get back to work the next morning.'

Dr Aparna Govil Bhasker

Let Go...If You Want to Survive

February 2002

My mother walked in with my dinner into the resident's quarters and found me crying inconsolably. I had lost my first patient, a young bride with 98% burns. Patients with such severe burns follow a very predictable clinical course. They are deceptively alert and conscious for a very short window. Sepsis then sets in in a flash and before one can realise, they are gone. As medical students, we are well versed about 'septicemia' and its sequelae. Our teachers emphasise on the gravity of sepsis in multiple lectures. Every medical book has multiple pages dedicated to this topic.

Yet, I was totally unprepared when I dealt with my first patient with severe septicemia which eventually took her life. I could not come to terms with the fact that a person who was talking coherently to me about her dreams and aspirations until one night before was no more the next day. The best medical care and most expensive drugs in the world could not save her. I grieved for her for a long time and even after 15 years sometimes I still think of her. I think of the myriad possibilities her life could have been, the family that could have been hers and maybe a career.

As I embarked on my clinical journey, I learnt the two very important lessons that day. First, that 'Doctors are not God' and second that 'Eventually at some point, you have to let go, that is the only way you can survive.'

April 2004

Medicine is a people's profession. As doctors, we meet people in some of the worst phases of their lives. We see them when they are at their most vulnerable and exposed. Back in 2004, as a surgical resident I was on night duty in the A and E. Like all on-call days that day also I had prayed to the Lord for a good night's sleep as I had a long day in the operation theatre (OT) the next morning. However, that night had something else in store for me. Around midnight, the emergency nurse informed me about a 23-year-old girl who had fallen from a running train while coming back from college and lost both her arms. We took her up for emergency debridement in the operation theatre. Unfortunately, none of the arms were salvageable and had to be amputated. She was in the hospital for months and every morning I would be at her bedside to dress her wounds. During those months, I saw her going through various phases swaying between depression to being hopeful and then delving back into depression. More than the physical wounds it was the emotional wounds that were laid bare in front of all us who were her caregivers. She would try her best to cope up with the pain and then would be bogged down with thoughts of what the future held in store for her. She was engaged to be married, 10 days from the day of her accident. Eventually, she broke her engagement as she could not allow herself to be a burden on another young life. What I saw in those four months was an entire life turned around. Hats off to her father who was a pillar of support not only for her but for the entire family. From afar I saw him build up her confidence bit by bit.

Human spirit and resilience are amazing at times. In due course of time, she was discharged from the hospital. After a year or so, she stopped coming to the hospital and all of us moved on with our lives at the hospital. Three years later, I was at Nagpur railway station waiting to travel back to Mumbai and I heard a familiar female voice making the train announcements for the station. I knew it was her! The moment I entered her office, the twinkle in her eyes and the smile on her face told me that she had eventually won the battle.

June 2016

'You doctors never listen to us. You should have got a postmortem done and there wouldn't have been any issue. Look, now you are here, wasting our time,' the police inspector on duty said to me, stealing a minute from interrogating a murder suspect. Another woman was screaming abuses from the next room while she was being questioned by the lady police officers for an alleged burglary. I cringed.

That night as I walked in the darkness, I felt the same darkness within. It was past midnight. My husband and I had left our three-year-old son at home and had gone looking for a police station near my hospital. I had not eaten anything the whole day. My mind was cluttered and I was a total mess.

All I could think was, this was not how it was supposed to be. Fifteen years ago, when I took the Hippocratic oath, I had never imagined that a day would come when I would be compelled to file a police complaint against a patient's family. Yet, here I was.

'This doctor kills people.' These words along with a surreptitiously taken picture of me in scrubs and a snapshot of my professional achievements together formed a social media creative. Another patient of mine had forwarded this image to me on WhatsApp, asking, 'Doctor, is this true?' The image had been doing rounds on Facebook accounts in a faraway foreign country.

As I stared at the picture, my face fell. I couldn't believe I was looking at my own picture. I will never forget that moment in my life. It was an antithesis to everything that I had ever wanted to be. Murderers kill people, not doctors.

The image had gone viral on the Facebook accounts in that country. I had no idea who was behind it and why they were sharing this image. However, sitting in my clinic, thousands of miles away, I could feel the hatred that they felt for me. That evening I returned home distraught. Soon, the heavy, looming sadness turned into acute depression and a sinking feeling that refused to go away. Somehow, the night passed. The next morning, I was all alone at home and I finally broke down.

As tears flowed, I cannot describe how I felt. Apart from the emotional setback, I had no idea about how to deal with this situation that I found myself in. I did not know what I should do next.

In addition to the personal anguish and pain, my reputation as a doctor was at stake. That one Facebook image threatened to destroy 20 years of hard work. In a matter of seconds, the image had been shared by thousands of people anywhere and everywhere. I was already proclaimed as the 'killer' and the onus to disprove it was on me. That day I realised that it takes years to build a person and a career and just a few seconds to destroy both.

It was at that moment that a close friend called me. He reminded me that I was not God. I had done the best for my patient. Things had not gone the way we had hoped, but I was being blamed for something that was not my fault. He urged me to be pragmatic, hold myself together and deal with the situation. The first thing that I needed to do was to go to the nearest police station and file a complaint in the cyber-cell against the defamatory post that was doing the rounds on social media.

One month ago, a foreign patient had arrived for an elective surgery. The 28-year-old girl was accompanied by her elderly mother. That day, I had three operations lined up. Her's was going to be my second surgery of the day.

The surgery proved to be challenging but things went well and there didn't seem to be any cause for concern. After the operation got over, she was taken off anaesthesia and we shifted her out into the post-operative recovery room. In the recovery, I spoke to the patient and told her that the surgery had gone well.

Then, I asked for her mother to come up to the OT so that I could apprise her of the daughter's condition. In the meantime, my colleague and I stepped out of the operating room to grab a quick bite. Ten minutes later, we heard the alarm for Code Blue in the theatre along with a flurry of activity in the recovery, which basically means that a patient has collapsed and needs resuscitation. It took me a second to realise that it came from my own theatre and we dropped everything and rushed inside.

My patient had suddenly become unresponsive and her heart rate was dipping rapidly. We wasted no time in starting resuscitation and the ICU team arrived within minutes and took over from us. For a moment, everything was a blur. I couldn't believe that the person I just had a conversation with was not responding anymore. I had a sinking feeling and it was one of those moments when deep inside, you know that you are fighting a losing battle and yet desperately hope for a miracle to happen. She seemed to stabilise temporarily as her heartbeat became steady and we shifted her to the ICU. During this chaos, her mother was on my mind all the time. In between struggling to keep her alive, I called her mother and spoke to her about her daughter's condition. I explained to her that though we were trying our best to do everything possible, her prognosis was poor.

Very soon she had another cardiac arrest and her heart rate started dipping. The ICU team resuscitated her once again but we could see that she was slipping away. She didn't survive the third cardiac arrest which occurred in less than an hour and a precious young life was lost despite all efforts. I was devastated. This was the first time in my career that I had lost a patient so suddenly after a surgery. Most likely causes for sudden death in such cases could be either a heart attack or a condition known as pulmonary embolism where a clot travels from the veins of the legs and gets lodged into the heart or the lungs. It is usually fatal.

None of us had ever imagined that this is how it would end. It felt like a personal loss and I couldn't help thinking about her poor mother. They had travelled all the way to India to get this surgery done in the hope of becoming better. I was worried about the mother and wondered how she would take the news of her daughter's sudden demise. How would she manage all alone in an unknown country? As I prepared to declare the death, I kept thinking about how I could help the mother to complete all the formalities that would be required now. I wanted to support her mother in every possible way in this difficult time.

I declared the death at 4.00 pm that day. As per the hospital protocol, cases of death soon after a surgical procedure have to be reported to the nearest police station. Getting a postmortem done is the norm and the only way to determine the final cause of death. By 4.15 pm, there were some five or six people who had collected outside the ICU and claimed to be the patient's relatives. The police arrived too and began their formalities. In another half an hour, a mob had collected outside the ICU. I was exhausted and was feeling extremely low. As I stepped out of the ICU, I had a feeling that it was not over yet. Until now, I had seen myself as a saviour and a fighter who had tried her level best to save a life. It was only then, that I realised that all these people who were assembled outside the ICU perceived me neither as a saviour nor as a healer. I was their culprit.

What followed for the next eight hours is something that I would never want to remember in my life. I felt like a convict who desperately tried to defend herself but failed because the verdict had already been passed. In those eight hours, I was cursed by so many people that a lot of those things are better left unsaid. I do not remember the faces of any of them. They clicked my pictures on their phones without my permission. They refused to get a postmortem done and finally settled when the hospital refunded the entire operation fee. I finally left the hospital at 2.00 am.

A month later, her family and friends initiated a nasty Facebook campaign to malign my reputation and labelled me a 'killer'. Although my heart was not into it, I was forced to file a police complaint with the cyber-cell to protect myself. I was lucky that the post did not infiltrate into the social media accounts in India and the damage was contained.

It is difficult to deal with a sudden death and the easiest way out is to blame someone. In this case, that someone happened to be me.

As a human being, I understand that it's extremely difficult to come to terms with losing a loved one but that day, all I wanted to do was hold her mother's hands and comfort her. Even though, I know that I did everything possible and had left no stones unturned in my patient's care, I was pushed into being defensive.

This brings me to a very pertinent question: Why is it that in every other profession, people are allowed to fail but doctors do not have this luxury? Right from medical school, we are taught to fight two of mankind's biggest enemies—disease and death—and I think we do a great job of it. However, at the end of the day, doctors are also human and while we win many times, sometimes we may lose too. Unfortunately, today doctors and hospitals are at their most vulnerable. All it takes is one surreptitious photograph or an offensive video for years of hard work to go down the drain in a second.

As doctors, we confront disease and death on a daily basis. People think that we get used to death and loss over time. Unfortunately, that is not true. There are many sleepless nights and often these cases stay in our hearts for life. For years we think about what we could have done differently to change the outcome. Grief is not a luxury that we are granted as many more lives await our care and we have no choice but to get back to work the next morning.

Dr Aparna Govil Bhasker is a bariatric and laparoscopic general surgeon practising in Mumbai. She has multiple publications and numerous book chapters to her credit. She is the managing committee member of many surgical societies and has a keen interest in clinical research. She is the co-founder of Debabrata Auro Foundation which was set up in 2016 to help the poor and needy.

Did You Know?

In a study of oncologists, researchers found that grief was considered shameful and unprofessional. Doctors in the study said they wrestled with feelings of grief but hid those feelings from others because showing emotion was considered a sign of weakness. The researchers reported that the impact of the unacknowledged grief was inattentiveness, impatience, irritability, emotional exhaustion and burnout. They concluded that the professional taboo around grief had negative consequences for doctors, as well as for the quality of care they provide.

Source: Granek, L. (2012). 'When doctors grieve'. www.nytimes.com/2012/05/27/opinion/sunday/when-doctors-grieve.html

Dear People,

'Yes she is working; no I do not know when she will be home; yes we are still married; no she is not imaginary-A doctor's husband.'

C.B. Bhasker

The Mr Behind the Ms

I got married soon after I returned from a stint in France as a management consultant. The piece of advice that everyone gave to me when I announced that I am marrying a doctor, that too a surgeon, was 'Have NO expectations'. They told me that this would ensure that I would never be disappointed. Over the years, I constantly trained myself to think that my wife was doing her best and that her work as a doctor took priority over everything else. This attitude also helped me to eliminate a lot of issues that could have stemmed from unmet expectations and disappointments over the years.

This brings back memories of many occasions when as a young couple, we would buy movie tickets and I ended up watching them alone. There were times when we were at the ticket counter and she would get a call from the hospital for an emergency and that would be the end of the movie plan. Not to mention the innumerable dinner plans that were cancelled at the last minute. We consistently missed celebrations like birthdays, anniversaries and weddings in the family and so on.

In those initial years, weeks would pass by without us meeting each other or having spoken to each other, despite living under the same roof. Being married to endless phone calls during the day and night and carrying the weight of the responsibility of someone else's health is not exactly in line with the common perception of a doctor's life of luxury and indulgence.

I repeat, I am not complaining.

When I meet people and tell them that my wife is a bariatric surgeon, I get mixed looks of fascination and curiosity. They covertly look at me from head to toe and try to size me up. Now, I have been and still am a fitness freak and a regular at the gym for almost a decade. Yes, there was a time when I was working for a start-up and the weighing scale was tilting dangerously towards the three-digit mark; so I guess it is only natural for people to ask me if I had gone under the knife (especially those who see me after a long time). Being married to a bariatric surgeon comes with its own challenges—and prejudices—after all.

As the years passed by, my wife and I forged a beautiful partnership. Like all married couples, we have had our ups and downs, but both of us have made an effort to understand each other. Both of us are ambitious people and very career-oriented. After we had our son, we finally found a balance between our professional and personal lives.

We have also learnt to share or give each other space whenever needed.

Before I got married, I always thought that doctors were immune to patients' fears and pain, as they go through this every day. I thought that maybe it stops affecting them after some time. I wondered if my wife too went through the same emotional arch. Over the years, I have seen her going through different emotions. She is elated when a critical patient does well. However, it is still difficult for her to adjust to the idea that sometimes, nature's forces are stronger and a doctor is, after all, only human. He or she can only try their best. Sometimes, the day does not unfold as you may have planned and life is always full of surprises, more so in a surgeon's life.

Most of our social get-togethers are with doctors. Being the only non-medical person in a company of doctor couples, I used to be intrigued by their discussions about patient care and stories from the hospital. Over the years I have started enjoying these meetings and narratives. My medical vocabulary has also improved by leaps and bounds. Being a part of the inner circle of doctors, I am privy to both sides of the spectrum and what I have realised is that doctors are heavily invested in the doctor-patient relationship.

Trust me, my obstinate mind did not think like this before marriage. I was a bit cynical. My perception of doctors has evolved as I changed the lens from a patient's son to a doctor's husband. Like an optician who changes the lens till the patient gets clarity and finds that 'aha' moment, my thought process has changed for good.

That brings me to the patient side of the story. The probability of finding at least one diabetic person in every family in South India is not very uncommon. In my family, it was my mother. She was diagnosed with diabetes almost three decades ago. By the age of 52, her kidneys had started giving up and every few months she would be admitted to the hospital. Her lungs would fill up with water and she would find it hard to breathe. These hospital admissions were becoming more and more frequent and almost every three months, she would be in the ICU for at least a week. Around this time, her haemoglobin dropped drastically and a surgery to remove her uterus was recommended by the doctors. It was a difficult decision for us. Surgery was necessary, but it could also tip the scales of the delicate balance that her kidneys were maintaining so far. Our worst fears came true as her kidneys did eventually let her down, soon after the surgery. Her recovery post the surgery was turbulent and she was advised regular dialysis. The word 'dialysis' meant the end of the world for my mother—and for all of us as a family. We were devastated and felt that all of us had failed her in some way. I felt anguished and even livid at the doctors and the hospital. I blamed the surgery for my mother's state. It was difficult to accept that to live, she would require dialysis on a regular basis. At that time, my mind could not fathom that this was the natural course of the disease and that she eventually would have reached this stage with or without the surgery for the uterus.

Soon, I realised that getting a slot for dialysis was not easy, even in a metropolis like Mumbai, which has so many multispeciality hospitals and standalone dialysis centres. With great difficulty, we would get the last slot at 8 o'clock at night. This despite my wife being a doctor at the same hospital. The only saving grace was that we did not get stuck in traffic jams while returning home in the middle of the night.

It was hard for my mother to get used to this new way of life. She had to undergo another surgery to create a fistula in her forearm that would facilitate dialysis. Till the fistula matured, she had to bear with the venous access in her neck. I remember the first time I saw her with the neckline; I had almost fainted. However, she was very brave during this entire period and after some months, she wanted to move back to her hometown, Puducherry. She would make the day trip to Chennai twice a week along with my father to get the dialysis done. Apart from the lack of good infrastructure in Puducherry, the other important reason to shift her dialysis to Chennai was that we had registered her for a kidney transplant there. The state of Tamil Nadu has the highest success rate for organ transplants. We were hoping to get a transplant for her at the earliest.

The world outside the dialysis room had a life of its own. While I would wait for my mother, I realised that these patients and their families were a very optimistic lot. Despite being physically weak, they would always wear a bright smile and a positive attitude. Being on regular dialysis is not easy. One needs to live with a lot of limitations when it comes to diet, medications, water and mobility. My mother is very passionate about cooking and loves to feed everyone around her. It would break my heart to see her eating bland, salt-less food day in and day out. An extra glass of water would be enough to tip the scales and make her breathless. The dietician gave us a list of what was not allowed, which seemed to be endless. I wondered if it was better to have a list of what was allowed—that probably would have been a shorter list.

Over a period of time, my father and I made a new circle of friends. The dialysis community was like an extended family to us. Sharing similar issues, coping with a loved one's illness and the endless wait for a transplant led to a different kind of fellowship. We would meet our dialysis friends much more often than our relatives. The nephrologists, the nurses, the support staff and the patients, all of us shared a certain camaraderie—the knowing looks, jokes and warm smiles because these were people who were familiar with 'the machine'. Everyone in the dialysis community had a story to tell. Some, like my mother, were rookies; others had been veterans in this place. But we all belonged. We were a part of the dialysis circle.

After a few weeks, I had to return to Mumbai. Her quality of life was not what I would consider real 'quality', but she was surrounded and taken care of by my doting father and my siblings. Despite our relentless efforts, she refused a potential live kidney transplant from any of her children, because she didn't want to risk our health. My mother is selfless. She is a pillar of strength who continuously inspires me not to complain. She was therefore registered for a cadaver kidney transplant programme.

The road to finally getting a kidney transplant done, however, was not easy. It took a lot of time and counselling by the doctors to convince my mother and my family to agree for the transplant surgery. My father and mother knew that there was no other option, but they were still very apprehensive about the surgery. We wondered if she would be able to sustain a major surgery. Her health was very delicate. I have always felt that one of the most challenging aspects of the doctor's relationship with patients and their families is to be transparent and educational about all matters related to health and wellness and yet lead them down the right path. It is important to educate patients about the risks involved without scaring them away. Yes, as patients, we get alarmed by even a risk of 1% and we can only hope that we do not fall in that unfortunate category. I always had reservations about the quality of life after the transplant, during the recovery period, the required anti-rejection drugs and their limitations. We had multiple sessions with the nephrologist and he allayed all our fears and concerns patiently. Medicine is truly an art.

Within a couple of years, she was on top of the recipient list for cadaver kidney transplant. We were mentally ready; in fact, we were looking forward to it. The first time we got a call from the hospital, I rushed to Chennai from Mumbai. At last my mother's woes were to come to an end. After due processes, we were told that the donor's kidney was not a match for my mother. Did we feel disappointed? Yes.

In the next few months, we got called to the hospital at two other instances. And each time we would drop whatever we were doing and rush to the hospital, hoping this nightmare would end soon. We hoped and prayed that the kidney would match and there would not be any last-minute surprises. One of the times, investigations revealed that my mother was harbouring some infection and hence was not fit for surgery. The next time, the donor's family decided not to go ahead with organ donation at the last minute. We had to control our distress every time and hope that the next call from the hospital would come soon. Every time I returned to Mumbai hiding my disappointment.

During this period, I was also a witness to patients who underwent a transplant only to find that their bodies had rejected the donor's kidney and they were back to square one. I also noticed a few who silently lost their lives during dialysis.

I wondered why subject the patient to the pain of surgery and drain their financial resources when the outcome of the surgery was not certain. I guess the human body is too complex. Even an automated manufacturing plant cannot guarantee a 100% defect-free output. As an expert from the automobile industry, I have witnessed numerous callbacks of vehicles for faulty parts or components that need to be replaced. Unfortunately, the stakes in the human body are much higher. We have to take our chances in the hope of a better life.

Three months later, we got another call from the hospital. We kept our fingers crossed and, this time, before I could reach Chennai, the surgery was completed. Her recovery was longer than expected, but she was relieved that she would not have to undergo any more dialysis sessions. It has been four years now and when we look back, it looks like a long and arduous journey for her and us. We were in it together and we never lost hope. In business consulting, when we advise companies, we are responsible for their financial health. Companies reach out to us to ensure that we diagnose and prescribe what needs to be done. Good consultants base their decision on quality evidence and that is where science comes in. We already know whether we can help them sail ahead or bail them out from a tough situation, or if it is too late already.

I feel doctors face similar dilemmas when they meet patients needing surgery. The intention is to make every patient's life better. Doctors often decide to do certain procedures because it's what is usually done, it is what they were taught, it sounds logical or because it fits with their own observations. At times, too much importance is given to skill sets and not enough to the decisions behind them. It is often said that any good doctor can operate, a better doctor will know when to operate and the best doctor will know when not to operate. Having said that, I do understand that when it comes to human lives, decisions cannot be taken at the push of a button. It is way more complex. Balancing the scales of emotions and evidence is a tightrope walk. I respect the medical fraternity for that.

In our case, the doctors guided us through one of the most difficult periods of our lives. The doctor-patient relationship was strengthened. Today, my mother does not trust anyone else except her nephrologist and even when she travels, she prefers to video chat with her doctor and take his advice for the smallest of concerns. Last but not least, I believe that it is faith and trust in this relationship that can help the patient to move mountains and overcome challenges.

C.B. is a management consultant. He heads the business advisory services of IPSOS, which is a multinational research and advisory firm in India. A management graduate from ESC Grenoble, he assists start-ups and entrepreneurs on their business strategy and for raising capital. He is an avid reader and a fitness enthusiast. He devotes a significant amount of his time for philanthropic activities through the Debabrata Auro Foundation.

Did You Know?

In an Indian survey conducted to assess the burnout among medical practitioners it was revealed that 45.02% (n = 217) and 65.98% (n = 318) of the participants scored high on the emotional exhaustion and depersonalisation scales respectively, 87.14% (n = 420) scored low on the personal accomplishment scale and 62.86% (n = 303) and 11.41% (n = 55) had medium and low scores on the satisfaction with the medical practice scale. This study also showed a higher prevalence of burnout among female doctors as compared to male doctors. A high burnout is seen more commonly in female doctors in India, probably because of higher expectations in the domestic settings, causing a discrepancy in their work-life balance.

Source: Langade, D., Modi, P. D., Sidhwa, Y. F., et al. (2016). 'Burnout syndrome among medical practitioners across India: a questionnaire-based survey'. Cureus, *8(9).*

Dear People,

'Being a doctor gives us the privilege to meet many different types of people, each very different from the other.'

Dr Debraj Shome and Dr Stuti Khare Shukla[1]

When Aspirations Meet Reality

It is said that beauty lies in the eyes of the beholder. Well, not always. As a surgeon practising in Mumbai, India, I come across many patients for whom glamour is not just a luxury but a source of living and, hence, a necessity.

A couple of years ago, a popular Hindi film actor walked into my cabin. He was suffering from frontal baldness (called androgenetic alopecia in medical terms). It is a genetically inherited condition and hence usual therapies like dietary supplements, oils, shampoos, hair salon products, etc., fail to work in this condition. It is one of the most common types of baldness in middle-aged men, now also afflicting younger men.

The actor was wearing a suave Armani suit and a pair of Gucci shoes but the most noticeable part of his personality was his down-to-earth attitude. He told me that he had tried every possible hair-loss therapy, including a failed hair transplant two

---

1 The cases discussed here are from Dr Debraj Shome's experience and Dr Stuti Khare Shukla has helped him narrate these.

years ago. Although he had come to me for a hair-loss treatment, I was still a little taken aback when he took off his wig to show me the patch of frontal baldness. I had seen him on screen for years and this was not the image that I was used to. I found out that he had lived with a wig for more than a decade, hiding his real self from everyone around him. Clearly, this was affecting him. I routinely come across men and women who develop severe psychological issues due to their baldness. Hair loss is a superficial problem, but its effects run deep.

The actor had lived in embarrassment and fear for a decade. During shoots, he would be concentrating on the wig than on the stunts. He was always worried, dreading the fact that one day, the wig would simply fall off and people would come to know his well-kept secret. Once, while performing a stunt, he fell and in trying to prevent the wig from falling, he ended up dislocating his shoulder. He lost that film, but more than that, it caused him immense pain and stress. One indeed does end up paying a high price for stardom.

He blushed as he started talking about an incident that occurred during a shoot in Manali several months ago. For the first time in his life, he had truly been in love. As he spoke about his feelings for the girl, I realised that there was a diehard romantic lurking underneath his tough exterior. 'After all, true love has no reasons; if it does, then it is not love,' he said. I was surprised to hear this from the man who was routinely in news for his affairs with leading actresses. Perhaps he was unlike the 'Casanova' image that the media had built for him.

The girl—a journalist who had come to interview him—had knocked on his door and he was blown away by her exquisite beauty. 'No movie star came close to her loveliness,' he said. She had doe-like beautiful black eyes and her voice was the most melodious he had ever heard. It was love at first sight.

The romance started with text messages, followed by phone calls and dinner dates. The chemistry was undeniable but there was an impediment in their fairy-tale romance. The actor was wary of being intimate with his partner. He was not able to feel fully free. It was the wig. Whenever they met, his focus would be the wig than the woman in his life. She, on the other hand, was unable to understand his predicament and started feeling a little unworthy. He felt like a failure because despite being madly in love, he was not able to express himself the way he wanted to. 'It was affecting him much more than any failed dance sequence or an action stunt in a movie,' he said.

There was only one way out. A successful hair growth treatment would help him regain his confidence and solve the problems that emerged from it. We began our treatment which is more innovative and advanced than stem-cell hair therapy, PRP and, in many cases, works better than hair-transplant surgery. We administered the QR 678™ hair growth injections on the scalp and after just four sessions, we could see the hair growing. After eight sessions, the bald patches started getting covered with hair. The results were overwhelming! When after eight months, this handsome man stopped wearing a wig, my satisfaction knew no bounds. What made me happier was his regained confidence. He became joyful and he could focus on his shoots without being bothered about the wig falling off. Of course, his relationship with his lady love improved as well.

I might have learnt and mastered the art of plastic and cosmetic surgery from some of the best teachers across the globe, but there are a few things which only life can teach.

That same day when I met Mr Actor, I also met three acid-attack survivors, one after another. What started out as an education in problems of aesthetics and looking good, started to become one of the most humbling and gut-wrenching days of my life. The three young women would have never imagined that their destinies would so cruelly intertwine and they would end up in the waiting room of my office with their faces scarred and disfigured with severe acid burns—all on the very same day.

They came from different parts of India, from different communities and different socioeconomic backgrounds. Yet their stories were strikingly similar—an obsessive stalker, unsolicited advances and constant persuasion which finally culminated in an acid attack. Why? Just because their refusal came as a blow to a man's ego and his false sense of entitlement.

Nusrat, the first survivor who met me, was a young girl from a lower middle-class Muslim family in Saharanpur, Uttar Pradesh. She had dreams and aspirations just like any other girl her age. She was a student, hoping to make a mark in her chosen field of law. Sohail, who studied in the same college, had taken an interest in her and had begun stalking her day and night. He made sure he tracked Nusrat's every movement. Nusrat had dismissed his suggestion to strike a 'friendship' several times in the past. She wanted to focus on her studies and career. She belonged to a conservative family and spending time with the opposite sex was not appreciated. However, Sohail was persistent. One day, when she was returning home from her college, he followed her and stopping her midway, tried to manhandle her. Nusrat was shocked and scared. She reflexively slapped him and ran into the safety of her home. What Nusrat didn't know was that this slap would cause her lifelong agony.

A few thousand miles away in Adilabad, Andhra Pradesh, Malthi, a spirited 22-year-old student of commerce, was only a few months away from getting married—a day she had been looking forward to ever since her engagement a year ago. However, Malthi had an ex-boyfriend who refused to leave her alone. As soon as he came to know that she was engaged to be married, he started disturbing her with constant phone calls. Malthi was his 'property' and he refused to accept that she would soon be married to someone else. He would follow her to the college and harass her continuously. She could not talk to her parents about this as they didn't know of her past relationship. One day, the boy cornered her in the middle of the road and disfigured her face by throwing acid on her.

Radhika, all of 21, was the sole breadwinner of her family. She had lost her father at the tender age of eight and as the only child, her sole mission in life was to earn enough to make ends meet and look after her mother. The two women lived all by themselves in a small apartment in Delhi. Radhika was a beautiful, intelligent girl and her father had dreamt of making her a doctor but financial burden crippled the family after he passed away. Her mother had to take up odd jobs and finally, Radhika had to drop out of school at the age of 16. She started working as a beautician at a local beauty parlour. As time passed by, Radhika became even more beautiful. Many young boys from the neighbourhood approached her and proclaimed undying love for her, but she never showed any interest. Looking after her mother was her only priority. She also hoped to own her beauty parlour one day and was working hard towards that goal. Of all the boys who pursued her, there was one particular boy who didn't want to take a no for an answer. Raju refused to believe that Radhika was just not interested. He was under the delusion that someday his persistence would win her over. As days went by and Radhika continued to display her increasing annoyance with him, he decided that she needed to be taught a lesson. He vowed that he would shatter her pride in her good looks. He achieved his goal by throwing acid on her face, permanently scarring her—physically and emotionally.

The unfortunate truth is that these are just three out of the thousands of women in India who have had their faces cruelly disfigured in an acid attack, destroying their lives and identities, just because some man could not take no for an answer.

That day when Nusrat had left college for home, she had not imagined in her wildest nightmares that a split second would turn her entire life upside down. Concentrated sulphuric acid was thrown on her face—an act of revenge meant to destroy her.

Her mother told me later that she was mortified of every man she saw and hardly spoke to anyone. Although her parents were brave and had accepted that their daughter would probably never look normal again, they were horrified by the mental trauma she was going through. One devilish act by a wicked juvenile had impacted so many hopes, endless dreams and multiple lives.

It was even more startling to hear that the mother of the perpetrator of my second patient, Malthi, was entirely unperturbed by her son's horrific actions. Not only did she wholeheartedly defend her son in the court, she questioned Malthi's character as well. She targeted her dark complexion and accused her of trying to trap her good-looking son. It was even more disheartening to hear how one woman could be so blindly judgemental about another.

After meeting these women, I was compelled to think about the bitter realities of our patriarchal mindsets. Unfortunately, it is true that some people in our society think that women are objects to be owned, that they do not have the right to make a choice or say 'no' to a man's unwelcome advances.

As a society, we aid, abet and nurture patriarchy in our boys by failing to inculcate the values of respect and wisdom for the other genders. In the land where we worship goddesses, we teach our daughters to conform to societal norms, rather than teaching our sons the meaning of consent. We hold on to stereotypes when it comes to women and cry foul if they try to break them. It is appalling to see that while sleeping pills require signed prescriptions, it is abysmally easy to procure industrial-strength acid in the market.

That day, as I saw the three young survivors together, a cruel truth dawned—that these crimes are not one-off incidents; neither are they restricted to a particular community or region of the country. They are astoundingly commonplace and could happen to anyone.

Each of these three girls had filed a police complaint but, shockingly, all the three accused men were out on bail, probably leading normal lives, while for these girls, every moment of existence was a struggle.

Disfigurement by acid is quite different from other injuries, which is why it is so commonly used in revenge crimes. The damage that acid wrecks is intense and irreversible. The acid eats away at the skin and muscle tissue and, sometimes, even seeps down to the bones. Not much can be done immediately after the attack, except for washing the area and applying emollients to soothe the skin to some extent. As most of the blood supply to the area is also damaged, there is little scope for skin grafting. In cases like these, the goal of a plastic surgeon is to try to restore as much functionality of the damaged facial features and organs as possible and make it, to put it bluntly, look 'less disfigured'. Treating an acid-burn patient evokes a rare kind of helplessness because, despite advances in medical science, there is absolutely nothing you can do to restore a face to what it was.

The physical pain of having acid melt your skin may subside with time, but the emotional and psychological trauma of losing your identity stays for life.

Several NGOs have come forward to help such victims, in terms of education, career and ensuring that they have a future. In fact, Debabrata Auro Foundation, an NGO started by Dr Aparna Bhasker and me, is involved in helping and treating acid-attack victims. In my opinion, while treatment and rehabilitation in the case of acid attacks are important but prevention is a must. We, as a society, must learn to respect women for what they really are, accept their choices and decisions, and treat them as equals.

The life of a facial plastic surgeon may look glamorous and lucrative on the outside, but it does not come without its share of heart-wrenching moments. I come across a large tapestry of patients—some who come to me to improve upon what they have and others who come to me with the hope that their shattered life will be stitched back into normalcy, or some semblance of it, with a surgery. It is the latter kind whose stories tug at the heart and sometimes bring tears in the eyes. They are the ones who can make the best of doctors feel helpless in the face of cruelty that humanity is sometimes capable of.

Having treated thousands of patients in my 14-year-long career, I humbly acknowledge that as surgeons, we are not God and that no matter how good a surgeon I am, or how hard we try, we may neither make someone look just the same as before nor make someone look the way they want to look like. I often tell patients that while medical science has made immense progress, no doctor knows everything and may certainly never know everything. We are merely scratching the surface with our knowledge of the human body. We are not God but merely an instrument of God, trying to do the best we can. However, we may try our best but not everyone can and will be cured. That is the sad reality of medical science. And no matter what one does for a living, it might never be as difficult as being responsible for the life and death of another human being, which is typically an everyday job for a surgeon.

It is this extremely varied tapestry of patients we see in a day that makes our days truly worth looking forward to—all in a day's work for a surgeon!

Based in India, Dr Debraj Shome is a surgeon, specialised in facial plastic surgery and facial cosmetic surgery. He is the co-founder and director at The Esthetic Clinics, which has multiple centres across the country. Dr Shome has received many awards from numerous agencies and is known for his breakthrough innovations in facial plastic surgery. He is the co-founder and director at The Esthetic Clinics, which has multiple centres all over India. Dr Shome has received many awards from numerous agencies and is known for his breakthrough innovations in facial plastic surgery. He has

more than 55 research papers written in top peer-reviewed international publications along with a US patent to his credit. He is the inventor of the QR 678 hair growth formulation. He was the first recipient from Asia and the youngest globally to be awarded the prestigious Davies Foundation Grant Award by the Royal College of Surgeons, Glasgow, in 2010. Besides clinical work, Dr Shome is the Director of the Debabrata Auro Foundation and dedicates a lot of time to philanthropic activities for the betterment of society.

Dr Stuti Khare Shukla is a dermatologist who has been involved in a number of campaigns against female foeticides and child abuse. She is also a fitness enthusiast and a trained Kathak dancer. Dr Stuti was a Fellow at The Esthetic Clinics, when she assisted her preceptor Dr Shome in writing this chapter.

Did You Know?

In 2016, India recorded 300 acid attacks but the actual number could exceed 1,000, according to Acid Survivors' Trust International, based in the United Kingdom, as most acid attacks go unreported. Acid is easily available in the market for Rs 16 to 25 per litre. There is no legal restriction imposed for buying or selling acid. The aim of most acid attacks reported is to disfigure, and not to kill. Until 2013, it was very difficult for the prosecution to hold or put a strong case against the accused as the Indian Penal Code did not define the term 'acid attack'. It was only in 2013 that the Supreme Court decided to add article 326A and 326 B to deal with acid attacks.

Sources: https://www.usatoday.com/story/news/world/2017/07/27/acid-attacks-women-india-survivors-fight-back/486007001/
http://jurip.org/wp-content/uploads/2018/03/Siddharth-Baskar-1.pdf

Dear People,

'Care for your fellow beings, whether they're patients, doctors or just any ordinary human beings. You never know what they may have gone through because everyone is fighting a battle that you may be unaware of.'

Dr Dheeraj V. Mulchandani

When a Doctor Becomes a Patient

I was just out of medical school from the University of Pune in India when a couple of friends and I started an internship at a nearby hospital. As interns, we were being paid a princely sum of ₹2,200 per month and would get free accommodation and food. Life was good, or so I thought. One evening in March 2002, I was completing rounds and getting ready for my night shift. I was walking along a dimly lit corridor when suddenly, I fell on the ground. I thought I had tripped but when I looked around, there was nothing on the tiled floor. I sat up in bewilderment, trying to fathom the reason for this fall. The next day, after washing up and getting ready for the regular shift, I was walking towards the hospital, which was about 900 metres away from our hostel with two friends of mine, when I fell right in the middle of the road. Again, I looked around and could not understand why I had fallen. This continued to happen at least once daily over the next few days. Once, I even fell down the stairs while carrying tea up to my hostel room.

Over the upcoming weekend towards the end of March, I took a leave of absence and returned to Mumbai to investigate the problem. I was taken to an orthopaedic surgeon who thought it was a knee problem. He examined me and suggested an MRI. It turned out to be normal. He then suggested that we should see a neurologist as well. The neurologist was a senior gentleman who did the necessary clinical examination but could not figure out any problem. We then decided to get a second opinion and got an appointment with another doctor, Dr Wadia. He too subjected me to an examination but it was different. He, unlike the others, took me into a private examination room, spoke to me like I was already a doctor (which I was, but wasn't made to feel like one at my other examinations), asked my permission to touch my muscles, requested me to disrobe, cared about my expressions and was gentle up to the hilt. In a matter of 15 minutes and in a single meeting, he had taught me the art of physical examination—something I had not learnt in five years of education.

When he was done with his examination, he advised an X-ray and MRI of the spine, as well as routine blood work and gave us a follow-up appointment for the next week. The next morning, I had just finished my shower when I fell again—this time in the bathroom. Possibly the slippery bathroom floor, I thought to myself, while trying to get up, only to realise that I couldn't. There I was, on the floor of my bathroom, naked as a newborn baby, unable to even reach my towel on the hook, crawling my way towards the door. I pulled myself up using the sink and the commode and somehow got to my knees. I grabbed my towel and crawled out towards the bed in my room. Then, I shouted for help.

My parents came running in, trying to make sense of what was happening. I was lying there on the ground alongside my bed, in my towel, dripping wet, unable to lift my legs. I was lifted up to the bed. My dad, who is a general physician, started examining me. The look in his eyes spoke volumes. Just like that, I had turned into a paraplegic (paralysed below the waist). My mother had tears in her eyes but still, she was the stronger one emotionally. I could see that. An ambulance was called, Dr Wadia was informed over the phone and all arrangements were made to admit me.

Even before I could savour the feeling of being a recent graduate of medicine and relish being a doctor, I had become a patient. A lot of people have asked me what I felt in those moments when I realised I could not walk. The answer still eludes me. I don't know what I was thinking. I am sure it wasn't about not ever being able to walk again. I remember feeling helpless because I needed people to dress me up and take me around in a chair fitted with wheels since we didn't have a wheelchair. I was taken down four floors by elevator and was out in the compound as soon as the ambulance arrived. My mom could not climb on to the high ambulance steps; my dad wasn't in a state to do so and he just kept repeating that he couldn't. I now realise that he was not in a mental state to accompany his paraplegic son. Luckily, a steadfast family friend was right there and she came with me in the ambulance.

The hospital process began which I will try and recount here as accurately as I can from the perspective of a patient. The resident medical officer came in and took a short history to make the case paper. The nurses came in to start an IV access line and take my temperature and blood pressure. All this was mechanical at best, with hardly any conversation and explanation. We were soon shifted to the scan room where the MRI scan was done and routine blood work was drawn. Somewhere in-between, I realised that I needed to use the bathroom and it dawned on me that for the first time in my adult life, I couldn't go to the washroom by myself. Slightly embarrassed, I asked for help and was made to wait for the orderly to come and assist me to the urinal. This was perhaps when it suddenly hit me—that I was now dependent on others for even my most basic needs. I was supposed to pass urine—with a sheet covering my modesty and turning to one side—into a metal container that was allegedly clean, only to try and get it out without dropping or spilling anything, to be handed over to either a stranger or my mother.

The horrific dependence continued but the cause remained undetermined. The scans showed some swelling around the spinal cord at the cervical and lumbar levels. The doctors would see me, discuss things among themselves and leave with hardly a word to me. Once in a day, Dr Wadia would come in and assure me that they were working on my case with the utmost dedication and would soon figure out what was going on. These visits usually lasted about five to seven minutes at best. I was never made a part of these discussions, either as a patient or a doctor. Perhaps, they didn't know how to explain that they had not found a reason for my illness yet.

Over the next few days, I was subjected to at least three lumbar punctures (tapping the spine for fluid) for various reasons. Almost all were inconclusive, but each and every one of them was painful. The local anaesthesia only dulls the pain; it doesn't really take it away. I was also subjected to an electromyography (EMG) and to date, I think it remains the most painful test I have ever undergone in my life.

The physiotherapist who was now treating me, was excellent at her job. She explained everything to me in detail but failed to emphasise how much it would hurt. She went on to insert long thin needles into my right leg muscles and applied a small amount of current to see the response. I was satisfied that this was going to be easy and proceeded to relax. She finished with my right leg and moved to the left. As the first needle pierced my skin, I felt excruciating pain, the likes of which I have never felt before. She was surprised but apologised and said that we had to do the other muscles of the left leg. I didn't have much of a choice so I consented. I had tears flowing out of my eyes the entire time.

We found out that I had spastic paralysis, the cause of which was still unknown. Absence of pain in the right leg was a sign that the spine was affected severely. Another MRI was performed and it was found that the swelling had somewhat increased and my lateral spinothalamic tract, which controls sharp pain and temperature sensations, was completely damaged. From that day onwards, I had no temperature or pinprick sensations below my thigh on my right side.

Sometime around the 15th day of my stay in the hospital, my bladder function started deteriorating. I was voiding small amounts frequently. More tests to check the function of the bladder in evacuating urine (voiding cystometrogram) were ordered. A catheter was inserted into my urethra, under somewhat sterile conditions, at the radiology department. It was only mildly painful and this was not because of the local anaesthetic jelly but because by now, the pain sensation had reduced right up to the groin. They pushed water in through the catheter, asked me to hold as long as I could, then void. I think I failed miserably the first time; so, we did it again. A diagnosis of neurogenic bladder was stamped on the paper. In my mind, as a patient, I just kept thinking, another notation on the chart without a real reason.

Since they couldn't determine the cause for anything, and the swelling continued to increase, I was put on steroids along with other medicines that would help me void completely. I was also made to undergo a CT scan which revealed some lymph nodes in my chest. A differential diagnosis of sarcoidosis and tuberculosis was put up. This posed a difficult dilemma for the doctors. If it was sarcoidosis, steroids needed to be continued, but if it turned out to be tuberculosis, the steroids could actually deteriorate my condition.

It was close to a month since I was in the hospital. I figured since all I had was time on my hands, I might as well try and figure out what was wrong with me. I read up the Harrison's Principles of Internal Medicine and came to the forlorn conclusion that perhaps there really wasn't a clear-cut answer after all. That was the day I realised that doctors don't always have the solutions. At the same time, I swore to myself that if I ever made it out and began practising as a doctor, I would be upfront with all the patients I have.

Since we were getting nowhere, the doctors proposed a radical option. I was to be subjected to a thoracoscopic biopsy of the lymph nodes to once and for all determine the cause of my condition—assuming the lymph nodes were related to the swelling around the spinal cord. I was wheeled into the OT and transferred to the table. The operation was delayed just a bit because the shaving orders weren't carried out. The barber was called into the OT and my chest was shaved right there. I was made to inhale that sweet gas that puts you to sleep so well. When I awoke next, I could barely breathe. I remember seeing my dad outside the OT and I kept mumbling 'It's hurting, it's hurting.'

Within the next three days, the reports came in. The lymph nodes were inflammatory in origin, with predominant lymphocytes. It definitely wasn't sarcoidosis; so, the other option was quickly accepted and I was started on antitubercular treatment. A diagnosis of myelo-arachnoiditis was finally made, although the cause could never be determined.

I was discharged the next day and luckily for me, the football world cup was on. So I had plenty of entertainment. I was instructed to take about 14 tablets a day, two injections of streptomycin and lots of physiotherapy and exercise. I followed everything dutifully. My bladder got better but my bowels were an entirely different matter. Now that I couldn't get off the bed, I needed an attendant to offer me the bedpan when required. If at all this was delayed for whatever reason, I ended up passing stools on the bed on more than one occasion. One of these embarrassing episodes happened when some of my friends had come to visit me.

Doctors worked with me daily to get me back onto my feet. Slowly, I started to kneel on my own, then stand with wall support, then use a walker to walk about the house and use the washroom. An achievement that I will never take for granted again. Then, very slowly, we moved to steps and staircases. My friends kept coming in and spending some time with me. My neighbours, who had now gotten used to seeing me walk in the passage, would always encourage me.

I spent my 22nd birthday with my friends at home watching the finals of the football world cup between Brazil and France. I was lying on the bed and my friends had a ball. I was happy. Despair never got to me in these past few months. I wouldn't let it. I truly believe that this episode helped me get stronger.

Eventually, I moved on from crutches to a walking stick. I could climb up and down a few stairs. I applied for a transfer of my internship—which I was yet to complete—to Mumbai. I was posted at GT Hospital, via the Sir JJ Group of Hospitals, as a special arrangement, since it was closest to home. I restarted my internship in August 2002 and went to work using a walking stick. It was a sight to marvel at. I was happy that my co-residents didn't just let me sit about; they asked me to do collections, paperwork and rounds just like the other interns, but they were a lot more patient with me. Finally, by June 2003, I could walk independently without the use of a cane. I completed my internship, got my MBBS degree and learnt much more in this period than through my entire five years of MBBS.

The lessons learnt stay with me even today. They have helped me deal with difficult patients much better. The Bible says, 'Physician, first heal thyself.' While most people think these words mean that the doctor must look after his/her own health, the truth could not be further from that interpretation. The proverb was intended to criticise, to advise one to focus on one's own defects rather than criticising the defects in others. My experiences taught me this in the hard way which eventually helped me become a better human being and a better doctor.

One of my patients, for example, had a long-standing history of fever lasting over a month. We just could not figure out the cause. I patiently sat him down and explained that sometimes we don't have the answers and we have to keep looking. I had to narrate my whole story to him for him to believe me. Thankfully, he got better soon but we still don't have an answer to his question. Only now, he accepts it without a doubt.

During this entire ordeal, I learnt compassion, I learnt patience, I learnt to be thankful for what we have, I learnt to listen to patients, I learnt to include them in discussions, I learnt to involve them in decision-making processes and I learnt empathy. I gained about 20 kilos because of the steroids and also learnt that appearances hardly mattered—as long as I could walk and use the washroom. I learnt how to walk again right from scratch, just the way a child does and most importantly, I learnt to love. The woman who eventually became my wife stuck by me through all of this. She stayed even when other friends stopped visiting. She kept coming home, encouraging me to step out, went for movies with a man walking with a stick, didn't care about the stares and was my reservoir of support, just like she is now. If there was anything that helped me fight more than my family's support, it was hers.

I can now run a 10-kilometre marathon, albeit a little slowly. I play cricket every Sunday. I swim, I jog, I play sports with my children. I am almost back to normal. I still don't have sensation in my right leg for temperature and pain. What I do have is a deep confidence in myself because I was pulled out of a seemingly impossible situation. Life is unexpected, so please live it to the fullest. Care for your fellow beings, whether they're patients, doctors or just any ordinary human beings. You never know what they may have gone through because everyone is fighting a battle that you may be unaware of.

Dr Dheeraj V. Mulchandani is a practising general surgeon in Mumbai. With over 15 years of experience in the healthcare field, seven of which have been in administration, Dr Mulchandani believes he has a mature and responsible approach to problem-solving. He considers careful attention to detail, effective communication and proficiency in technology as few of his best assets. He is an active blogger and has contributed to many publications and books. He has developed a love for running and does it at least three times a week.

Did You Know?

Studies have found that doctors who have assumed the patient role show more empathy and possess better communication skills. Role reversal represents the fundamental skill of connecting with others through self-awareness, self-regulation and empathy. The situation for the doctor who becomes a patient may be disconcerting, but the 'do no harm' nature of medicine and the generally accepting demeanour of patients render the relationship between empathy and role reversal especially harmonious. Although it is comfortable and convenient to stay on one side of the relationship, grasping an emotional representation of the other side is essential. We all desire to be understood, but to be understood, we must first seek to understand.

Source: https://www.mdedge.com/psychiatry/article/133387/practice-management/when-doctor-becomes-patient

Dear People,

'We, doctors, can make such a difference by just going the extra mile.'

Dr Gabriela Casabona

Love and Science Can Break Limits

Carol is an ambitious and optimistic 27-year-old woman with a beautiful bright smile. She lives with her husband and a young child and loves her career as a psychologist. A normal life like any of us, you would shrug and say. However, her life was quite different until a few years ago. On a busy Monday morning in June 2015, 25-year-old Carol came to see me at my office in Sao Paulo in Brazil. I looked at her—the right side of her face was asymmetric, distorted and severely scarred, and her right eye watered incessantly. I learnt that this was because she had undergone 18 reconstructive surgeries on her face over the past 17 years.

When Carol was just eight years old, she and her family met with a tragic car accident. The mishap not only killed her parents but left her with permanent scars that she was still battling. After years of multiple surgeries on her face, she was finally referred to me by an oculoplastic surgeon, who has known me to provide creative and non-invasive combination treatments for facial scars.

Carol's case was very challenging. The deep layer of tissue around the sides of the lower eyelid was densely stuck to the bone right below the lateral corner of the eye, where the upper and lower eyelid meet.

The malposition of this tiny but important area had led to a retraction and deformation of the whole lower eyelid. This gave her eye a pulled appearance and it was also the reason why her right eye continuously watered. What was worse was that as hard as Carol tried, the eyelid would not close completely.

Before she came to me, Carol had undergone three surgeries for this and had taken many steroid injections to fix the problem but much to her disappointment, nothing had worked. In addition to the scarring on her face, the constant watering from her eye was highly unnerving and was greatly impacting her career as a psychologist.

I studied her case for a month, using magnetic resonance imaging (MRI) pictures and other scans. My primary goal was to restore the position of the lateral canthus and also enhance skin elasticity and appearance by treating all the layers from fat to the skin itself. I decided to try a new device that could rearrange collagen fibres (the main structural protein found in skin and other connective tissues) to about 3.0–4.5 mm deep in Carol's eyelid. I planned to use this along with other devices to soften the hard and fibrotic tissue of the eyelid and smoothen the discolouration of the area.

Carol had only one request—she was petrified of more surgeries and didn't want to be sedated during the procedure. Well, I thought that was an easy request to attend to. On the day of the treatment, an extremely strong numbing cream was applied all over the right side of her face and kept for 40 minutes. As we waited, my assistant prepped for the procedure and lined up five different devices that we would use to reduce the incessant watering from her eye and to improve the appearance of the scarring.

When she saw all the preparation, Carol was very nervous and started to cry. I gently held her hand, 'I hope this is the last time,' I said to her, softly. It got us chatting about life and how the unpredictable can transform our lives to make us who we are today.

As soon as the numbness set in, we kicked off the first step of the treatment. This was the most crucial one because we were going to use a very modern microfocus ultrasound technology that heats the tissues up to 65 degrees in different depths to try to soften and regenerate the hard tissue (fibrosis) that was pulling her lower eyelid down. Carol felt a slight discomfort but 'nothing compared to so many other procedures before this,' she said, prodding me with confidence to continue.

We then had to smoothen the dark areas (hyperpigmentation) surrounding the scar and shut the big blood vessels visible through the thinned-out skin grafts she had.

It was then time to treat the scar and the retractions seen in the skin of the lateral cheek—and it wasn't going to be easy. The scars had an abnormal growth and looked very lumpy and red among some whitish areas. If one could look inside this kind of scar, one would see a lot of fibres gathering together in a very disorganised way. To try to organise the tissue to make the skin look normal, I chose to use a very well-known laser called CO2 that has the ability to coagulate tissue and, as a result, it brings new fibres, therefore, new fresh tissue, which then results in a more natural look. This laser requires eye protection; so, we needed to put a metal shield lens to protect Carol's eye (as the area was very close to the eyelid). The procedure would involve the strong smell of CO2 burning the skin and then many passes to resurface the surrounding area. Once I was done, I took the shield lens off her eyes and realised Carol was crying. Instinctively I thought, 'Was she in pain?' But no, she wasn't. She was suddenly overwhelmed by the memory of all the trauma she had been through and could not hold back her tears.

I applied a cold soothing ointment on her skin and we left her to rest for a while with some motivational music playing in the background to cheer her up.

After she got some rest, Carol was soon ready to get started with the last step, which was micro-needling. Micro-needling is a process where fine needles are used to create tiny punctures in the top layer of the skin which then trigger the body to create new collagen and elastin, thereby rejuvenating the skin.

It was while I was performing the micro-needling when I felt that my eyes were moist. Suddenly, I realised how terribly lonely this young girl must have been since her parents died in that car accident 17 years ago. She had undergone so many surgeries on her own with no one beside her. I took a deep breath and grasped the weight of the responsibility and expectation she had placed in me. At the same time, it was heartening to realise that she still had the hope to become better.

Quickly wiping my tears, I said to her, 'Carol, we both know that when we face challenges, we all have two choices: Face it and wink, or surrender. I want you to know that you are not alone anymore. I am here for you.'

After the procedures were completed and she was given all the care instructions, Carol left after giving me a warm hug.

The next morning, however, she came rushing into my office. She was terrified that she looked like a monster. Her face was swollen with crust all over and the retraction of the lower eyelid appeared worse due to the swelling of the posterior and anterior lamella under the eye (the layers of skin, fat, muscle and bone that constitute the eyelid). My staff and I calmed her down. We showed her pictures of pre-and post-blepharoplasties (plastic surgery of the eyelids) that had been performed with CO_2 laser, explaining step-by-step how her scars would heal. Soon Carol was not just calm but was smiling!

As we wanted her to heal as soon as possible, we decided to use a protocol that consists of using an old technology used by dentists for healing teeth inflammation and has been used for various other inflammatory conditions. The diode light with low energy is cold light and some spectrum of that can be used as a healing booster.

Five days post the procedure, after daily care with low energy healing lasers, Carol's face was almost completely healed. The hypertrophic scars were flattened and less red. The skin surface was smooth and the discolouration had improved significantly despite post-treatment redness in some areas. The best part was that her right eye had stopped watering. Her lower eyelid was 30% higher than when she had first come to me and it was enough to normalise the drainage of her tears so that she wouldn't have incessant watering from her eye, all day long.

It has been two years since the procedure and Carol still comes by to my office every six months. Other than a little occasional watering from her eye, her face has completely healed. She is now a confident young woman leading a normal life like she always wanted to and doing everything she loves to do, including furthering her career as a psychologist in Sao Paulo.

Whenever I think of Carol, I remember her condition (watering of the eye with severe self-esteem impact) and how impossible it seemed to help her at the beginning. I am reminded that if we deeply understand the mechanisms of what we do even if there are no precedents, we can be successful. Every time I remember what we could achieve in her case without any surgery, I am reminded of the powerful new tools in our armamentarium that are available today. And every time I think of how well she overcame it all, I am reminded of how we can make a big difference in someone's life with a meaningful conversation or, sometimes, with just a reassuring smile. As doctors, remembering this becomes even more important. It is amazing how we have the power to heal the body, and sometimes, also the soul.

How a conversation can sometimes help the healing process reminds me of another patient, Bianca—18 years old, beautiful, and with a body that would make a Victoria's Secret model envious.

Bianca used to be a very happy, athletic and outgoing teenager. By the age of 14, however, she had a bad flare of Atopic Dermatitis (a condition that makes the skin red and itchy) which was treated by a general practitioner with pulses of corticosteroids orally. One of the collateral effects of those drugs is the trigger of acute and severe stretch marks. As soon as it started to appear, she looked for treatment elsewhere but for two years no one could solve or even make it more than 20% better. She was devastated and could not answer when her friends would ask her with an amazed look: What happened to you? She was also relentlessly bullied that pushed her into attempting suicide twice. If you saw her, it looked like she had been in a fight with an animal where she had acquired these linear stretch marks, from her back all the way to her lower legs. The scars varied in length and depth but they had one thing in common—they were all blood red.

Striae is the medical term for stretch marks and these initially appear as raised, asymmetric, blood red lines called *striae rubrae*. Typically, these tend to lighten and flatten over time. Bianca was one of the most severe cases I have seen in my career as a dermatologist. For the last three years, she had undergone more than 15 different treatments at some of the best clinics in Sao Paulo but had experienced unsatisfactory results. When she came to me, I saw a beautiful but profoundly depressed girl, who was pleading for help. She seemed to have lost all hope. As a doctor, this case was a great challenge for me because, honestly, I also didn't know what treatment could help her.

Most doctors, traditionally, tend to replicate what they were taught and trained for in medical school. But when a case such as Bianca's comes to us, it sometimes prompts us to think of an unconventional approach to help our patients.

One day, not long after I had first met Bianca, I was reading a clinical paper on the complications of fillers (absorbable products that are used to restore volume or to enhance volume especially on the face). Some of them can lead to collateral effects such as inflammation, oedema and allergy, and some can leave a yellowish look if injected very superficially. I was studying about fillers to discuss on a board of adverse events when an idea struck me—why not use the adverse event of one procedure to treat another?

I called her and explained my idea to her. I would use a diluted dermal filler, which was more superficial, to improve appearance and atrophy. This is a special kind of filler because it not only can give volume but also stimulates new collagen fibres around it. As an adverse event, this dermal filler would give a yellowish look to the skin which was exactly what I was looking for: appearance improvement and effective collagen stimulation. The main frustrations of *striae* treatments are the colour and the permanent atrophy that is hard to improve. With this filler, I could use the superficial injection of the *striae* (scar-like) to replicate the adverse event of yellowish discolouration which combined with the white or red colour of the *striae rubrae* would make it look more like regular skin colour. There would also be the advantage of using something very superficial that would give the immediate correction of atrophy (depression and gap in *striae*) and help stimulate new collagen and elastin fibres around the area injected in the long term.

The treatment plan I advised for Bianca was to combine two different ways of stimulating collagen for improvement of atrophy and depression of *striae* area: the process mentioned above and micro-needling. Her first session would consist of both treatments and two more months of micro-needling alone over the course of three months would follow. During the first session, she walked into the office happy and hopeful at the possibility of getting better. Her spirit and mood were infectious, and it inspired me. She was more confident than I was that the treatment would work.

I wanted to be sure of every little detail; so I took pictures of her scars myself, not leaving it to an assistant. I lay her down and applied numbing cream to the affected areas. During the next 40 minutes, while we waited for the numbness to set in, Bianca and I talked about various things—her aspirations and dreams, her boyfriend and parents. It was interesting to get a peek into her life and understand the kind of person she was, things that impacted her and how she had chosen to deal with adversity.

Forty minutes later, as my assistant took off the gauzes with the numbing cream, Bianca joked, 'Wow! I don't look like a zombie anymore!' That made us all chuckle.

We began the procedure after cleaning the area. The injection started and as the needle pierced the skin, the liquid came out, and together we saw the immediate improvement of the colour and texture of the *striae*. I glanced at Bianca and she looked at me incredulously and smiled. After numerous injections on the buttocks, inner thighs, knees and posterior leg, I asked her to stand so I could have a look at the progress. I choked with emotion at what I saw—the colour was 40% better, and the texture or depth of the scars was 80% better in the treated areas. It was working.

The next step was aimed at improving skin thickness and boosting what had already kick-started (neocollagenesis and neo-elastogenesis). As she was being prepped for the procedure, Bianca said quietly, 'What doesn't kill you, makes you stronger.' We had never spoken about her suicide attempts, but her statement acted like a foot in the door. I wanted an opportunity to understand this girl and her fears better. 'Why did you try to kill yourself?' I asked. 'I was so lonely and felt even more so when people would look at this,' Bianca replied, pointing to the stretch marks. 'Everyone believes that I am exaggerating and always just says "It will be okay." I would feel better if people just recognise my horrible condition and stay on to help me fight it,' she said simply.

I was speechless at that moment, but I agreed with her. It may be simple to think that one can disregard what people around us believe or say, but one cannot deny the pain it causes. I looked her in the eye and said, 'We are in this together now and if it does not work, we will keep trying.'

After saying that, I went back to the task at hand. This part of the treatment was a little scary—a vibrating pen (dermapen) with a lot of needles on the tip is rubbed on the surface of the skin, causing pinpoint bleeding areas and the blood is left on the wound to work as a healer. So, we just covered the area with a sterile plastic band and left it for about four hours before showering it. That was the end of the first session of Bianca's treatment.

The next day, my assistant received a frantic call from her. She wanted to know if it was normal to feel a burning sensation all over the treated areas. 'It is absolutely normal,' we reinforced and told her again that the sensation would last for three days, and mainly when she showered. A month later, Bianca returned for her second session and bowled me over with her confidence. She undressed and pointed out to me the areas that were 100% better, the areas that were showing 60% improvement and the areas that were better by just 20%. It looked like she had created her own scoring sheet, I joked. The mood carried through the session and the procedure went off well. A month passed and it was time for Bianca's next session. But when she didn't turn up, I called her. I heard an excited voice at the other end, 'I am in Barcelona having fun at the beach but I promise I am protecting my "areas" from the sun!' She laughed. I hung up very happy that this experience had changed her way of dealing with her life.

Three days later, Bianca returned—nicely tanned on her lower legs and upper body, but completely pale in all the areas that were being treated. I was amazed by her commitment to my instructions. She underwent the last and more aggressive session of micro-needling and everything went smoothly and as per plan.

I then saw her after a month when she was waiting for me with a book in her hand. Handing it to me, she said, 'I want you to look at it. This is what this treatment has given me.' When I looked at the album, I saw dozens of pictures of the sunrise, surf trips and beach parties. I was overcome with emotions and couldn't stop the tears that rolled out of my eyes. I hugged my young patient. Her progress and thrilled face had made it all worth it. Bianca was 85% better, according to her own stringent scoring method, and was anxious to continue the treatment. She reaffirmed my belief that we, doctors, can make such a difference by just going the extra mile. She taught me that challenges are truly opportunities in disguise and also inspired me to try the treatment on other patients and, later, publish a paper about this innovative and effective combination treatment for stretch marks.

Dr Gabriela Casabona is a dermatologist practising in Brazil. She has dedicated the first 10 years of her career to mastering cosmetic rejuvenation of both face and body. She spent much of the last five years in many training programmes in the US, Latin America and Europe, furthering her expertise in skin cancer surgery, Mohs surgery and honing her reconstruction skills (especially oculoplastics). Dr Casabona is presently an international speaker for Allergan Medical, Merz Medical, and also a medical consultant and speaker for Mesoestetic Spain.

Did You Know?

Surveys tell us that patients want physicians who can skillfully diagnose and treat their sicknesses as well as communicate with them effectively. Research clearly demonstrates that effective communication is indispensable to successful diagnosis and treatment.

Source: DiMatteo, MR. (1998). 'The role of the physician in the emerging health care environment'. West J Med, *1998 May; 168(5): 328-3*

Dear People,

'The patient-doctor relationship can be hard and complicated, but when it goes well, it has its own kind of magic.'

Dr Jesse Berry

Do What You Love

I knew I wanted to be a paediatric ocular oncologist and treat retinoblastoma from the very first time I saw Sarah, who suffered from this childhood cancer.

As an intern in New York, I was young, impressionable and wide-eyed as I sat next to the senior physician on the ocular oncology service. I watched Sarah play—she was a gorgeous two-year-old, the rare toddler who passes right through being cute to being truly beautiful. She had long blond hair that ended with bouncy round curls and the most beautiful blue eyes I had ever seen.

I listened as the senior physician explained to Sarah's father that she had retinoblastoma, a cancer growing on the inside of the eye. Left untreated, it would escape the confines of the eye and kill his child. As he said this, I realised that one of her eyes was just a bit too sparkly. As Sarah played with her building blocks, it became apparent that the light reflex in one eye was somewhat off. It was whitish-yellow and almost glowed as she bobbed her curly head around. The senior physician explained that the cancer was too advanced to try to salvage the eye—the vision and all the ocular structures had been destroyed already. In order to save her life, it would be essential to remove the eye through a surgery called enucleation. On hearing this, the father turned pale and trembled just a little. He looked as if the senior physician had, instead of speaking to him calmly, slapped him straight across the face. Quite clearly, it was the most heart-wrenching moment of his life but he took a deep breath and agreed to the physician's advice. That day, with a heavy heart, he took Sarah home to prepare her for surgery.

The next morning, dressed in blue scrubs, we waited at the entrance of the main operating room. The father lovingly carried his perfect daughter—already in her surgical gown—in his arms, squeezing her closer with each step. And then, with a steely resolution, he handed her over to the physician. Of course, he knew she would come back cured of the cancer that was destroying her eye and risking her life. However, there's no denying the pain he must have felt as a parent, knowing she would come back, with one less big blue eye. I was rapt, of course, with fascination for the kind of cancer that hides in sparkly eyes and presents only by peeking through pupils and causing a certain glow. What also really moved me was that in such a short span of time, the senior physician had gained absolute trust and understanding from her father.

How did he inspire such confidence in Sarah's father? How did he quickly and quietly—but so strongly and soundly—build such a beautiful patient-doctor relationship? How did he convince the father to hand his daughter over to a near-stranger to perform a major surgery? I always knew that this special relationship, created by an intersection of the skills of a doctor with the life of a sick patient, was a critical reason I had chosen to pursue medicine. That day, Sarah was cured of cancer, and I found my life's passion.

Sometimes though, the disease may not follow a textbook course and despite our best efforts, curing every child may not be possible. That's when you find yourself at real odds with your passion, your training, your white coat and even your humanity.

This brings me to the story of Joseph. A story I will carry with me in my heart for my entire life.

Joseph was a rambunctious two-year-old toddler who was brought to the emergency room by his mother. She thought something was wrong with his head since he wasn't as playful as he used to be and had lately started walking into walls. He was scanned in the emergency room and while his brain was perfectly fine, both eyes were filled to the brim with cancerous masses. On the same day, he was seen by the ocular oncology service and found to have extremely advanced retinoblastoma in both eyes. The tumours pushed up against the lenses of both the eyes and none of the normal structures in the back of the eye were visible—no retina, no optic nerve, nothing; it was all consumed by the tumour.

Joseph was started on a three-drug chemotherapy regimen within 24-hours of walking into the emergency room. Normally, in response to the chemotherapy, tumours are seen to shrink at each subsequent visit. Joseph's tumours, however, did not budge and showed no response to chemotherapy. In fact, after the fourth cycle of chemotherapy, the tumour actually started increasing in size in one of the eyes. To prevent the disease from spreading, that eye had to be removed and a slew of new treatments was started for the remaining eye. Over the next few months, Joseph underwent treatment after treatment, finally, culminating in an external beam radiation therapy.

However, within a month, the tumour started to grow again. Whatever set of mutations were in this tumour were absolutely unstoppable: every conceivable therapy known to treat retinoblastoma was thrown at the remaining eye and the tumour just laughed at us. Maybe, it even snarled.

Walking into the room to tell Joseph's parents that his second eye had to be removed, is something I will never forget. Clearly, with all that tumour in his eye, he saw very little, but he had stopped walking into walls and I remember watching him reach for a large red truck after the radiation therapy. As I went to open the door, I felt a wave of nausea bubble up and tears come to my eyes. Joseph wasn't my own child, of course, but he was my patient. I had fought for him. I had used everything inside me, my entire well-honed skill set, to save his eyes. However, it was time to accept that his disease was stronger than the best therapies available. I let go, pulled my shoulders back, put the white coat on, and opened the door donning the mask of the strong doctor his parents expected to see.

There was complete silence in the operating room during Joseph's surgery; not a single word was spoken from the beginning to the end. Afterwards, I squeezed his parents' hands and said at least this would be his last eye surgery. No more trauma from all the treatments, the examinations under anaesthesia and the visits to the hospital. They took their blind son home that night. And I took my white coat home, took it off and cried.

You can't save them all, every doctor knows this, but it still hurts.

Sometimes, the hardest lesson to learn is when to stop the fight. We must be brave, try new things and fight harder, but it is the utmost challenge for the doctor to know when to stop the fight so that continued therapy does not harm the patient. It is up to the doctor to weigh the odds, to know the risks and the benefits and to know when to call off the fight. But no matter how much experience doctors acquire, it remains the most difficult aspect of our job.

This is best exemplified by another patient of mine called John. Like about 10% of patients with retinoblastoma, John came from a family of retinoblastoma survivors.

His grandfather had been treated with bilateral radiation and his father was treated in the early days of chemotherapy and met with good success in one eye but the other eye had required enucleation (surgical removal) in order to cure him of cancer. A little rebellious against his disease, John's father smoked, scoffed at sunscreen and absolutely refused prenatal genetic screening for his child. So, John, given his inherited genetic risk for developing retinoblastoma was screened for the first time when he was three days old. Initially, he had two small tumours in one eye. We still tested his blood, but given that he had developed tumours, we already knew he carried the same mutation as his father and his grandfather had before him.

Luckily, the tumours were small enough and could be treated with laser. However, with time, more tumours formed and involved both the eyes. Chemotherapy was initiated and John responded beautifully, needing just a few sessions of laser after chemotherapy to stabilise the tumours.

Over the next year, John was watched carefully, with multiple examinations under anaesthesia. He did well and did not develop any new tumours nor did the old ones recur. For almost a year, John was stable. But cancer is sneaky; it can nap for months and then wake up with a roar. One day, John came for an examination and there was a massive tumour recurrence in one eye. It was so significant that past photos were searched for any sign of this lurking threat but nothing was found. The cancer seemingly slept soundly and then leapt without warning into a full-blown growth.

We had reached a common crossroads in the care of patients with retinoblastoma: Do we stop fighting to avoid putting the child through more treatment and perform surgery to remove the eye? Or do we fight more, fight harder, use new tools and do whatever it takes to save the eye, all the while knowing there is an active cancer residing there, which, at any minute, could spread to the orbit (the area around the eye), the brain or throughout the body?

We decided to fight. He had already been through a lot, but he had responded well each time, so it seemed reasonable to try again. John's father, with one of his eyes lost to retinoblastoma, was not ready to accept the same fate for his son. We tried a localised method of giving chemotherapy directly to the eye, but to no avail—the tumour only grew larger. And then one day, it suddenly appeared to have turned a corner and started responding to laser therapy. So, we lasered more and harder to kill this tumour, striving to overtake an eye that we were fighting to save. To my complete joy, it worked!

The tumour shrunk with every laser session until it became a tiny fibrotic scar with no sign whatsoever of a lurking, active cancer. I was certain that we had won against the retinoblastoma. I felt sure since we had used our best tools and well-honed treatment protocols and saved his eye. Alas, we celebrated a little too soon.

One day, John's dad noticed that John was not moving his eye very well. He came to us and we scanned him immediately and there it was—a large tumour lurking in the orbit.

It was biopsied and, of course, there were no surprises—it was undoubtedly a retinoblastoma. And so, the fight continued. John went through more cycles of chemotherapy, spanning another six months of his life, and then radiation therapy spanning nearly the rest of that year. He responded well to the treatment and currently, he is all right. There is no evidence of cancer lurking in his body on clinical or imaging evaluations—but we will all hold our breath for a while longer knowing that it can rear its ugly head at any moment.

As one of his many caregivers, I still struggle with his fight. Did his cancer recur because he has a genetic mutation in all the cells of his body that predispose him to retinoblastoma, osteosarcoma and many other cancers? Or did the cancer recur because we tried too hard to win another battle in what is a very long war? No one, including me, will ever know for sure. But John taught me that sometimes there is a benefit to calling off more fights, even if at that moment it may feel like you are waiving a white flag against this foe named retinoblastoma.

Thankfully, for every patient you carry in your heart out of pain, there are a few more you carry there out of joy. This is critical for the survival of both the profession of medicine and for the patients who need our care.

One such patient who brought a lot of joy to me was a young boy called Sampson. Like Joseph, Sampson was a playful, happy baby boy who presented such an advanced cancer that the chance of saving either one of his eyes was always very low. Even at the outset, it was a gamble to treat him. His parents were resolute in the conviction that an alive but blind Sampson would always be preferable to losing their son. Having done their research, they suggested bilateral enucleation to us if that is what was needed to cure him of retinoblastoma. We proceeded with treatment cautiously, and at every step, he did well. After every chemotherapy session the tumours responded and with every laser treatment, they shrunk further. His retinoblastoma had read the textbook. When Sampson was pronounced cured, there was general cheering from the nurses, staff, anaesthesiologists and, of course, the oncology team who had cared for him for several years and watched him grow from a baby to a young boy in spite of his disease.

His parents told me that each night he says his prayers for his mom, his dad and his grandparents and then adds: 'May God bless Dr Berry too.' My heart bursts with joy every time I remember that.

And then there are the birthday parties.

I didn't realise that for parents of a child with cancer or any serious illness, birthdays have a whole different kind of meaning. It is not as much a celebration of birth, as much as it is a celebration of survival.

Violet, a sweet girl with strawberry blonde hair, taught me that. Violet was born premature and spent the first few months of her life being poked and prodded by doctors (as was necessary to save her life, but no less stressful for her parents). And given how small and young she was, she required frequent eye exams to monitor for normal retinal development. But the doctors found something odd in Violet's eye. First, it was called a haemorrhage, then a scar from a typical retinopathy of prematurity—a common disease of among premature infants—then a type of macular dystrophy called Best's disease. Finally, the doctors decided none of this was correct and much to their chagrin, it was found out that Violet was suffering from retinoblastoma. You can imagine her parents' exasperation. After enduring months of tests and treatments, their daughter was almost healthy enough to go home, except for this ever-changing diagnosis that labelled her as a cancer patient at such a tender age.

I was, admittedly, equally sceptical about the diagnosis as I walked in to examine Violet. Just a glimpse into her eye was enough to make it clear to me that Violet did indeed have retinoblastoma. Luckily, I was able to gain the trust of her parents, who had been given so many wrong answers. This tumour had been diagnosed early and along with this, a small tumour in the other eye was also treated. Overall, she did very well with good vision in one eye. Although, it has not been without the typical ups and downs that come with the management of cancer, particularly managing cancer in children. So, when Violet turned three, I was surprised to receive an invitation to her birthday party. The invitation was pink (obviously!) and princess-themed (again, obviously!) and it seemed like a huge birthday party for a three-year-old.

On the back of the invite her mother had written: 'Dr Berry, thank you for giving me the gift of Violet's birthdays.' Yet again, tears flowed from my eyes. This is what I love about this field, what I feel so passionately about—the ability to give these children the opportunity to have themed birthday parties, year after year!

The patient-doctor relationship can be hard and complicated, but when it goes well, it has its own kind of magic. Unfortunately, there is no magical formula that I can share with you to make it happen more easily. On some days it seems effortless, while on other days, building trust can seem to be the most arduous task on this earth. This is heightened even more in paediatrics, when the primary relationship is to be formed with the parents of a sick child, as much as with the child herself. I still haven't entirely figured out how that senior physician did his little bit of magic, which inspired me so much. As for me, I do believe that parents can feel my passion for caring for children with retinoblastoma. Like so many surgeons and doctors, my love for it is palpable and it wraps around us both, enveloping us in a special sphere of trust wherein I say: I will take care of your child as if she were my own.

Dr Jesse Berry is the Associate Director of Ocular Oncology at the USC Roski Eye Institute and Children's Hospital, Los Angeles. She is the founder of WOO, Women in Ocular Oncology, and the meeting host for the 2019 International Society of Ocular Oncology. Her clinical expertise includes retinoblastoma, melanoma, anterior segment, other intraocular and external tumours. Dr Berry enjoys travel, exploring cuisine, yoga, fashion blogging and exploring the greater Los Angeles area.

Did You Know?

In a study, it was found that doctors experiencing grief in a medical context is considered shameful, unprofessional and a sign of weakness. Most doctors hide these feelings from others. The study reported that oncologists struggled to manage their feelings of grief with the detachment they felt was necessary to do for their job. More than half of the participants reported feelings of failure, self-doubt, sadness and powerlessness as part of their grief experience and a third talked about feelings of guilt, loss of sleep and crying.

Source: Granek, L., Tozer R., Mazzotta P., et al. (June 2012). 'Nature and impact of grief over patient loss on oncologists' personal and professional lives.' Arch Intern Med, *172(12): 964-966.*

Dear People,

'Medicine is a noble profession but it is still a profession and doctors, like the others in society, need to be remunerated fairly for their talent.'

Dr Kamal Mahawar

Each One of These Grey Hairs Has a Story to Tell

'Did the registrar think much of Mrs Das (name changed)?' I asked the nurse in the emergency surgical assessment unit somewhat flippantly. I was only a senior house officer (fairly junior in the hierarchy of surgery) but a little too sure of my diagnosis. I was confident that the patient had biliary colic (stomach pain that you get from gallstones) and it was only a matter of time before an ultrasound would confirm this. In the meantime, she just needed some pain relief medication. In my mind, no other differential diagnosis was possible.

'Did she not have free air under the diaphragm?' the nurse responded, 'She was just wheeled into the OT.'

I had a sinking feeling as it dawned on me that I had forgotten a very basic tenet of general surgery—one must perform a chest X-ray to rule out perforation of a peptic ulcer in every patient who has upper abdominal pain.

A more diligent doctor in the hospital's accident and emergency division had, in fact, requested it. But in my imprudence and arrogance, I had ignored another basic rule—I had failed to even check the X-ray. If not for that registrar, the diagnosis would certainly have been delayed, worsening the lady's outcome. A perforation can make a patient sick very quickly and a significant number of patients die from the sepsis (progressive severe infection) that can set in due to delays in diagnosis and treatment.

I went to the OT. The registrar and the consultant surgeon were performing the surgery. It was like any other day in the OT—the same passing of instruments, two nurses talking to each other in a somewhat hushed tone in a corner and anaesthetists concentrating on their monitors. The consultant acknowledged my presence and asked me to scrub in. The surgery was successful and the lady was discharged to go home a few days later. I must have treated countless patients with the same illness in my surgical career but I have not been able to erase this grave error on my part from my memory.

One hopes that instances of personal failings will reduce as the years go by, and they do. However, things do go wrong from time to time and as a surgeon, it is difficult to not blame yourself when that happens. You tend to forget the achievements as you walk through the corridors of the hospital, making a number of split-second decisions on a daily basis, but tend to always remember the things that didn't go right. Irrespective of whether you are at fault or not, you mentally relive those cases again and again. I constantly ask myself: 'Could I have done that better? Why did it happen? How will I prevent it from happening again?' I have learnt that sharing instances of my own personal failures is often the best way to teach juniors. I know of some very generous colleagues who would even falsely admit to mistakes committed by others to make them appear human. I don't need to do that; I have enough of my own.

The problem is that medicine is not an absolute science and many a times there are no clear answers. You read scientific literature to see if others have encountered the same problem. You speak to senior or junior colleagues hoping to get an explanation. And if no one else in the world has encountered it, you publish it in peer-reviewed scientific journals so that others might learn from your experiences. As a result of this churning, you gradually become a better doctor. But another day comes and you learn an entirely new lesson. 'Each one of these grey hairs has a story to tell,' I would often fondly tell my juniors.

I am not sure how many patients know that each year, millions of medical articles are published by hundreds of thousands of doctors from around the world. We do it in our free time—in the evenings and over the weekends. When others are spending time with their families, many doctors are thinking about how they can deliver better care for their patients. One sees the time we spend in hospitals and clinics, but a typical doctor also needs to spend hundreds, if not thousands, of hours every year to simply keep abreast with all the latest developments and new literature. Those who take slightly more interest in academics and research end up getting consumed by it. There is little else left in their life. In return, one may be invited to deliver a lecture at a conference but more often, you get nothing in return, except the satisfaction of making things better than you found them.

Medicine is a noble profession but it is still a profession and doctors, like others in society, need to be remunerated fairly for their talent, the long, arduous education and training, and the unpredictable and erratic working hours. However, in India, there is non-existent infrastructure and few jobs reward doctors adequately for their effort. There's an added expectation of working in rural facilities for meagre wages where basic equipment, medicines and support from other healthcare professionals are lacking. Unsurprisingly, many Indian doctors either migrate abroad or resort to whatever it takes to establish themselves. As a result, numerous questionable practices have crept into the medical profession and dented the doctor-patient relationship.

If you think about it, the exchange between a doctor and a patient is remarkably simple. Patients must have faith in us; of course, remunerate us and we, on the other hand, should deliver professional care with empathy.

Every seriously ill patient is an emotional and a professional challenge for doctors. And sometimes, despite our best efforts, the disease gets the better of us. However, the failures don't leave us. Like a detective, you try to play the scene again and again in your head, trying to find an explanation. You try to think scientifically and objectively, detaching yourself from the patient, but then at the end of the day, you are only human.

'She is younger than me and has two kids,' you think. 'Doctor, I will not die, will I?' The weight of these expectations echoes in a doctor's mind all the time.

Even now, some two decades after I began my surgical career, every single surgical complication keeps me awake for nights, therefore, affecting my whole family. 'Complication management surgery has to be got right'—one of my teachers used to say and I now regularly impress that upon my juniors, 'This is the patient's last chance. Good surgeons not only have a low complication rate but they also manage complications well.' I make sure my patients know that I care and when I take their consent for surgery, I tell them, 'Approximately 1% of my patients with this operation will develop a complication serious enough to need a re-operation, but that is when you and I will be tested. In such an eventuality, I would need you to maintain trust in me and if God is kind, I'll get you out of there.'

One day, I received a large envelope with some money in it and a note that I could donate it to any charity of my choice. A 70-year-old patient, who had already thanked me with a box of chocolates and card, had sent it. You would think that I must have done something really good for her. Why else would she be so happy with me? In fact, when I operated her for the first time, it hadn't gone very well and to solve the complication, I had to perform a re-surgery.

The ensuing complication was followed by several long meetings and discussions in the presence of the patient's children (and grandchildren). I explained, in great detail, what had gone wrong and what I would be doing to correct it. The danger was much more and we were fighting for her survival. Therefore, my patient and her family needed to know precisely what had happened and what I was going to do to set it right. They also had a right to know my usual results in a similar scenario so that they could still have confidence in my care. She kept her faith in me, I tried to maintain my professionalism and the end result was satisfactory.

That day, I received one more thank-you card. 'I nearly ruined your statistics,' it said. Another patient had sent it and it immediately transported me to the night when I had treated her. It was Saturday and she was the first patient on my list that day. After finishing all my surgeries, I went to the ward for my customary evening ward round. These rounds rarely took more than a few minutes as, by and large, patients were fine at this stage and too drowsy to talk. However, things were not as smooth that day.

'Dr Mahawar, you should go home,' the patient had remarked as it was getting close to 9 pm. I had already told my family to leave for a planned get-together without me.

'I will be late, very late,' I had told my wife over the phone. After 15 years of marriage, a surgeon's wife gets used to these one-liners. It usually means I am not in control anymore and circumstances will decide when I'll get home.

'Come straight to the restaurant, if you can,' my wife had said.

'Did you hear me?' my patient asked again, having failed to obtain any response to her suggestion that I should go home.

'Yes, sorry. I would rather be in the hospital today. In case you decide to ruin my statistics.'

I was somewhat jokingly referring to my complication and re-operation rate which are the numbers on which a surgeon's performance is measured. Although every month I examined my practice and complication rates, I wasn't going to do it that night. In fact, something about the patient told me that things were not right. My priority at that point was to understand what was happening to her. She looked pale and was bleeding.

My experience had taught me that many of these patients only have transient post-operative bleeding that would usually settle without any need for further operation. I also knew that she would be best managed if I stayed in the hospital to supervise the efforts of juniors and nurses. Eventually, the scan showed that she only had bleeding in the abdominal wall from one of the port sites. We managed to treat her without any further operation and she went home absolutely fine. And I went straight to the restaurant that night. I made it in time for some laughter and delicious Indo-Chinese food.

In my numerous years of service, I have missed numerous family dinners to face adversity, death and dying. I have missed the personal time required for recuperation for more suffering and sorrow. From my college days, I recall the fatigue and frustration of being a doctor, but never for once have I doubted my purpose or my calling as a doctor. At times, it's difficult to be a doctor but then good relationships with my patients nourish me and remind me that I am, first and foremost, a healer who people come to when they can't go to anyone else.

Dr Kamal Mahawar works as a consultant general and bariatric surgeon at Sunderland Royal Hospital in the north east of England. He takes a significant interest in

the research of bariatric surgery and regularly writes on related topics. He has co-authored over 100 peer-reviewed articles and multiple book chapters. His book **The Ethical Doctor** ***was published by HarperCollins in 2016.***

Did You Know?

The primary pressures on physicians' lives include the emotional toll of constantly working with sickness and death, the responsibility for decisions that can cause pain and suffering, and the high expectations of demanding patients in an era where medical knowledge is far from unlimited. Spouses and children of doctors have always been envied for their high status, their high income and their high-achieving style of life. However, according to researchers, life in the medical family isn't always a permanent vacation. These investigators have found that the stress in doctors' lives can be damaging not only to their children and their marital partners but also may affect everyone else in the quality of patient care and the level of medical costs.

Source. McCue, J.D. (February 1982). 'The effects of stress on physicians and their medical practice'. N Engl J Med, *306(8): 458–463.*

Dear People,

'The best medical treatment in the absence of faith between the patient and the doctor can fail to produce the desired objectives'.

Dr Lalit Kapoor

Brave Patients and Rogue Patients

A 30-year-old real estate agent was travelling in a Mumbai local train when he slipped and fell between the edge of the railway platform and the train. He came under the train and both his legs were crushed completely. To save his life, we had to carry out above-knee amputations on both legs. It was a great misery but to this day, when I think about that man, I vividly remember what he said when I informed him that he had lost both his legs.

'It is my karma,' he said, 'And I must come to terms with my destiny as early as possible.' His instant acceptance of the inevitable was unbelievable. He said nothing was to be gained from shedding tears over what was irreversible and it would be far more productive to think about what had to be done. 'The earlier we thought about it,' he said, 'the better'.

I had read the British writer Somerset Maugham, who was also a medical practitioner, on why he thought doctors ought to be good writers. Doctors see patients when the mask of pretence slips off. They get to see the real person, his/her pain, suffering and fears. As doctors we are exposed to unedited human behaviour, and this affords observant and humane doctors an opportunity to chronicle fascinating stories of not only love, courage, faith, fortitude and determination, but also those of connivance, ungratefulness, greed and viciousness.

In the case of this patient, I saw those words play out. Here was a young man who had lost both his legs in a railway accident and within a few hours of coming out of surgery, he had not only accepted the inevitability of his fate but was ready with questions about his future: When will I be discharged from the hospital? How soon can artificial limbs be fitted on me? Which is the best artificial limb centre in the country? How soon will I be able to get back to work?

When I saw him the next morning, he told me he had already made some enquiries and gathered some valuable information: (a) Being an amputee, he would now come under the disabled category and would be entitled to some special benefits from the government, including special loans, tax concessions and so on. (b) He would be able to import a specially designed car which can be driven by amputees and he would be able to do so without having to pay import duty. (c) He had found out that the army artificial limb centre in Pune was the best in the country and he planned to go there as soon as possible.

He had initially planned to develop a plot of land and now, seeing no reason for delay, he decided to pursue it as soon as he recovered. The more I listened to him, the more I marvelled at how easy he made it sound. As if losing both his lower limbs was a trivial issue and not significant enough to come in the way of his future plans. Who would say that it was only the second day after the catastrophe had struck?

I had never come across anyone with such fortitude and strength of character and his determination and tenacity left me speechless. It was a humbling experience and a revelation that acts of heroism were not limited to the battlefront.

Since then, I have realised that a lot of humbling lessons in life are learnt at the bedside of patients. In *Harrison's Principles of Internal Medicine*, I had read that the true physician has a Shakespearean breadth of interest in the wise and foolish, the proud and humble, the stoic hero and a whining rogue. He cares for all patients. In a practice spanning nearly half a century, I too, have had my share of opportunities to peep into the complex recesses of the human mind and have come across many memorable patients.

However, sometimes, I also come across patients, who I take the liberty to place in the 'rogue' category; Mr Anil Srivastava (name changed) was one of them.

The 67-year-old man brought his 85-year-old mother to the hospital with a complaint of mild slurring of speech and some degree of disorientation. She was admitted to the ICU, necessary investigations were ordered, and treatment was commenced. He declined to consent to a CT scan of the brain, citing that his mother was too old for such expensive investigations. He also refused a specialist consultation by a neurologist and almost forced the general physician to treat a neurology patient. The treating doctors had no option but to record the lack of consent in the case file and continue the treatment to the best of their abilities under the above constraints. On the third day, the patient's condition started worsening and she lapsed into unconsciousness. Srivastava then asked for a CT scan and demanded that a neuro-physician examine his mother. Unfortunately, she was deteriorating rapidly and was not in a state where she could be taken for a CT scan. She passed away before the neurologist could arrive at the hospital.

After a few days, Srivastava asked for an appointment with the team of doctors to question them regarding the cause of his mother's death. He kept coming to the hospital and insisted on cross-examining the doctors each time. The team of doctors was extremely patient with him and answered all his queries. Slowly but surely, his nefarious plans started surfacing. He claimed that his mother had died due to the negligence of the doctors. He also alleged that the doctors had erred in not doing a CT scan of the brain and had not even bothered to refer the patient to a neuro-physician. On being reminded that it was he who had refused consent to call a neurologist and perform a CT scan, he flatly denied it. We were appalled when he said that the entry of denied consent in the case papers was a fabrication. If that wasn't bad enough, he went so far as to accuse the doctors of having killed his mother.

Later, he filed a police complaint against the doctors for criminal negligence. He wrote multiple letters to the health minister, the chief minister and the prime minister, alleging gross medical negligence leading to the death of his mother. He demanded that the doctors be jailed and he be granted a compensation of Rs 20 lakh for the loss of his dear mother. He also complained to the Maharashtra Medical Council and demanded disciplinary action against the doctors. In addition to all of the above, he filed a case in the consumer forum as well.

During the course of events, one junior doctor had become friendly with Srivastava, and when asked why he was hounding the doctors, the man confided that he wanted to build a temple in the memory of his mother and that he was hoping to conclude with an out-of-court cash settlement to withdraw all the cases.

Srivastava did not succeed in his plans and all complaints were later dismissed. However, he managed to cause immense mental trauma and harassment to the doctors. We also lost both time and money expended on the case.

Such patients cause incalculable harm, not only to the concerned doctors but to the entire healthcare system, which, in turn sadly, impacts the patients themselves. These incidents, in fact, have formed the genesis of the system of defensive medical practice—as a result of which millions are wasted in doing unnecessary investigations as a precautionary measure to preempt any future litigation. In fact, many doctors, especially those who have had a similar experience, view every patient as a potential plaintiff and prefer to indulge in defensive practice to play safe.

Both the real-estate agent and Srivastava exhibited contrasting behaviour which impacted the resulting doctor-patient relationship. It taught us that odd or disreputable members exist everywhere. That, in no way, means that the whole community—of doctors or patients—is disreputable. It also led us to explore what has now become a belief: there is a compelling need to bring together the various facets of human behaviour pertaining to the practice of medicine. This finding must be used to underline the importance of a sound doctor-patient relationship and how it can speed up care.

One must remember that doctors, too, want patients to recover and recovery is difficult if the treatment is approached with suspicion and distrust. The doctor-patient relationship today, therefore, needs faith from both the doctor's and the patient's side. Faith is an important ingredient in the process of healing. So much so that the best medical treatment in the absence of faith between the patient and the doctor can fail to produce the desired objectives.

Dr Lalit Kapoor is a practising general and GI surgeon for more than 40 years. A gold medallist in surgery, he is the Medical Director of Shakuntala Memorial Hospital, Mumbai and chief surgeon at Suchak Hospital, Mumbai. He is the founding member and past president of the Association of Medical Consultants, Mumbai. Dr Kapoor is a proponent of practising medicine ethically and upholding

the highest traditions of the profession. He is an author of the widely acclaimed book, Better Safe than Sorry—Medico-Legal Do's and Dont's. *He has also held editorial positions for various publications of AMC and IMA.*

Did You Know?

While absolving a doctor from Maharashtra of the charge of medical negligence after 20 years of an incident in which a road accident victim succumbed to injuries at a hospital, the apex court held that 'it is not possible for any doctor to assure or guarantee that the result of treatment would invariably be positive and the only assurance which a professional can give is that he is professionally competent, has requisite skill and has undertaken the task entrusted to him with reasonable care'.

Source: https://indianexpress.com/article/india/supreme-court-absolves-doctor-of-medical-negliegence-charge-after-20-years-4606044/

Dear People,

'As your generation continues to build machines based on intelligence, remember that as human beings, we are built on emotions.'

Dr Marcus Ranney

The Future of Doctor-Patient Relationship

Health Story 2033

The telepod opened on the 18th floor. I stepped out into the freshly cleaned, sparkling white hallway, the walls of which reflected the sunlight streaming in through the floor-to-ceiling glass windows. I looked at the London skyline. It was a sight which never ceased to amaze me—no matter how many years I have been greeted with this morning view.

I walked down the hallway towards the operating theatre block. Casper, my digibot, hovered over and greeted me. A bald football-sized metallic sphere hovering four feet above the ground, Casper's smooth aerial movements were accompanied by a low-pitched humming of its internal motors and processor.

'Good morning Doc,' the female programmed voice said.

I just had the personality module upgraded to make it more affable. The last one sounded like the gruff voice of the terminator, which was a wee bit off-putting when it would interact with my patients.

'It's a lovely morning indeed, Casper. How's my day looking?' I asked.

As Casper ran through my schedule and updated me on my shift, I decided to take a detour and pop in and say hello to my friend James. He was visiting our hospital from New York to work on a complex case and I hadn't seen him since we were young doctors, still wet behind the ears.

'Good morning James! How are you, old fellow?'

'Dr Ranney—ding dong,' he responded with an old joke of ours from our younger days. He said this whenever he saw something or someone he liked.

I shook his hand and we walked over to his counsel where his cobot had already begun its work. He was in town to perform a rather complicated pancreatic resection on a patient of ours and rather than do it remotely from New York, 3,500 miles away, had decided it would be best to be in the same building as the patient.

'Wow,' I said. 'Pretty neat-looking cobot you got here! It looks like the new Raphael 3000.'

Indeed, it was. The term 'cobot' was shorthand for 'collaborative robot' and came into our parlance a few years ago. First used on the automated assembly lines of car-manufacturing plants around the year 2020, the idea was to have robots work closely and in tandem with human beings, rather than replace them. There was a political motive behind developing these types of robots that particularly needed human collaboration: society had increasingly become fearful of unemployment and redundancy with technological advancements. Nevertheless, these machines were particularly useful for complicated tasks, surgery being one of them.

'It's great!' James said. 'The software allows me to programme my entire surgical plan beforehand, even taking into account unforeseen errors and likely complications. I can then run the plan through the M&M (morbidity and mortality) algorithm, and it throws up sections of the procedure which I need to pay close attention to. Everything else is on autopilot and I don't even need to be in the room for it. Frees me up to have coffee with an old friend.'

We spent the next 15 to 20 minutes catching up on old times and as we did so, I could see Casper's monitor from the corner of my eye. The screen mounted on her front started to change colour as an indication that I was running late from my programmed schedule. It's okay, I thought to myself. After all, it was many years since I'd seen James and I don't know when I may have the chance next.

'Doc, may I suggest we make our way to the consulting deck?' Casper said, in the most restrained voice I've ever heard from her. The upgrade clearly did more than just change the voice modulation. It appeared to have upgraded the personality too. I realised that time was moving faster than expected, so I warmly hugged Jim goodbye and promised to meet again soon. I was sure I saw Casper smile when I finally said goodbye.

'What's the plan Casp?' I asked my assistant, seeing if she would respond to a slang greeting.

She didn't. So, I asked again, using the full name.

'Your avatar has started consulting already, Doc. You have 14 patients to see today, only two of which need your personal attention.'

Three years ago, in the year 2030, technology reached the point of Singularity (the S point). You may remember this was a cause of great concern for academics and entrepreneurs in the early part of the 21st century, as they feared that machines would take over the Earth. Thankfully, this did not happen. The Singularity was the moment when computers became smarter, or rather more intelligent, than human beings. Artificial Intelligence, or AI, has always been feared as people assumed that at some point, consciousness would enter its ability. Thankfully, this did not happen. Turns out, we still haven't been able to crack the hard problem of consciousness and even in 2033, it looks like a very far-fetched idea.

The advantage of surpassing the S point was that computers could self-generate their own algorithms on a scale which humans could not even begin to comprehend. As these machines grew smarter, one beneficial effect was their ability to mathematically measure our personalities and reduce all our decision-making abilities to a complex set of algorithms based on our neurochemical pathways (which acted as a surrogate marker of our behaviour). These personality 'drives' could then act as digital avatars of our real selves and perform lower functional tasks that we weren't interested in or didn't have the time for.

For me as a doctor, one of the biggest advantages of creating a digital avatar was to handle the mundane task of seeing patients all through the day. It allowed me to spend more time to see the most critical ones or those which interested me the most. It sure was an expensive way to generate more time for me to pursue my interests and for leisure. There were, of course, minor glitches with the system, and patients could sometimes tell that it wasn't the real me they are consulting with, but the system captured all the data and automatically made its way to my clinical dashboard for my review and final sign off on all decisions being made. The more I trained the system and accepted and rejected outcomes, the better it got in understanding my decision-making tree and ultimately my personality.

'That's great, Casper. So, I have time to download this month's education credits to my neuralink interface.'

It is in 2033, as it was in 2018. Doctors, as with almost all professions today, needed to continuously expand their knowledge. The rate of change was so high that if you didn't keep up to date with new developments, you could very quickly find yourself obsolete. The advantage, however, was that unlike the old days which involved hours of reading, the neuralink interface would automatically download all the relevant data and information into parts of my brain called the hippocampus and memory cells of the frontal cortex. Think of it as a Dropbox account for my memory. All it involved was plugging my interface online via the CNS uplink plug on a regular basis and then as I would drift off into a deep sleep for 20 minutes, the software would go about its business.

I awoke to a heavy knocking on the door. I was still in a daze from having gained consciousness sooner than expected, and then a little concerned about probably having to repeat the download owing to the abrupt closure of the link. As I opened the door, a grey figure walked into my suite. His face looked familiar and I racked my hippocampal cells to try and place him. The curtain of haze lifted and suddenly I leapt from my sofa.

'Professor Stewart!' I exclaimed.

'Yes, Marcus. Good to see you, young man.'

I couldn't believe it. Professor Stewart, or the 'Prof' as we used to call him, was my very first clinical lecturer in medical school. One of the most intelligent people I had ever met in life, he exuded old-school medicine. A knowledge bank of cases, he had pretty much seen every type of pathology imaginable and in addition to being an encyclopaedia on the subject himself, he had the best bedside manner I had ever seen. All topped off with a suave Scottish accent, which would make any patient swoon.

'How wonderful to see you Prof! It's been close to 25 years.'

As I invited him in and he sat down clumsily on the chair, I noticed how time had not been kind to his body. As we spoke about what brought him to the facility, he described his personal journey over the past few years. Unfortunately, he was diagnosed with a bone-marrow tumour a few years ago, and whilst he tried multiple rounds of nuclear therapy and personalised regeneration based on his own stem-cell-developed marrow transplants, the disease had taken its toll. He was visiting the regeneration department to participate in the new mitochondrial rejuvenation trial, to see whether it would delay the inevitable, but his hopes were not too high.

I sat there and sadly listened to this hero of mine. He was slowly succumbing to a disease we knew so much about in theory but were unable to translate our knowledge into any practical improvement. It was at that moment that the irony of my day occurred to me.

I had spent every effort possible in avoiding physical contact with my patients, leveraging technology wherever I could. With robots and AI, my life had become as sterile as I could make it and my only physical interactions that day were with two ghosts from my past. What had happened to me? What was happening to my profession? My mind travelled back into the past, to the first time I met the professor. I was in my early 20s and like everyone that age, I thought I could do it all. Prof had asked me to examine this young patient who had come in complaining about pain in his abdomen. I immediately stretched out my arm and just before I could place it on his torso, the prof yelled *stop*! What proceeded was a detailed lecture on the importance of talking to the patient—the art of clinical reasoning and history-taking, as he called it. It was indeed a sight to marvel at when performed correctly. As I would watch him over the next three months, I learnt so much of what being a doctor really meant and how much could be achieved by just knowing the right question to ask.

What had become of the time-honoured, almost sacred bond called the doctor-patient relationship? What purpose does it serve in healing and recovery and does it still exist today, in 2033?

'Prof,' I asked, 'what do you think about how doctors today interact and engage with their patients?'

What followed was an intense dialogue about how disappointed he had become. Not because he thought that we were not diagnosing patients correctly but because he felt that the art of healing was lost somewhere in this onslaught of technology.

As we spoke, I began to realise the certain practicality which exists in having an effective relationship with one's patients, allowing the doctor to tease out clinical details; an ability which, of course, would have been much more essential in the days before modern-day diagnostics. But that was not the entire truth. This relationship is much more complex. I realised that it is a synergistic relationship, in which the doctor also gains as much from the exchange with another human being.

My professor reflected on his own personal experience and told me about how and why he had come to see his doctor. At a time when he was physically in pain when his morale was at its lowest and he felt the most vulnerable, all he needed was another human being who could show some empathy and comfort him. Trust, after all, is the foundation of any successful relationship. Trust is either built through a personal history of knowing the doctor or trust in the profession itself. But with this technological revolution and the disappearance of the doctor from the medical scene, where had this trust migrated? It had not been translated to the machines and neither to their manufacturers.

'So, what has happened to the relationship?' I asked. 'How could I compete with a computer which is smarter than me?'

Today, machines know on a second-by-second basis what is happening in the internal chemistry of my patients. Machines can also review the latest research and publications in real time. They can arrive on a probability-based assessment of the patient in a fraction of the time that it would ever take me. Haven't we, therefore, become stewards of these machines? They were meant to augment our abilities not replace us—or so we all told ourselves.

'They cannot replace you, Marcus, because you are human. And in my moment of fear, in pain and suffering, it is the warmth of another like me in which I find my greatest solace,' the Prof replied.

'As your generation continues to build machines based on intelligence, remember that as human beings, we are built on emotions.'

He stood up and I helped him to the door. He hugged me warmly and, in that moment, we both knew that it would be the last time we would ever see each other.

Casper helped me go about the rest of my day, ensuring I managed to complete all my tasks that afternoon. There was, however, one big difference that day—I decided to see all my patients myself.

Dr Marcus Ranney completed his bachelor of science and medical degrees from University College Medical School, London. His research expeditions have led him to climb the sides of Everest, skiing in the Arctic and the European Alps. After practising clinical medicine in London, in 2011, he made the transition to Mumbai where he has worked in the healthcare and life sciences industry as a strategic advisor and venture capitalist. Marcus is currently General Manager of Thrive Global in India, a US-based behaviour change technology and media company. As a futurist, his current research is focused on what the future of health and society will look like in 2030.

Did You Know?

The human body is such a complex and dynamic entity—each one being unique—that medicine will never become a mathematical problem where data can be crunched to produce the single right answer. AI will increasingly inform and improve this decision-making process—a process that must be guided by physicians. The great challenge going forward is in recognising and nurturing this irreplaceable human element and to train doctors to work with machines without becoming too reliant on them.

Source: http://www.medicineatmichigan.org/forum/2018/fall/ai-and-irreplaceable-human-element

Dear People,

'Doctors pay commercial rates for all amenities and yet Indian society expects its doctors to be completely altruistic.'

Dr Mitalee Shome

When the Saviour Himself Is Sick

Doctors. The very word conjures images of some of the most important experiences of life—some that are meant to be relished and others that are better forgotten. As a young girl, I always looked up to our family physician. There was something magical about him. The pain seemed to disappear the moment he would walk in. The cool touch of his hands on my forehead, asking me to stick out my tongue like Goddess Kali while making a weird gurgling noise or palpating my liver while I lay down flat on the bed—these are all photographic memories that I cherish to this date.

That was the era when doctors relied more on their clinical skills than on investigations. I had full faith in him and trusted him implicitly. He could never be wrong. My family physician, too, strongly believed in building a relationship with his patients. He was a keen listener, engaged his patients in conversation and asked questions. He would talk at length to his patients before recommending any investigations. As an older patient, this is something that I really miss in the doctor-patient relationships of today.

Most of the times, a doctor enters the patient's life during a period of extreme stress. This relationship is akin to a roller-coaster ride, enjoyable at times and tenuous at others. I have been fortunate to experience the beauty of the former. As a young girl, I didn't know that my life was destined to revolve around doctors. Eventually, I got married to one and today, I am a proud mother of one of the most renowned facial plastic surgeons in the country. My husband was a member of the old school of physicians. He trusted his fingers much more than any high-flying pathological or radiological test. His clinical sense was astute and eight times out of 10, he hit the bull's eye when it came to diagnosing an ailment. It was no wonder that his patients trusted him blindly and had full faith in his diagnosis. He was a friend, philosopher and guide to most of his patients. He cared for them deeply and at times, they would approach him with their personal problems too. Night or day, they knew he would be by their side whenever they called. He was their saviour.

I still remember December 1992. India, at that time, was a very different country to what it is today. Indians hardly had any choices in consumer products. We had black and white televisions and Ambassador cars. Growth rates were low, television channels were few, and thus, people too had lesser wants. The doctor-patient relationship was very different from what it is today. Doctors had more time, while patients had more trust and respect. It was in this backdrop that the worst communal riots in India's history broke out, tearing through the fabric of our nation. Mumbai was amongst the cities worst affected. It was a time of deep distrust, where even neighbours stopped trusting each other.

For my husband, it was an inordinately difficult and testing time. There were patients of different religions who needed looking after. While there could be no discrimination medically, society itself was deeply fractured and was looking at doctors treating people from 'the other religion' with deep distrust.

I remember how my husband volunteered to care for injured patients at this time. I remember how he would return home every night and cry. He had seen bodies with dismembered limbs but more than that, he saw how people had lost all humanity and become devil incarnate. He spent hours counselling people that neighbours and friends for life couldn't just become enemies overnight. He carried the deep scars of this episode for the rest of his days. He understood that being a doctor was a big responsibility. Being a doctor meant he was the health caregiver, philosopher, guide and teacher all rolled into one! This is what he professed to do in the rest of his career.

Patients loved this attitude of 'giving' in my husband–this attitude of giving time freely while charging very little. After all, this is what Indian society seems to expect from its doctors—give all and expect very little in return! I wonder if this is possible or even plausible in today's day and age. Medical education today costs huge sums of money and effort. Doctors pay commercial rates for all amenities and yet Indian society expects its doctors to be completely altruistic.

However, my husband believed otherwise. He continued his work as service until one day, the saviour himself was diagnosed with lung cancer.

It was the cold and dreary month of December 2008. We had returned from a family wedding in Kolkata and the cold and cough was inadvertently attributed to a change in the weather. However, a nagging cough that my husband developed refused to go. A visit to the chest specialist did not solve matters. It only diverted our focus with temporary relief. Despite a full course of antibiotics, the cough was relentless. The signs were ominous and the next logical step was a CT scan of the chest, which he himself suggested. It confirmed the worst and he was diagnosed with stage four lung cancer, which had spread to multiple organs.

We had no option but to gear up for the imminent trial. Mental agony, emotional distress and financial calculations hit us hard as we struggled to cope with the crises. I was shattered. I felt that this was a full stop to my otherwise peaceful and happy life. The whole world turned topsy-turvy and meaningless. I was in denial and terribly lonely. I started questioning whether being altruistic to patients and being left with a miserably low bank balance was really worth it. We did not even have money for our own treatments when we most needed it.

My husband was unruffled. Even if he was affected, he did not show any traces of it. He had accepted the verdict as God's will. It was beyond my understanding how he could be so calm and composed during this period of crisis. I would lay awake night after night with a million thoughts running through my mind. To be honest, I sometimes even thought that maybe my husband was selfish and uncaring. I thought, 'How could he not be worried about me and our child?'

I was angry at God for being so cruel. Time and again I asked Him, 'Why me?'

The nightmare had only just begun and God had decided to test me and my strength even further. My son, who was in the USA at that time, could not come to terms with the diagnosis of lung cancer in his seemingly healthy and fit father. A liver biopsy (to get a sample of the tissue from the liver spread of the tumour) was suggested by the treating doctors to confirm the diagnosis. However, what should have been a simple procedure turned out to be a nightmare. The young and inexperienced doctor who took the biopsy punctured the portal vein (a large blood vessel next to the liver) and the whole abdomen was filled with blood. His blood pressure dropped and he went into a shock. He had to be shifted to the ICU immediately. It was unbelievable that a simple procedure such as a biopsy could push my husband into such a critical state. It shattered all my faith and belief in the medical fraternity.

Complications can occur after any procedure. For the medical fraternity, these are mere statistics and may be counted as being within the permissible rate of 1 to 2%, but for the patient and their families that one complication always amounts to 100% agony. While undergoing treatment, not much is in our control. We can just grit our teeth and grab the next feasible option. When it came to my husband's health, I had to force myself to look ahead. 'Now what'? I asked the specialist. 'If he survives this, then we will start treating him for cancer,' the doctors said. This was the biggest 'if' I had ever heard in my life.

Sleepless nights, tears and hopelessness followed with prayers. At that time the love and support of family and friends gave me the strength and will to survive. The week in the ICU was a trying time but the efficiency and professionalism with which the case was handled, along with God's will and blessings, got my husband back on his feet and reinforced my belief in the healthcare system. Once he was discharged from the hospital, we visited the oncologist to chart the future course of action. The oncologists were extremely sceptical, as chances of survival with stage four lung cancer were less than six months. My son who was a doctor and I decided to fight, no matter the chances.

Six cycles of chemotherapy were prescribed.

The real test started now. With the first cycle of chemotherapy came the after effects—nausea, lack of appetite, low platelet and haemoglobin count and immense physical discomfort. The treating oncologist was quite positive about the outcome. A man of few words, he would never really say much to us. I was looking for reassurance but, unfortunately, our doctor friends had already pronounced my husband's death sentence. No one thought that he would live beyond six months.

During those days, my platter of suffering was full. It felt like I was fighting a losing battle. Despondency had become second nature to me. However, when I look back, I realise that when the Almighty puts you through trials, He also gives you the strength to sail through the storm. Sometimes, we just need a sliver of inspiration to lift our spirits and mine came from none other than the person we were fighting for: my husband. He amazed me with his grit. A man with tremendous willpower, he decided to live for and in the present. As always, his patients remained his priority. It was as if nothing had changed. He would brave a chemotherapy cycle, sport a mask to avoid infection and reach his clinic the next day. No amount of persuasion could dissuade him from the call of duty. 'My patients are waiting, they are sick and in pain. Let me go and see them,' he would say. This was a doctor who was fighting the battle of life and death himself. Practising medicine was his purpose in life and he remained true to this purpose till the very end.

The oncologist treating my husband was no different. He was a big motivation. My husband's willpower, coupled with positivity and encouragement from his oncologist, rejuvenated my ailing husband. The inevitable was pushed into the subconscious.

When I think back, I am also reminded of small mercies: my son was being trained at MD Anderson Cancer Center (MDACC) in Houston. Some world-renowned names in oncology were among his friends. My son spent several hours exploring the latest in treatment research in lung cancer to ensure that his father got the very best possible treatment. One of the clinical trials being conducted had shown that in addition to the routine chemotherapy if thalidomide (an oral medication which stopped the cancer cells from developing new blood vessels and thereby decreased their nutrition) was added, the results of the chemotherapy were much better. However, in allopathic medicine, in fact, in life in general, we all know that everything has a pro as well as a con. We were extremely apprehensive about the efficacy of this new drug. Thalidomide is known to accentuate chances of gangrene in patients undergoing chemotherapy. This is where having a qualified doctor in the family helped us. My son said, 'I would much rather take that little chance that my father lives longer with thalidomide, even if he loses a leg in the bargain.' This statement gave me courage and the oncologists in India had no option but to comply and attempt the thalidomide trial on my husband. Our son took all the risks and waived off the same for the oncologists in a written submission to the hospital.

Lo and behold! It worked.

The second opinion of the oncologists from MDACC also proved to be a godsend. It gave my husband a fresh lease of life. I thanked the Almighty for being with me and sending me the much-needed help of angels in the form of doctors. The miracle of all this was that in three months, my husband became cancer-free. This was so startling that initially, the oncologist felt the positron emission tomography (PET) scans had been mixed up with some other patient's. Clearly, this result would not have been possible without my son's knowledge. In healthcare, knowledge may be the difference between life and death. These were the benefits of belonging to a family of doctors.

At the end of one year, the results were good and my husband was in remission. Our hope was rekindled, even though we knew that this was a temporary phase. Another year passed by. We went on holidays, trying to make him live every moment to the fullest. He seemed to enjoy every moment, without a care in the world. We were the happiest during that period, but it was very short-lived. The disease relapsed with a vengeance after a year. To make matters worse, he was found to be resistant to the older drugs and we started looking for newer avenues. It was a race against time.

Here again, our network in healthcare came to our rescue as we tried experimental drugs which had not received approval for use. The oncologists at MDACC were very empathetic and it spoke volumes about their commitment towards patients. Their second opinions were positive. Soon, help started pouring in from all quarters. Acupressure, reiki, prayers, blessings—it all followed. The treatment continued but the side effects came back fiercely this time. To divert my husband's attention from his physical pain, we took the doctor's permission to take him out on holidays, some long, some short. We went to the USA, Thailand and Hong Kong, where my sister and her family lived. He had decided to enjoy every moment as if there was no tomorrow. No one believed he was a terminally ill patient. He lived for three years and nine months after being diagnosed with stage four lung cancer. During this period, he was constantly in and out of the hospitals. Not once did he complain or feel depressed. Physical pain and discomfort could never bog him down.

The inevitable happened eventually. The end arrived. He developed jaundice and his abdomen was filled with fluid. Pain finally gripped the indomitable spirit and crippled him. He sensed the end was near. For the first time in all these years, I could see the pain in his eyes. Breathing was difficult. Nothing was helping. I wished and prayed for him to be relieved of the pain. We shifted him to the hospital. Here again, I realised the vagaries of the healthcare system. The day we shifted my husband to the hospital was a Sunday. No senior consultants were available that day. To make matters worse, the oncologist himself was abroad for a conference. The junior doctors in the hospital clearly did not have the same amount of expertise. They were confirming treatments with my son who, being a facial plastic surgeon, was hardly the best intensivist For such a critical patient. That night, my husband slipped into a coma. The next day he was relieved of all pains and worldly cares.

I realised again, painfully, that healthcare can never be perfect because it depends so much on the individual brilliance of doctors. We may have the best processes, but how will we ever replace the acumen, skill and experience of a great doctor? Maybe, that night, we would not have lost my husband if the chief oncologist was in the country. But then again, would my husband even have lived till that night had some other brilliant doctors not intervened?

It was a trying time. The help and support I received from all the doctors who treated my husband will remain with me forever. I also realise now why my husband himself was so invested in his patients. Medicine is not a mere profession. During sickness, not only the patient but the entire family looks up to only one person after God and that is the doctor. My husband understood this and always kept the interests of his patients above his own. I was lucky to have similar doctors by my side during my husband's illness. Long live their tribe, is all I pray.

Dr Mitalee Shome is an MPhil and PhD in English Literature with over 40 years of teaching experience in English Literature. She has taught over 12,000 students on subjects like English and business communication. She has presented around 50 papers in national and international seminars and published 17 papers in academic journals, books and magazines. Presently, apart from teaching, she imparts training in spoken English, writes and edits content for different corporates. Dr Shome has been awarded by multiple agencies for her path-breaking work. She also dedicates a lot of time for philanthropic work through the Debabrata Auro Foundation.

Did You Know?

During the 1970s and early 1980s, descriptive studies provided evidence that family members of the cancer patient also suffer from stress. These studies, conducted in spouses (primarily of breast cancer patients), documented that partners often experience sleep disturbances and eating disorders, heightened anxiety and depression, a pervasive sense of helplessness and fears about cancer and its treatment. The illness causes a ripple effect that results in changes to the family's identity and to daily routines. These changes have long-lasting effects, regardless of the outcome of the disease. Although the effects generally are perceived to be negative, involving different types of losses, it should be remembered that many families describe the positive effects and resulting strengths of coping with the crisis of cancer.

Source: http://www.cancernetwork.com/oncology-journal/crisis-cancer-psychological-impact-family-caregivers

Dear People,

'Easy access to Googled medical information, much of which is less than authentic, has put a lot of doctors on the back foot as they try to regain the confidence of their patients for whom the internet is always right.'

Dr Mohamed Rela and Dr Ashwin Rammohan

The Doctor-Patient Relationship

A Sisyphean Endeavour?

An optimal doctor-patient relationship requires both emotional and cognitive components. Still, the impact the doctor-patient relationship has on the patient, the physician and the medical profession as a whole has never been analysed adequately. Sadly, even the media in its hunger for sensationalism often fails to paint the true picture, especially from the healthcare providers' point of view.

We distinctly remember two incidents where the patients' families responded in completely contrasting fashions during the difficult phases of the patients' recovery. While both of them recovered and went home, their behaviour—and its impact on the medical team which took care of them—highlights the difficulties faced by medical professionals today.

Agam Seth (name changed), a 37-year-old man, was suffering from multiple infections and had developed a tendency for bleeding as a result of a failing liver. A thorough evaluation revealed that chronic alcohol consumption had resulted in an end-stage liver disease leading to a liver transplant. His wife volunteered to donate a part of her liver to save her husband's life. After numerous tests, systematic and comprehensive evaluation and appropriate legal documentation, she was deemed suitable for organ donation.

A few days later, Seth underwent a liver transplant. The operation was uneventful and he was later transferred to the liver transplant intensive care unit for further monitoring and support. Unfortunately, his new liver graft functioned poorly and his post-operative recovery was complicated. Soon, his condition started deteriorating and he needed additional support to maintain his heart, lung and kidney function. As he progressed on to multi-organ failure, he had to be put on dialysis, plasmapheresis (a process of removing blood plasma), clotting support and high broad-spectrum antimicrobial agents. He continued to remain in the ICU with round-the-clock intensive monitoring and we ensured an open channel of communication with the patient's relatives. We kept them informed of his fragile condition at every stage.

While Seth continued to remain critically ill in the ICU, a different drama was unfolding outside the hospital. It could well have come straight out of a Bollywood movie. One fine day, a mob of over 50 antisocial elements appeared from nowhere, wielding makeshift weapons and accusing the hospital of extracting money from the patient's family in the name of treatment. They alleged that the hospital was deceptively keeping a dead person in the ICU. The mob was headed by a stranger, who had now magically turned into a close relative. He attempted to hold the hospital to ransom, with threats of damage to property and life. This gentleman repeatedly iterated that he was willing to spend any sum of money to get his so-called 'brother' cured. But now that the patient had died, he was well within his rights to demand a full refund from the hospital. He also tried to extort large sums of money to placate the irate crowd that had collected outside the hospital. Eventually, the police had to be called to control the mob and provide protection to the clinical team. We held a series of detailed meetings with this man, his associates and the patient's actual family in the presence of the police. Not surprisingly, he was quick to rattle off his numerous political affiliations.

In the meantime, multiple visits to the ICU by various 'relatives' confirmed that the patient was, in fact, alive, but on life support. The hospital refused to be blackmailed into providing any financial reparations and, as expected, the gang grudgingly dispersed, obviously disappointed at the lack of the promised windfall. Over the next two weeks, the patient's condition dramatically improved and, much to everyone's relief, he was transferred out of the ICU in a fortnight.

In a surreal turn of events, when it was time to pay the bills, his wife turned around and filed a lawsuit, claiming that the patient was being detained in the hospital illegally. Clearly, this baseless allegation was made with the sole intention to evade payment of the bill. The patient not only refused to bear the expenses incurred in saving his life, but he also had no iota of gratitude towards the untiring and selfless efforts of healthcare professionals.

One fine morning, he disappeared from the hospital ward, never to be heard from again. We sincerely hope that he remains well wherever he is and continues to be on regular medications and necessary follow-ups in view of his post-liver-transplant status. Such incidents, however, create rancour and leave even the most ungrudging doctor saddened and under-appreciated, despite all the hard work put into saving lives.

Liver transplantation, especially living donor liver transplantation, sits at the pinnacle of all surgical endeavours. Despite its many benefits, the flipside of liver transplantation in India is the high cost and the paucity of public sector funding for this operation. Most middle-class families end up spending their entire life's savings to allow for a new lease of life for their loved ones. At times, when the post-transplant recovery does not progress as desired, the escalating costs of the treatment may push the already stretched-out family against the wall. While the high cost of treatment leads to increasing financial burden, the critical state of their loved one doubles their anguish, understandably making them react to the whole conundrum in an adverse manner.

Nathan (name changed), a 60-year-old man with a penchant for Indian sweets, came to us with progressive signs of liver failure. He was diagnosed with end-stage liver disease and was advised to undergo a liver transplant. Despite having very strong family support with numerous relatives coming forward to donate a part of their liver, he opted to be listed for a deceased donor (cadaveric) liver transplant. After nearly six months, Nathan received a compatible liver from a brain-dead donor. He underwent a transplant and though the surgery was a technical success, he developed primary non-function, which is a well-recognised condition known to occur in about 5% of all deceased donor liver transplants. In these cases, the new liver fails to function after transplantation. As a result, Nathan was kept on multi-organ support and remained critically ill over the next few days. It was soon obvious that the new liver was not going to function and the only option was an urgent second liver transplant before his condition became irreversible.

The patient's relatives were updated at every step regarding his critical condition and after multiple detailed discussions, he was listed for a super-urgent retransplant—with a hope that another whole liver might become available within the next

24 to 48 hours. However, this didn't happen. Simultaneously, willing family members were evaluated as partial live liver donors. His college-going daughter turned out to be a good match. Nathan underwent a retransplant the next day and received the right lobe of his daughter's liver. The operation was uneventful and the post-operative period smooth for both the donor and the patient. Soon, both were discharged from the hospital in excellent condition. Through this difficult period, the family and the doctors had developed a sense of camaraderie, successfully working towards a common goal of getting the patient better. Nathan remains well to this date and has become our good friend.

The stories of Agam Seth and Nathan show how each patient is different, as is each doctor, but modern healthcare has vastly changed the scenario. With continuing advances in technology and expertise, modern science is able to answer many unsolved questions. This has led to an escalation in patient expectations, sometimes way beyond what science can actually deliver. Coupled with skyrocketing costs of healthcare, the time-honoured doctor-patient relationship that was based primarily on trust, empathy and respect is now gradually attaining a transactional nature. Today, it is a much greater challenge for clinicians to lead a patient from this confusing gamut of sentiments on to the road to recovery and cure.

The historical model for the doctor-patient relationship involved a patient's complete dependence on the physician's professional authority, leading to a paternalistic model of care. This model evolved towards shared decision-making and drifted further towards a system where it has been reduced to a mere product to be delivered. Easy access to Googled medical information, much of which is less than authentic, has put a lot of doctors on the back foot as they try to regain the confidence of their patients, for whom the internet is always right.

Though the endeavour remains Sisyphean in nature, the utopian median, like the stories of Seth and Nathan show us, lies somewhere in between. Utopia for us would amalgamate all that has developed in the healthcare industry—not only the technological progress but also the increased awareness among patients. The future, therefore, lies in collaboration and we envision a time where each new patient and doctor form a special and individualised relationship filled with competence, trust and empathy for each other.

Dr Mohamed Rela is a world leader in the field of liver transplantation. He is the chairman and director of the Institute of Liver Disease and Transplantation at Gleneagles Global Health City, Chennai. He is also the professor of HPB and Liver Transplant Surgery, Institute of Liver Studies at Kings College Hospital, London. In a career spanning three decades, he has performed over 4,000 liver transplant surgeries around the world and has more than 600 publications to his credit. A team led by him performed a successful liver transplantation for a five-day-old girl, giving him an entry into the Guinness Book of Records in 2000. In his non-surgical time, Dr Rela delves into Tamil literature and Renaissance art.

Dr Ashwin Rammohan is a liver transplant surgeon and the director of Academics and Research at the Dr Rela Institute and Medical Centre, Chennai. He is also a consultant at the, Hepatobiliary Pancreatic Surgery and Liver Transplantation Gleneagles Global Health City, Chennai. He has over 60 international peer-reviewed publications, 50 abstracts/presentations in national and international conferences and two research theses to his credit. He is the International Surgical Advisor to the Royal College of Surgeons and Physicians of Glasgow, UK and a

faculty for the Postdoctoral fellowship in Minimal Access Surgery at Dr MGR Medical University Chennai, India.

Did You Know?

A 2015 survey by the IMA suggests that as many as 75% of doctors in India have faced some form of violence at work. Doctors faced maximum violence when providing emergency services with as many as 48.8% of such incidents reported from intensive care units or after a patient had undergone surgery, the study said. Escorts of patients committed 68.33% of the violence.

Source: Dey, Sushmi. (2015). 'Over 75% of doctors have faced violence at work, study finds.' The Times of India. *http://timesofindia.indiatimes.com/india/Over-75-of-doctors-have-faced-violence-atwork-study-finds/articleshow/47143806.cms*

Dear People,

'Doctor-patient relationship is one of the most enduring, endearing and satisfying relationships where we learn to listen and see not only with our ears and eyes but also with our hearts and minds.'

Dr Nitin Kadam

The Bitter-Sweet Pill

The first time Sagarbai came to my office, her weathered and creased face made her look much older than she was. She was from the Wasmat *taluka* in the Marathwada district of Maharashtra. Her village, Chudawa, was underdeveloped and struck by drought. Her only son, Amrut, 27, had just been diagnosed with kidney failure. He didn't think he would survive but Sagarbai did. Amrut's wife had been unable to bear the stress and had left him, leaving behind their three-year-old daughter, Sandhya.

Sagarbai, on the other hand, refused to give up and was determined to save her son. She had been told that only a kidney transplant could save her son's life. Sagarbai used this piece of information as her armour and made her way to our hospital from her village—which was 350 kilometres away—with her ailing son. The fact that she could not afford the treatment did not deter her in any way.

When the nephrologist and I met Sagarbai and Amrut, we explained that Amrut needed a compatible donor and that the surgery would be complicated with limited chances of survival. Sagarbai listened to us keenly but her hope didn't diminish. She told us that she had two perfectly functioning kidneys and that she could easily be the donor. We told her that donating her kidney would mean that she would have to maintain aseptic precautions at home and take lifelong medication. Unless she could figure out how to do that, we could not go ahead with the surgery. However, Sagarbai pleaded with us and asked us to proceed. She was sure that she would manage everything else. In that moment, I knew that I was dealing with a person whose determination and willpower was unparalleled.

Soon, the nephrologist and the transplant team started the arduous procedure and the transplant of the kidney from mother to son was successful. A few days later, when Amrut was shifted to the general ward, his three-year-old daughter Sandhya visited. When it was time for her to go, she refused. She didn't want to return without her father and grandmother who were equally thrilled to have her around. The little girl kept crying and would not leave. The matter was brought to my attention but before I could take a call, the nurses told me that they were willing to take care of the little girl until her father was discharged. I wasn't sure whether they had come to take my permission or inform me but I knew I had no choice. The nurses poured their affection on the child. They brought her clothes; the social worker gave her colouring books and crayons and other staff members got her toys and dolls from their homes. Soon enough, she became a part of our hospital and showered the staff with affection.

The day before Amrut's discharge, Sagarbai came to my office, beaming with happiness. She was grateful for our work. I told her that she would have to look after herself, her son and return for regular check-ups.

Meanwhile, I discussed their case with the managing committee of the hospital's trust and they agreed to provide lifelong financial support for Amrut's medical needs. Their hospital bill, too, was completely waived off. When Sagarbai heard this, we expected her to be grateful and leave gracefully, instead, she was offended. She came to the billing department with her life's savings tied in a cloth bundle—old worn-out notes amounting to ₹3,000, two tarnished silver coins and a small idol of Lord Ganesha. Her logic was simple: she had saved money for an emergency and now that her son was back on his feet, the hospital should accept it. I shall never forget the dignity Sagarbai showed that day.

It's been four years. Sagarbai regularly follows up with us every two months when she comes to collect her son's medicine. He's back to work, his wife has returned and they've been recently blessed with another child. Sagarbai is very happy that her family is together again. On her recent visit, she was accompanied by her chirpy, little granddaughter who was jumping around in my office. Sagarbai had also brought a sack-full of peanuts for her staff. They were from the farm where she worked as a labourer—perhaps she was paid in kind. Sandhya, now seven years old, is a bright student. She dreams of being a nurse someday and making sick people better, just like the nurse 'aunties' who treated her father.

In my 35 years of practice, I have been lucky to meet some inspiring people, especially patients like Sagarbai who are selfless despite not having much themselves. However, hospitals, on the other hand, are finding it challenging to deliver quality healthcare at an affordable price. Despite that, the way the healthcare system is presented by the media is just one side of the coin. On the other side are heart-warming stories of nurses and doctors taking that extra mile to save someone's life and bring joy to a patient.

When I was a young medical graduate, I used to spend most of my time reading books. One day, my elder brother suggested that I use my free time to do something worthwhile for the people of Nanded, my hometown. At that time, coincidentally, I was reading a book about the life and journey of Dr Ida Scudder, founder of the Christian Medical College and Hospital, Vellore. Dr Scudder's journey and my brother's advice encouraged me and a like-minded doctor to start a mobile clinic in Nanded. We bought a van, some commonly needed medicines and medical supplies, and set off.

Every morning we went to the various villages in the vicinity and addressed people's primary healthcare needs. We would see patients, talk to them, give medicines, offer vaccination, do simple dressings and suturing and return home in the evening. We became regular with our mobile medical aid and people in the community started appreciating our efforts. Along the way, a philanthropist donated his house to admit and care for patients. That's where we started the journey of setting up a rural healthcare centre in the village of Nila, 11 kilometres from Nanded. There were no healthcare and education facilities in this marginalised region, hence the new centre was able to offer services not only to Nila but to people from adjoining regions as well.

It was these early efforts that taught me that if one is persistent, patient, sincere and focused, no goal is impossible. Especially in the medical field, we need to be continuous learners, keen observers, and earnest and ethical in our conduct. Here, the doctor-patient relationship plays the most important role. It is one of the most enduring, endearing and satisfying relationships where we learn to listen and see not only with our ears and eyes but also with our hearts and minds.

This reminds me of an incident that is forever carved in my memory. At a multispeciality hospital outside Mumbai, a world-renowned surgeon from the US was performing a complex surgery. As it was part of a three-day international conference which included live operative workshops, the audience was watching the surgeon with rapt attention. A question-answer session was planned after the surgery. After the operation, the doctor from abroad de-scrubbed and went to change to get ready to go to the conference hall. When he came out of the theatre, he could not find his shoes. Everyone assumed that the housekeeping staff had kept them away and a mini search party went looking for the missing pair of shoes. It would be immensely embarrassing for the hospital if the dignitary's shoes were not found. The administrative staff was rushed to the nearest shoe outlet to get a new pair of shoes for the doctor. After all, no one could let him walk around barefoot. In the meantime, the doctor was offered a pair of shoes by someone else so that he could attend the Q&A session while the search for the missing shoes continued.

The search had now extended into the patient's waiting area outside the OT. During this commotion, a frail old man appeared and innocently asked what it was that everyone was searching for? Was it, by any chance, a pair of shoes? Suddenly, everyone's focus shifted to the man. 'Yes. Yes,' everyone replied in chorus. With all gazes fixed on him, he put his arm in a cloth bag hanging on his shoulder and like a magician brought out the shining pair of missing shoes. We enquired why he had taken them in the first place. In a very matter-of-fact way, he said that he was the grandfather of the child who had been operated. Ever since the child was born, they were making rounds of various hospitals for his grandson's treatment. Finally, the child had received the treatment he needed. In the old man's eyes, the doctor was no less than God and so he wanted to take the doctor's shoes home to keep them in his temple.

Each time I remember this incident, it makes me smile. As a doctor, helping someone through the challenges of a serious illness is a privilege and when a patient is so grateful that he/she starts to worship the life-giver—if not as God but as someone in his shoes—it strengthens my belief that the doctor-patient relationship is healthy, strong and will survive for many years to come.

Dr Nitin Kadam is a paediatrician and a professor of paediatrics. He is the Medical Director of MGM's New Bombay Hospital, Vashi and a trustee of the MGM Trust. MGM Trust runs medical colleges and hospitals with over 2000 beds in the state of Maharashtra and has treated 21 billion patients since its inception in the 1980s. He has more than 60 publications in national and international journals. He has received several prestigious awards for his contribution to healthcare as well as for development of hi-tech affordable and quality healthcare and bringing it within the reach of the masses. Humble to the core, he strongly believes that the blessings of innumerable underprivileged patients are the force behind the success and sustainability of their hospitals. He is also a keen sportsman, writer, reader and a patron of fine arts.

Did You Know?

India was one of the first countries to give its citizens national healthcare as a uniform right. However, in the present scenario, Indian rural healthcare faces a crisis unmatched to any other social sector. Nearly 86% of all medical visits in India are made by ruralites with a majority still travelling more than 100 kilometres to avail healthcare facility of which 70–80% is borne out of pocket, landing them in poverty.

Source: Kumar R. (2012). 'Academic institutionalization of community health services: Way ahead in medical education reforms'. J Family Med Prim Care, *1(10): 9.*

Dear People,

'Medicine is not mathematics and a single formula cannot be applied to everything. Every patient is different and there are multiple factors that need to be considered before arriving at a conclusion.'

Dr Olithselvan A.

Transforming Lives in the Midst of Riots

Three years ago, a 20-year-old girl walked into my clinic with her mother and elder sister. The moment I saw her, I sensed high anxiety around her. My intuition was proved correct when I saw the huge stack of medical files that she was carrying. We introduced ourselves and started talking about the reason why she was at my clinic.

Her problems had started about a year ago when one of her aunts was diagnosed with autoimmune liver disease. Autoimmune liver disease occurs when the body's immune system turns against its own liver. In particularly bad cases, it can progress to cirrhosis of the liver and eventual liver failure. The cause for this disease is still unclear, but it is said to occur due to an interplay of genetic and environmental factors.

The girl was very close to her aunt. She would accompany her for doctor visits and listen carefully to what the doctors had to say. She was tech-savvy, young and it was no surprise that she started looking up the internet for more information about autoimmune liver disease. For this generation, life without Google is unimaginable, but as doctors, we routinely face the perils of this kind of information overload. After the Google search, she decided that she must get an anti-neutrophil antibody (ANA) test done on herself too. Unfortunately, as luck would have it, the ANA test turned out to be positive, albeit in very low titres.

This was just the beginning of a never-ending wild goose chase. She first consulted the same doctor who was treating her aunt. Though she did not have any symptoms related to liver or any other autoimmune pathology, the doctor ordered an extensive panel of tests to rule out autoimmune disorders and liver pathology. As expected, all the tests turned out to be normal. It certainly did not help when during the consultation, the doctor told her that the possibility of her having an autoimmune disease could not be ruled out fully and that there was a chance that she may develop it in the future. This so-called honest opinion from the doctor who, incidentally, was not a specialist but a general physician, created mayhem in her young mind. It led to many sleepless nights and all of this when all she had done was accompany her aunt to the doctor.

Her entire outlook towards life changed and she began to relate every minor symptom to autoimmune liver disease. Once a brilliant student, who topped her class in every exam, she was now hesitant to even attend classes. She worried incessantly about her health and in the process, her dreams about her future were completely shattered. She constantly thought about the financial burden that her family would have to bear if she developed an autoimmune disease. This worsened the insomnia and led to severe clinical depression. Her family was devastated to see her in this state. Once a young, enthusiastic and brilliant girl with a bright future, she was now struggling to get through each day.

Her family consulted specialists along the length and breadth of the entire country. Every visit resulted in a new list of investigations. She even underwent liver biopsies on two occasions. It still beats me why anyone would advise a liver biopsy in a patient with normal liver function tests. These array of tests and consultations worsened her psychological status even further. She was convinced that she had an unknown disease, which no doctor was being able to diagnose. Her worst fears had come true.

I carefully looked through the entire bunch of notes and test results and patiently ran through each and every symptom that she complained of. Right from the beginning, I understood that this was a patient who needed my time much more than my intellect. It took me a long time to explain to her that the ANA test should be performed only in a relevant clinical context. The test being positive by itself (especially in low titres) did not signify much. Even if the tests meant something, the chance of her developing any kind of autoimmune disease in the future was very minimal. God forbid, if something were to develop, we would have to cross that bridge when we came to it. There was no way of predicting if and when this would happen and how it would manifest. I patiently explained to her that the probability was equivalent to the chance of having a road accident. We all know that we have to die one day, but that does not mean that we stop living. It was pointless to live in constant fear of a medical possibility, which might never arise.

She started visiting me every month and, in every visit, I would drive the same points home. I ensured that she did not undergo any further tests during this period. This went on for about three years. One day, after yet another counselling session, I just took away all the medical files from her and told her in an affirmative tone that it was time she started living her life. We would tackle the problems as and when they would occur. For now, she needed to stay away from hospitals!

I got the feeling that she finally believed in what I had been telling her for more than three years. For the first time, I saw a slight hint of a smile on her face. After that, I did not see her again in my clinic, but her family kept in touch with me regularly. They told me that they had finally got their daughter back. It has been four years and she has not seen any doctors. She is back to being her normal self before the dreaded ANA ruined her life. It's always a pleasure to receive her greeting cards on every occasion. Her most recent New Year card read: 'Myself and my entire family's best wishes and love to you and your family on this occasion. A great doctor, wonderful human being, completely empathetic, undoubtedly idealistic and with a radical approach towards establishing medical ethics and humanities in India. A fatherly person, a kind teacher who taught me the true value of life than merely living.'

Though I have not seen her for a long time, I know she is doing well now. Her medical files are still in my clinic cabinet and I hope that I never need to open them again.

In this era, where half-baked knowledge from the internet is available to everyone, people often feel that this knowledge is sufficient to self-diagnose and treat medical conditions. Internet knowledge can never replace the expertise of a specialist, which has developed with years of experience. *Medicine is not mathematics and a single formula cannot be applied to everything. Every patient is different and there are multiple factors that need to be considered before arriving at a conclusion. People also need to understand that every investigation has limitations and it can never be accurate enough or permanent enough to diagnose or rule out a condition. Ordering more tests is not equal to a better diagnosis. Unfortunately, in this day and age, doctors are compelled to get more investigations done in view of the increasing number of litigations against the medical fraternity but a balanced approach is, nonetheless, essential. Nothing compares to the physical presence, knowledge and healing touch of a doctor as my following experience will demonstrate.*

One day, we received an intimation from TRANSTAN, the Tamil Nadu government's transplant authority, about the availability of a liver from a deceased donor. The organ was allocated to one of our patients in Salem, Tamil Nadu. This particular patient had been on the waiting list for two months. He was a 55-year-old man who was diagnosed with end-stage liver disease and had suffered through many complications and multiple hospital admissions. With each passing day, his condition was deteriorating rapidly and his only chance of survival was a liver transplant. Our team and the patient's family understood that he would not survive for more than a few weeks if the liver transplant was not carried out at the earliest.

When we received a call regarding the allocation of a liver to him, it was as though God had finally answered our prayers. The donor organ was allocated to our hospital in Salem but, at that moment, the patient along with our team of doctors was in our flagship hospital located in Bengaluru. As per government regulations, the donor organ could not be shifted to any other hospital within or outside the state. Therefore, the recipient had to be taken to Salem. As a liver transplant is an extremely time-sensitive affair, this had to be done as soon as possible.

We had to urgently travel with the patient to Salem so that the surgery could take place. This involved a three-hour road journey across the border of the states of Karnataka and Tamil Nadu. Under normal circumstances, this is something we routinely did at least two to three times a month. On this day though, the situation was extraordinary. There was a huge protest in both Karnataka and Tamil Nadu over a disagreement about the distribution of the waters of the Cauvery River. Both the states were engulfed in violent protests, which were particularly severe around the border regions. Kannadigas living in Tamil Nadu and Tamilians living in Karnataka were particularly targeted. Protestors were stoning and burning the vehicles of both the southern states. The police were not allowing any vehicles, including ambulances with Karnataka number plates, to drive into Tamil Nadu or vice versa.

It was under such circumstances that we had to travel to Salem from Bengaluru. The potential danger to the lives of the doctors, the patient and his family was clear. A mob does not differentiate between normal individuals and patients in times of such difficulty but we had run out of options. We spoke to the patient and his family and made them aware of the situation and the danger that lurked on the journey. They also knew that this was the last chance to save his life as they had seen him deteriorate rapidly in a short span of time. If this chance was missed, they knew, it would probably be the end. It was therefore that they agreed to travel with us across the border to Salem for the surgery. We were a mixed group of doctors: three doctors in our team were Tamilians and one was a Kannadiga. This had a special relevance because mobs on either side of the border were targeting and unleashing violence on people of the other state. We knew that our life was in danger in both the states. However, as doctors, we also understood that this was the last throw of the dice to save this patient's life. The fear, however, was that if we decided to accept this challenge, it might cost us our own lives. Despite that, there was no question in our minds and we unanimously decided to take this challenge.

Our team of doctors accompanied the patient in an ambulance till they reached the outskirts of Bengaluru. Once we reached, the police did not want to take any chances by allowing an ambulance with a Karnataka state registration number across the border into Tamil Nadu. We were asked to stop the ambulance about a kilometre before the Tamil Nadu-Karnataka border. Left with no other option, we took the patient out of the ambulance and strapped him in a wheelchair. We then walked and pushed the wheelchair for a kilometre on National Highway 7 under the cover of darkness and crossed the border to enter Tamil Nadu. This was the longest one kilometre of my life. We tried our best to stay calm and convince ourselves that we were going to be fine. We were intentionally crossing in the middle of the night so that the risk of mob violence was the least. When the cops manning the border saw us, they were dumbstruck. A team of doctors pushing a patient on a wheelchair to enter Tamil Nadu in the middle of the night was not a sight they had expected.

An ambulance with a Tamil Nadu registration number was waiting for us on the other side of the border. We breathed a sigh of relief as we got into the ambulance and drove for another two hours to Salem to reach the hospital. The surgery started around 4 am and was completed by 2 pm the next afternoon.

Later that evening, when the patient was stable, he was extubated and taken off the ventilator. His blood test reports were up to the mark and showed that the liver transplant was a success. In the night, when the entire team gathered for dinner, we sat back and pondered upon what it had taken to make this transplant happen. Was it absolutely necessary for us to undertake this life-threatening journey? Should we have risked our own lives to save a patient's? What would have happened to our families if anything happened to us? Would we do this again in a similar scenario?

The only answer to all the above questions was a unanimous and resounding yes. It's moments like these that require stepping up and feeling the gravitas of the white coat. It's not merely a profession, it's a calling, a mission, or perhaps even devotion. It requires unparalleled involvement, commitment, respect and willingness to help all other people.

Therefore, we would trudge on numerous life-threatening journeys to save lives. We would do it again and again for we are blessed and proud to be in this noble profession of saving lives. In this particular case, the patient recovered quickly after the liver transplant and continues to visit us for follow-ups. A member of his family usually accompanies him and, each time they come, the midnight adventure flashes across my mind. However, the moment I see him and his family member, there's not a shred of doubt in me that the effort was—fully and undeniably—worth it.

With over 20 years of experience as a hepatologist, Dr Olithselvan A. is currently practising at Manipal Hospital, Bengaluru. He is credited with establishing the first liver transplant centre in western Tamil Nadu. He is an expert in dealing with cases related to liver transplantation evaluation and post-liver transplant care; cirrhosis and end-stage liver disease; acute liver failure; and jaundice evaluation and treatment. Dr Olithselvan is a member of General Medical Council, UK; Royal College of Physicians, UK; International Liver Transplantation Society; and Indian National Association for Study of the Liver. His passion is to offer the best treatment in the most cost-effective manner in India. This emanates from his observations that these treatments are highly expensive overseas.

Did You Know?

In the horrifying violence that followed the Partition in 1947, the angry mobs didn't even spare hospitals. When an Amritsar hospital was attacked by a Hindu-Sikh mob, Dr Purushottam Dutt and his brother, Dr Narain Das, took out their guns and confronted the assailants and did not allow them to touch the Muslim patients in their hospital. In another incident, a Muslim doctor in Amritsar, Dr Abdur Rauf, saved 200 non-Muslims who were cornered in the Katra Karam Singh locality. Asked to decide on their fate, Dr Rauf invoked Islamic teachings of moral conduct to counter those who wanted to avenge the mistreatment of Muslims in other parts of Amritsar. His words led to all the non-Muslims being set free.

Source: https://www.thebetterindia.com/67924/unsung-heroes-partition-india-pakistan

Dear People,

'The law of nature is creation and destruction. In between these two extremes is the role of medical professionals.'

Dr Pradeep Chowbey

Dharamshala to Dharamshala

The Journey of a Thousand Miles

Ever since I was a child, I would spend my time at my father's dispensary, manually mixing medicines on cue for his patients. It was this early stint that established the choice of career for me long before I knew the real responsibilities of a doctor. In 1977, I arrived in New Delhi from a small town in Madhya Pradesh because I had landed a job in a hospital.

My childhood dream of becoming a surgeon was coming true. As the journey began, I realised how excruciatingly challenging yet immensely rewarding medicine can be.

On a usual day as the surgical registrar at the Ram Manohar Lohia Hospital in New Delhi, I got a break from rigorous night duties and continuous shifts that often ran through 48 hours. I vividly recall that chilly winter night. Cold winds had taken over the city, but I was lucky to be comfortable and cosy in my hostel room. Fortunately, no emergency duty was scheduled.

As I was about to retire for the night, I heard a knock on my door. One of the ward boys wanted me to come down and see his five-year-old son who was admitted to the hospital for severe dehydration earlier that day. I tried to explain to him that I was not the right person to treat a case of dehydration, but he insisted that my healing touch would be enough to cure the child. I was persuaded by his faith and I reluctantly stepped out and followed him through the fog that had set in.

As I stood before the little boy hooked to the drip, I casually picked up the reports, looked through them mindlessly and affirmed to the father that the right treatment was being followed. Moving to touch his forehead, I rested my hand there for a few seconds. There was nothing more to be done. The ward boy thanked me profusely as I hurried to get back to the comfort of my warm room to catch up on some much-needed sleep.

The next morning, I learnt my first lesson in the power of faith and compassion; the father came looking for me with a sort of reverence and the news of his son's quickened recovery. As a young doctor starting out in his career, this was the first of many such incidents that kept reaffirming the importance of practising compassion. Through the years, I realised that serving patients involves spending time with them, holding their hands and sometimes talking about things that are important to them. Since then, I have strived to treat every patient with an added dose of compassionate care.

As the years progressed, I grew as a medical professional and established a dedicated centre for minimal access, metabolic and bariatric surgery. It was here that I matured as a surgeon and began to understand the nuances of surgery. Initially, my field of interest was hepatobiliary, pancreatic and breast surgery and I was keen to treat cancer via surgical oncology.

Unfortunately, cancer affects every organ of the body and always appears to be a step ahead of medical intervention. Each surgery brought a new wave of helplessness and thoughts of futility and after a few years, I was completely disillusioned. Surgical care in cancer came with the cost of tremendous post-operative pain and discomfort, both for the patient as well as the doctor.

In the initial years, I was constantly struggling as people associated 'surgery' with something dangerous, something to be feared. It sparked a negative feeling in most patients and drove them towards alternative and conservative courses of treatment, which often failed. It was challenging to make people see that the surgical removal of organs affected by cancer was positive, a way to cure the body rather than destroy it.

The inability to alleviate post-operative suffering from large incisions of surgery left me with a void. However, in 1989, after a decade spent in conventional open surgery, I came across a surgical demonstration that altered my path forever. At a conference of the American College of Surgeons in New Orleans, I witnessed four cases of endoscopic gallbladder surgeries that seemed nothing short of a miracle.

What astonished me was that the patients were walking the very next day and subsequently recovering within the next few days to resume work and daily activities. Quick recovery time, less post-operative pain and no large incisions—this was something my dreams were made of. I gravitated towards this new procedure called laparoscopy. It was my higher calling. Three small punctures of laparoscopy, as opposed to larger incisions of oncology, could go a long way in making countless lives back home easier. It was meant to be!

Each time I thought of the possibilities, I was torn between continuing with oncology or battling the learning curve of laparoscopy. It was a difficult decision, considering a shift in speciality after almost a decade in surgical oncology but it seemed imperative. Like a phoenix, I was reborn from the ashes of mutilating surgeries with large incisions to the kind cuts of laparoscopic surgery.

Initially, there was immense resistance from the senior surgical community. However, a change was on its way and I had already chosen my path. At that time, it seemed unnatural, impractical and prohibitively expensive. It also led to a lot of mockery but despite the initial expenditure involved, I believed laparoscopy was the best solution for the masses: those who worked on daily wages and suffered losses due to months spent in recovery after surgery. Since I was committed to making a difference for my people in delivering the best healthcare possible, I was always up for a debate.

As the years passed by, laparoscopy was widely adopted. The initial inhibitions waned with each successful operation and the perspective gradually shifted towards acceptance and positivity. There was always a certain calmness that patients experienced post a laparoscopic surgery, which was very different from the post-operative course of open surgery. Gradually, patients, too, developed confidence in the procedure and that helped yield far better results when it came to recovery. Over the next few years, I trained countless surgeons across the country. And thus, it began—the laparoscopy revolution in India.

However, in recent years, despite the medical advances, we are witnessing a disturbing trend in the medical fraternity where patients are distrustful of doctors. It is disconcerting for older doctors like me who learnt the ropes from their seniors. I used to observe how gently my father interacted with each of his patients and that taught me what the doctor-patient relationship should be. However, striking the right balance can be intimidating and, often, there is no balance. Over the years, I have realised that the doctor-patient relationship is based on empathy and trust. For it to work, patients must have faith and medical professionals must have the singular objective of curing and managing the ailment.

For a surgeon, however, technical challenges are not the most important. The management of personalities and circumstances can make or mar a surgeon and his practice.

Add to that the pressure of protocols and it is a different ball game altogether. In March 2001, we received a call from the Rashtrapati Bhavan to schedule a visit as the then President of India Shri K.R. Narayanan had complained of acute pain in the abdomen. He was in his early 80s and had a history of cardiac bypass surgery along with a number of other co-morbid and complex medical conditions. I had been appointed as the honorary surgeon to the President of India in 1997, and this for me was indeed a call of duty. I was briefed about the complications while being escorted to the residential wing. On examination it was instantly clear that the pain was due to stones in the gallbladder. The investigations revealed that small stones had slipped into both, the common bile duct and the pancreatic duct.

In the midst of all the chaos, decisions had to be taken regarding his prior commitments and schedules, the most important was that of hosting the prestigious and much-awaited Padma Awards that were to be held on that very evening. Considering his health and condition at the time, I took an extremely calculated risk of allowing them to proceed as planned. After suggesting that I be present throughout the ceremony, the president geared up for an uncomfortable evening loaded with painkillers that would eventually make him drowsy. As the ceremony commenced, I took a front row seat and anxiously watched the proceedings, looking for hints of fatigue or pain. He conducted the situation with utmost grace and charm and as the function drew to a close, we all breathed a sigh of relief.

Within the next few days, the scheduled surgery took place under stringent protocols. The president, however, was a source of encouragement and composure for the entire team, letting each one of us know that he was confident about our capabilities as pioneers in the field of surgery. Taking longer than usual, the surgery inched towards a close and once the sutures were firmly in place, we knew he was on his way to a speedy recovery.

After being discharged, he walked out comfortably, greeting the media and extending an invitation to each of the team members for an evening at the Rashtrapati Bhavan. He personally invited everyone, from the topmost consultants to the lift operator and the technicians who wheeled him into the operation theatre. He greeted us with his typical soft and generous demeanour, humbly meeting each one of us and gifting us wrist watches as a token of his appreciation. It was, indeed, an evening we cherish till date.

This brings me to my next story, seven years later. In October 2008, I was delivering a lecture in Japan when I received a phone call from India. I was requested to urgently tend to an unnamed VIP patient who was reluctant to opt for surgery to cure a severe case of gallbladder stones. I suggested that my team of doctors were available in Delhi but the caller insisted on my presence. After a lot of reluctance, he finally revealed that it was His Holiness the Dalai Lama who was struggling with acute abdominal pain.

The flight back was unnerving. I didn't know the magnitude of the task that lay ahead or the impact it would have on me. When I landed in Delhi, I headed straight to the monastery in Dharamsala and geared up for an audience with His Holiness. Suddenly, the restless energy that had taken over throughout my journey was replaced by calmness. I caught a glimpse of him at the end of a long corridor. He was waiting to meet me outside the preaching room. As I quickened my steps towards him, his face became clearer. Although he was a little weary from the pain and discomfort, his eyes twinkled with happiness and beautiful wrinkles formed at the corners as he smiled. He greeted me warmly, clasping my hands and leading me to the king chair, where he sits to deliver his sermons. 'Today you will advise me what to do, so you will sit in my place and I will listen to you,' he said with a chuckle, sitting on the sofa meant for visitors.

I uneasily perched myself up on his chair. This time, I was up for the placebo effect as, contrary to what one might believe, there was no magical transformation. Despite that, a sudden clarity took over and I did what I knew best, thinking about the treatment of a patient with gallbladder stones. Within a matter of a few minutes, I explained to him that the body works round the clock and like a machine, it's prone to wear and tear. If one part of the mechanism stops working, then the only solution is to remove it from the system so that normal functions can resume. Listening in complete silence, he said, 'If you say so. I think we can set a date and go ahead with it.' The date was set for 9 October 2008.

When His Holiness got admitted to the hospital, there were no traces of anxiety or stress. In fact, when he was wheeled into the OT, he had a sense of composure that helped us concentrate better. When we anaesthetised him and gained access into his abdominal cavity using needles and insufflators (where carbon dioxide is used so that space can be created during laparoscopic surgery), we witnessed something we had never seen throughout our careers—all the monitors went blank without any explainable reason. There was silence for the next few seconds, but no one panicked or said a word—it felt as if time had stood still. When the screens flickered back on, we continued on without any mention of the event. Looking back, it feels like an unreal memory, lingering on without a logical or technical explanation. The rest of the procedure went on smoothly.

The experience of being in such close proximity with His Holiness the Dalai Lama taught me the true meaning behind practising compassion. His presence radiated an unmatchable aura of love, happiness, harmony and brotherhood that cut across age, race, culture and belief. I had witnessed a rare divinity.

However, I must say that a clinician's intention is always to save a life, irrespective of who lies before them at the operating table. The law of nature is creation and destruction. In between these two extremes is the role of medical professionals. The medical profession in its true sense is always trying to find a path for disease management that is against nature. As clinicians, our intention is to reduce the suffering, enhance recovery and aim to cure whenever possible. However, we must not forget that the ultimate winner is always going to be Nature (God).

My life came to a full circle when I started my professional career and stayed in a dharamshala in Delhi and then had the honour of operating on His Holiness the Dalai Lama and spending precious time with him at his abode at Mcleodganj (Dharamshala), Himachal Pradesh, atop the mountains. The journey has been gorgeous, filled with blessings, love and happiness.

Dr Pradeep Chowbey has pushed the envelope in laparoscopic surgery in India. Currently, Executive Vice Chairperson of Max Healthcare, he established the Minimal Access and Bariatric Surgery Center at Sir Ganga Ram Hospital in New Delhi in 1996. It was the first-of-its-kind minimal access and bariatric surgery centre in Asia. Dr Chowbey has had the honour of operating on Shri K.R. Narayanan, former President of India, and His Holiness, the Dalai Lama, for laparoscopic gall bladder surgery. With over 72,000 surgeries to his credit he is featured in the Guinness Book of Records 1997 and Limca Book of Records 2000–2017 (consecutive years) as the first endoscopic surgeon performing most number of minimal access surgeries.

He has authored more than 200 clinical publications and several book chapters. He has also been at the helm of many national and international surgical societies as their president. In 2002, the Government of India awarded him the Padma Shri.

Did You Know?

Spirituality is recognised as a factor that contributes to the health of many persons. The concept of spirituality is found in all cultures and societies. It is expressed in an individual's search for ultimate meaning through participation in religion and/or belief in God, family, naturalism, rationalism, humanism, and the arts. All these factors can influence how patients and healthcare professionals perceive health and illness and how they interact with one another.

Source: Association of American Medical Colleges. (1999). Report III: Contemporary issues in medicine: communication in medicine. Medical School Objectives Project. *Washington, D.C: Association of American Medical Colleges, pp. 25-26.*

Dear People,

'Burn injury is a huge public health problem. In fact, more people die of burn injuries in India than malaria and tuberculosis.'

Pragya Prasun Singh

Scarred, Survived and Succeeded

I had a troubled childhood marred by sexual abuse. During those years, the only person I felt close to was my maternal grandfather. He was my pillar of strength and the one I have numerous fond memories with. However, my association with him was short-lived. When I was about to enter college, he suffered a massive stroke. It was heartbreaking to see him in such a miserable condition. The stroke left him paralysed and he could neither talk nor walk on his own. I devoted myself to his care during his entire treatment and helped with his physiotherapy for the next year. During that time, I matured as a person and realised that I could think beyond my personal trials. I found out that I was capable of taking care of my loved ones and that taking care of others dulled my own pain.

When I was 23 years old, I graduated with a degree in fashion management and got married to a boy of my parents' choice. Two weeks after my marriage, I was going to attend a campus placement interview at my college in Delhi but that same evening, my beloved grandfather passed away. I was reluctant to leave and wanted to be with my parents but they persuaded me to attend the interview. As per tradition, a newly-wed could not attend a funeral. Probably, I should not have listened to them and stayed back as no one could have imagined what lay in store for me that ill-fated night.

I was on a train to Delhi and around 2 am, I was jolted out of my sleep. I was in immense agony as I fell from the berth, only to realise that my whole body was blazing like an inferno. It felt like I was on fire. I lost consciousness. After many days, when I finally opened my eyes, I saw that I had been doused with acid by a heartless coward who wanted to marry me but my parents had not agreed. For 17 days, I swung between life and death in the ICU of the burn ward in a hospital in New Delhi. I had sustained 47% burns and acid fumes had penetrated into my lungs. Even the doctors had very little hope that I would make it.

Once my condition stabilised, I was shifted to the burns ward where I spent the next three months. In those three months, I witnessed many patients entering the burns ward screaming and leaving silently, shrouded in white. Every day, I saw different kinds of burn cases and heard stories which shook me from inside. Night after night, I heard the painful screams of other patients and sometimes the sounds of crying relatives, whose loved ones had lost the battle of life. I just could not comprehend why doctors were not able to save these patients. Some of the patients who passed away had comparatively minor burns than mine. Some died soon after surgery or after contracting some kind of infection. At times, I would be furious and would blame the doctors for not being able to save these precious lives but the truth dawned on me soon. The problem is that our country does not have good infrastructure for treating burn patients.

Burn injury is a huge public health problem. In fact, more people die of burn injuries in India than malaria and tuberculosis. As per the data extrapolated from the information received from three major government hospitals in Delhi, approximately two lakh burn patients become disabled and 1.4 lakh people die due to burn injury annually. This comes to one death every four minutes due to burns. Sadly, burn injury is still mostly unrecognised in our country.

I remember another patient named Manju who was also a newly-wed like me. She had sustained burns when her clothes caught fire while making tea for her father-in-law. While my injuries were spread across the face, neck, hands, chest and back, Manju's injuries were confined to her chest and hands. Over a period of time, she and I grew quite fond of each other. She would smile whenever she saw me. I would always encourage her and tell her that we should be thankful to just be alive. We were lucky to have supportive husbands and families and we needed to live for them. We could not disappoint them by showing our pain.

Manju and my surgeries for skin grafting were planned in the same week. Manju got operated two days before me and when I heard that her surgery was successful, it increased my confidence. Soon it was time for my surgery. While it was successful, I was confined to the bed for almost 15 days after it. I also developed an infection in the donor area (the thigh region from where the skin is harvested) which required a change in dressing within a week. I will never forget how painful it was.

The pain of dressings was even worse than the pain of being scalded with acid. I would shudder at the mere thought of dressing and sometimes even beg the doctor to just kill me as I could not bear that pain any longer. Every day, I would pray that the dressing person would be in a good mood and would be gentle during the whole process. It took me 10 days after that dressing to walk and the first thing I did was to visit Manju in her room.

A shiver ran down my spine when I saw another patient on her bed. I found out that Manju had developed an infection and died five days after her surgery. I realised how lucky I was to be alive despite developing an infection at the donor site.

Manju's death got me thinking that I was sleeping on a deathbed. I didn't mourn her death, instead, I prayed to God to give me more strength. I started taking better care of myself, not just because I wanted to live but also because I did not want the efforts of my loved ones to go in vain. After all, they were also suffering along with me. My mother never gave up no matter what the doctors told her about my life after the acid attack. She didn't know that burns resulting from an acid attack could never look normal again. A single incident changed my life but I believe that, sometimes, it is better to have hope that stems from ignorance rather than despair that stems from knowledge.

My experience taught me that burn patients need much more effort when compared to others in a hospital. However, in India, doctor and nurses specialising in burns are overloaded with patients. The nurses in burns ward, who spend their lives in such miserable conditions, are never compensated as they should be. There is an acute shortage of burn units in private hospitals and there are hardly any separate wards for burn patients in paediatric age groups. The majority of the burn patients belong to the lower strata of society; hence, their paying capacity is much lower compared to patients suffering from other ailments. As a result, all patients are just dumped together in a ward where they become highly vulnerable to infections. A patient who has burns has no choice but to live with the stinking smell of his/her burnt skin till the wounds are healed but the nurses and doctors who have to stay and help them heal are never appreciated or compensated fairly for their work.

After three long months, I was discharged from the hospital and taken to Chennai for an eye treatment as the vision in my left eye was deteriorating. At the end of my tests, I was informed that nothing could be done to recover the vision in my left eye at that stage. Had I come a little earlier, things could have been different. I was extremely disappointed because at the previous hospital I kept complaining to the doctors about the deteriorating vision but they kept telling me that it was due to infection and it would improve later. They had said that my wounds took priority over the vision.

Now after hearing that nothing could be done to save my left eye's vision, my mind was flooded with questions. Perhaps I should have pushed the doctors in Delhi to take the eye issue more seriously. But how would I have known? I was not an expert. It's the doctor's job to give me the right advice. Of course, stabilising the patient after burn injury is their priority but was it right to neglect the eye?

While I was miffed with my previous doctors, the doctors in Chennai came as angels in my life. I was operated within three days of my consultation. The operation had to be hurried so that, unlike my left eye, we could save my right eye by creating a proper eyelid. Ever since the attack, my upper and lower eyelid had melted away and my eyes would remain open even while sleeping.

By then, I had developed the courage to accept it as a part of my fate and move on. In the next few months, I underwent multiple surgeries for my neck, hand contracture release and nose, chin and eyelid reconstruction. I continued to ask questions and that helped me care better for myself and accelerated my recovery process. Of course, doctors did not have as much patience with all others. It is understandable that doctors may not have that much time to interact with each and every patient. Doctors and nurses are already overloaded with work. Imagine one nurse for 30 patients? How much time can she afford to spend with each patient on counselling, along with doing her regular work?

During the course of my treatment, I had consulted and had been operated in a government hospital as well as some of the most reputed private hospitals in the country. I can confidently say that most hospitals were overflooded with patients and that they all lacked proper counselling facilities and guidance. The real patient care and a holistic approach to rehabilitation were missing. After witnessing the plight of several acid-attack and burn survivors, I was aware of patients who were in a much worse condition than I was. I was fortunate to get timely help and medical treatment, but many are abandoned by their own family and the society to suffer alone in the darkness.

I wanted to do my bit to help them in whatever way I could and started a non-profit to counsel and empower survivors by educational and vocational training and facilitating reconstructive surgeries and non-surgical cosmetic procedures. Today, I am proud of my accomplishment, contribution and reformed thought process: 'I am not a victim,' I say, 'I am an "ambassador". I have to fight for others who need my support at this moment and here I stand as proof that I'm not what happened to me, I'm not my face, I'm what I make of myself. I'm a story with a happy ending.'

Pragya Prasun Singh is an acid attack survivor turned activist and social worker who has been fighting for providing relief and rehabilitation to her fellow acid attack and burn survivors for the past six years now. She is the founder and secretary of Atijeevan Foundation, an NGO that apart from facilitating surgeries free of cost, it also provides avenues for income generation to several acid-attack and burn survivors by training them to create handicraft products. She has been coordinating with eminent doctors and hospitals from across the country for medical advice and treatment. A postgraduate in fashion management, she is the recipient of several Indian and international awards and accolades for her exemplary work in the field of social welfare.

Did You Know?

India has the highest incidence of acid attacks in the world, rising from 83 incidents in 2011 to 349 in 2015. The easy availability of acid is the primary reason for India's failure to prevent such attacks. Four years after the 2013 judgement when the Supreme Court ordered every state and union territory to outlaw the over-the-counter sale of acid, one can still buy a bottle without much difficulty in various places across the country.

Source: https://www.hindustantimes.com/india-news/four years after-ban-acid-sales-in-free-flow-under-supreme-court-nose/story-00tu9xW1AEFGwMChlrp7ML.html

Dear People,

'For them, we had changed from demigods to monsters. In our own mind, we had gone from hero to zero, fearless to timid, gutless and easily terrified.

Dr Rajiv N. Palvia

When a Mob Destroyed Our Hospital

On 24 January 2010, a 25-year-old man was brought to our hospital in Pen, a small town in the Raigad district of Maharashtra. He was injured while playing in a sports tournament and now complained of chest pain and severe backache. As our hospital was well-known in Raigad, he was transferred from Alibaug where his tournament had taken place. At the time of admission to the hospital, the patient was stable, his physical examination and ECG was normal. However, he did have a history of uncontrolled diabetes with diabetic retinopathy.

Treatment was initiated immediately. However, soon after, he developed severe chest pain and collapsed. An ECG was done and it showed an extensive anteroseptal infarct which means an obstruction of blood supply to the heart leading to a massive heart attack. All measures to resuscitate him failed and the patient could not be revived. Unfortunately, he was declared dead after half an hour and the police was informed as per the routine protocol.

While we had tried our best to save this patient, we could have never imagined the aftermath of this incident even in our wildest dreams. The news of his death spread like wildfire and in less than an hour a large mob of around 2,000 people assembled outside our hospital. We sensed danger and reached out to the police, requesting them to send their personnel at the earliest. But before the police could arrive, a few rogues from the mob barged in and started ransacking our hospital. They also threatened us with dire consequences. At first, the threats were verbal but soon the mob turned violent. Each and every instrument, furniture, electric appliance in OPD, wards, special rooms, ICCU, OT, labour room, casualty and laboratory was shattered. Someone started a fire in the chemist's shop and an LPG cylinder was thrown in the fire to blast the premises.

We were appalled and could not believe what was happening. A moment ago, the building was a hospital with admitted patients and their families. Now, it had turned into a war ground with everyone running to save their lives. We had to act swiftly. The police helped us to quickly evacuate the admitted patients from the ICCU and the wards. While we were busy protecting other patients, the mob had advanced to our residence on the second floor of the hospital where our families were present. Nothing was spared and a handful of policemen were totally helpless in front of the mob. Somehow, we managed to escape that night but not before risking our lives to save our families and our patients. The intensity of violence can be judged by the fact that apart from the police, nine vehicles of the Rapid Action Force had to be deployed in that small town of Pen for the next couple of weeks in anticipation of further violence.

In people's minds, we had changed from demigods to monsters. In our own mind, we had gone from hero to zero, fearless to timid, gutless and easily terrified. We escaped from our own hospital like fugitives and headed towards Mumbai. We knew that if we were found, we would be killed instantly. Even if we did escape death, we didn't have the answers to many questions: What next? What did the future have in store for us? What would we do in Mumbai? What if those people found us there? What if the police implicated and arrested us?

In the next few weeks many rumours were spread about the incident: the doctor killed the patient, the doctor gave the wrong injection, the patient had polytrauma and critical injuries were missed by the doctors. Most people found it very hard to believe that a 25-year-old could have a heart attack and die of it.

It was the worst day of our lives. Everything that we had worked hard to create over so many years had come crashing down in one evening. Not only was it a financial setback, but also an emotional and a reputational setback for us. It took us months to recover from the shock we experienced that night.

In Mumbai, we took refuge at our friend, Dr Manish Motwani's residence. He took great care of us and we shall forever be indebted to him for helping us during that troubled time.

Meanwhile in Pen, the deceased's family members, other villagers and local politicians were pressuring the administration to arrest us. The family was refusing to take the dead body after postmortem which, incidentally, had been performed 'on camera'. It was only after the intervention of the inspector general of police that the relatives agreed to take the body for final rites.

In order to save ourselves from this unpardonable maligning, we met the then Home Minister Shri RR Patil. He looked at the provisional report of the postmortem and assured us of police protection and strict action against culprits.

After that, around 40 people were arrested and charges were framed against them. Out of these, 10 were juveniles and were released. The remaining 30 were behind bars for around eight months after which they too were released. This was probably the biggest number of people arrested in India for vandalising a hospital.

Meanwhile, the case reached the sessions court in Alibaug. We, along with the police, identified the miscreants involved in the violence. Our ordeal continued as the court acquitted them citing that the doctors were biased in their identification. Our appeal in the High Court got rejected as they did not deem the case fit for appeal.

As I look back, I often wonder if identifying people who damaged our hospital in front of our own eyes is not enough proof for the court of law, then what is?

After a couple of years, we reopened our hospital but much to our chagrin, the environment remained hostile. People did not trust us anymore and the doctor-patient relationship was at its worst. Ultimately, we decided to close our hospital and shifted to Goa for further studies. I took up a senior residency post in urology and nephrology at the Goa Medical College.

As time passed by, slowly, I regained my self-confidence and lived what, in retrospect, was the golden phase of my life. I learnt windsurfing and scuba diving in Goa and extensively explored the state and its numerous beaches. It helped me heal internally and start thinking clearly. Slowly, I gathered the strength to begin all over again. After a few years, I came to Mumbai and started another multispeciality hospital in Navi Mumbai. My cofounders of the Pen hospital opened another hospital in Pen.

That incident taught us numerous lessons. One of the biggest lessons that I learnt was that though a few patients are troublemakers, the same is not true for patients at large. Even today I respect and have tremendous faith in the sanctity of the doctor-patient relationship. Similarly, the medical profession also has some black sheep but that again is not true for all doctors. This incident also made us realise the importance of money and the value of time. Today, we practise in a cosmopolitan area with tremendous positivity and respect from people around us.

Though this incident was very unfortunate, it forced us to look at life in a different light. It taught us that doctors, too, need to take a break and enjoy life. Life is unpredictable and we learnt to value it. It taught us to make time for our hobbies, our families, ourselves and realise that even for doctors, there's a life beyond treating patients.

Dr Rajeev N. Palvia is a gold medallist in surgery from Mumbai University. He is trained in bariatric (weight loss) surgery and minimally invasive surgery (laparoscopy and endoscopy). Dr Palvia has attended and presented papers in various national and international conferences. He is attached to various corporate hospitals in Navi Mumbai and is the Head of Department of Surgery at Yerala College, Kharghar.

Did You Know?

There exist no 'central' law in India for the protection and safety of the medical community. While it is a non-bailable offence to assault a uniformed public servant like a bus driver or a policeman, there is no distinct penalty for hitting an on-duty physician in a white coat. Such acts of violence go unpunished as, in most cases, the incident ends up as a compromise between the two parties, which encourages the occurrence of such incidents.

Around 18 states across the country do have such laws in place to protect medical personnel. However, they are usually not implemented efficiently and doctors are often left to face the wrath of unhappy kin of a patient.

Source:https://www.thestatesman.com/india/violence-against-doctors-on-the-rise-hospitals-need-better-security-measures-1502665989.html

Dear People,

'Ethics form the cornerstone of the doctor-patient relationship.'

Dr Ravi Wankhedkar

A Doctor Is Always a Doctor

The day 19 December 2009 is etched in my memory for two reasons. My wife Meena and I, along with a group of 20 other members of the IMA, Dhule, were on a cruise in Lakshadweep for a breather from our usual hospital routine. The other reason why I remember the day so distinctly is because it was also our 25th wedding anniversary. What made the day exceedingly wonderful was that 25 years ago, we were on the same island in Kadmat for our honeymoon. While the anniversary was a big reason why the day was memorable, the ensuing chain of events ensured that it was a day I'll never be able to forget.

The day started ordinarily—a sunny day, ideal for sunbathing. Some of us were relaxing on the beach, others were enjoying water sports. Suddenly, someone from the hotel staff came running towards us. 'Doctor Sahib,' he said, 'a man has drowned while snorkelling. Please do something'. Meena, the entire IMA team and I rushed to the spot where the body of the man was lying. He was not showing any obvious signs of life. There was no pulse and he was frothing at the mouth. Our picnic mood vanished and we started resuscitating him immediately.

Though the island was remote, it had an ambulance and a primary healthcare centre (PHC). After 10 to 15 minutes of continued resuscitation, the young man's heart started beating again. Fortunately, by that time the ambulance had arrived and we shifted him to the PHC.

At the centre, we managed to get help for basic life support and resuscitation. While his pulse returned, he wasn't breathing and continued to froth at his mouth. One of the doctors from our IMA group was an anaesthetist. He found a laryngoscope and immediately inserted an endotracheal tube (used to ensure the adequate exchange of oxygen and carbon dioxide). He then started artificial ventilation through an ambu bag. Meanwhile, another member of the team secured an IV line and administered injections of hydrocortisone and furosemide.

Once the man was partially revived and stabilised, we called his relatives to explain the condition. After some time, a young woman in her early 20s walked in and broke down the moment she saw him. We calmed her down and spoke to her in detail about his critical medical condition. She was his wife. They had recently got married and were in Kadmat Island for their honeymoon. It was a déjà vu moment for me. What if this would have happened to Meena and me 25 years ago?

I could understand the woman's plight and imagined how it must have felt to be all alone in an unknown place. I decided that we would do everything possible to save this man. Even though he was critical, I told his wife, there was a fair chance of survival if we could get timely care in an ICU with proper ventilation and monitoring. Meanwhile, I asked her to contact both their parents. She was in a state of shock and could not remember the phone numbers of the man's parents. Somehow, we managed to contact her parents in Lucknow who were aghast when they heard what happened and were clueless about handling a situation like this.

Eventually, we took charge and informed them that we would try to shift him to the nearest ICU, wherever we could find one. The problem was that we were stuck on an isolated island, with a patient who was oscillating between life and death, and with each passing minute, we were losing precious time.

As his condition required dire measures, we contacted the naval authorities to find out if he could be airlifted. However, due to technical reasons, it was not possible for a helicopter to land on a sandy beach. At the same time, we contacted the Starship Cruise Authorities to find out if one of the ships could somehow be brought near the island as this would allow him to be airlifted from the ship. However, since Kadmat was surrounded by a shallow lagoon, a cruise ship could not be brought near it. Besides, even if we were to find a way to take him to the ship, it did not have a helipad to facilitate the airlift.

The cruise, however, did have a dispensary, with standby life-support equipment, including a defibrillator and a ventilator. Our first goal, therefore, was fixed. We decided to take him to the dispensary on the cruise ship by a small boat. The ship's crew was cooperative and agreed to our suggestion. We shifted the patient on to the small boat near the seashore. Two doctors were with him during shifting and one of them continued ventilation through the ambu bag. Thus, the young fellow was set to sail over the same waters that had attempted to drown him a few hours ago. It was a sign. The circle was completed and I had a strong gut feeling that he would definitely survive.

Once we reached the ship, it was immensely difficult to transfer him as there was a significant height difference between the small boat and the cruise ship. After numerous efforts, we finally managed to get him shifted into the cruise ship dispensary. The dispensary was equipped but the doctor on duty was used to treating only minor ailments like seasickness and headaches. He had no experience in dealing with such critically ill patients. The anaesthetist with us read the situation and immediately took control of the ventilator tubing and put the patient on the ventilator. We then set up a 24X7 rotation to ensure that at least one of us would be monitoring him at any given point in time.

Our next goal was to shift him to a proper hospital. It was difficult to predict how many days he would need to recover or if he would recover at all. We contacted the nearest naval base in Mangalore. They were willing to have him shifted to their hospital but transferring him was a big challenge as airlifting was out of question. We had no choice but to request the cruise management if the cruise itself could be taken to the Mangalore Naval Base Hospital. They agreed. Saving the young man's life had become everyone's priority.

After numerous hours in the rough seas, the cruise reached the hospital at the Mangalore naval base. Their well-equipped hospital had great infrastructure and we knew that he would be in safe hands. The young man's family members also arrived in Mangalore on the same day. Until that time, we had been his caretakers, his relatives and his family. We had grown quite attached to him and wished to see him recover completely. However, our cruise was already lagging way behind schedule and we had to leave.

We left the hospital late in the night. It had been our wedding anniversary but Meena and I had not got a second to ourselves that day. When we finally got a moment, I looked into Meena's eyes. I was feeling a tad guilty for not being able to spend any time with her the entire day. 'Meena,' I said, 'I am sorry I could not give you time on our 25th anniversary but I hope you understand.' Meena looked at me, smiled and said, 'Ravi, you saved a life on our anniversary and that was the best anniversary gift that I could have ever received.'

As days passed, the young man's family constantly stayed in touch with us. They told us that his health was improving gradually. Very soon, he was out of danger. After he recovered fully, he and his wife, along with their families, came all the way to Dhule to thank us.

As our conversations spiralled on, we discussed how the medical profession has become investigation-centric. I told them that I personally believe that clinical correlation is more important. I don't believe in investigations where the outcomes don't match my clinical findings. Treatment must be customised for each patient and medicine must be person-centric, not investigation-centric. That's what we had done for the man.

I strongly believe that medicine is not only a science but also an art. Science merges with philosophy in a doctor's clinic. It's the intersection of medicine, philosophy and art that medical ethics are all about. Ethics form the cornerstone of the doctor-patient relationship.

The experience of saving the young man in Lakshadweep taught me what it means to be a doctor. A doctor is always a doctor. It does not matter if he/she is on a vacation, partying somewhere or going through some kind of personal crisis. A doctor must be ready to sacrifice everything at the call of duty.

Unfortunately, today, it is disheartening to see patients filing court cases or resorting to violence against doctors. After almost 30 years of managing hundreds of critical trauma patients, I can say this with authority—if a doctor can communicate honestly with the patient and his family, and take the time to explain the disease, its prognosis and, at times, his own limitations, then people are willing to accept even the worst. However, giving false hope and trying hard to impose one's greatness always creates problems. Complications are the reality of the medical profession and if they do happen, doctors must seek support and involve as many other doctors as possible. Sharing responsibility always decreases stress. It is the attempt to 'cover-up' which creates more complications.

Trust is the foundation of any doctor-patient relationship. Medical technology may change, the concepts about disease and therapies may change, but humanity and empathy are values which will always stay constant. Doctors who inculcate these values will always have a strong bond with their patients. In my mind, as my own relationship with the young man is proof, such a connection is very difficult to destroy and it overcomes any physical, chemical, financial or psychological force.

Dr Ravi Wankhedkar is a professor of surgery at SBH Government Medical College, Dhule. He is a practising general and anorectal surgeon with over 30 years of experience. He is the treasurer of World Medical Association 2019–2021 and is serving as the president of SAARC Medical Association 2018–2020. He was the national president of IMA in the year 2018. He is the National Chair of the UNESCO BIOETHICS programme and is the National Chairman of IMA Accreditation Council. He was awarded the Teacher of the Decade in 1999 and has received multiple other awards. In his free time, he enjoys trekking and farming.

Did You Know?

Traditional medical ethics, in normal circumstances, condemn the doctor who ignores the call for help. In *Law and Ethics for Doctors* (1958), Stephen Hadfield affirms that 'a doctor must give necessary treatment in an emergency unless he is assured that it can and will be given by another'. The ethos of the physician is rooted in the benevolent desire to assist people in medical need. That is the raison d'être of the doctor. In the language of virtues, the doctor who ignores a cry for help may display selfishness and cowardice and lack the virtues of benevolence and compassion.

Sources: Hadfield, S. (1958). Law and ethics for doctors. *London: Eyre & Spottiswoode, 41.*
Sokol, Daniel K. (2012). Law, ethics, and the duty of care. BMJ, *345: 680.*

Dear People,

'Understanding the physical state of the patient comes easy with diagnostic tools. Understanding and appreciating the psychological turmoil caused by the disease requires special efforts.'

Dr Reina Khadilkar

The Inheritance of Goodness

In the early 1990s, I was a junior resident in the department of surgery when a young girl was wheeled into the ward with 70% burns. In those days, our hospital was not equipped to handle such a severe case of burns and, even before I could examine her, I knew that the fate of the unfortunate girl was sealed. As I conducted the examination, I heard her feeble voice ask me if she would survive. As a doctor, I had to keep her morale high and I said with a smile, 'Only if you allow me to dress the wounds every day without making noise and take all the medicines we give you'. 'I trust you, doctor', she said. Despite the fact that burn dressing is one of the most painful procedures, the brave girl did not utter a word for the next few days. Her faith in my ability to heal her and her trust that I would help her see through this traumatic episode kept her smiling through the next few harrowing days. Eventually, we lost her, but her belief in my words and her ability to face the situation at such a tender age stayed with me for a long time. It was through her endurance that I learnt the amount of trust people place in a doctor, the responsibility of words and how faith can see you through the most difficult times.

My role as a doctor has always been beyond the conventional medical-school format. My childhood was spent in the world of hospitals, patients and medicines. My parents were doctors and I lived through their stories as I saw them build a practice in the small town of Aurangabad in Marathwada, having refused a great opportunity to work in the UK.

'Every patient who walks through the door of my hospital is the invisible form of Lord Vitthal, the favourite deity of Maharashtra,' my father, Dr Shrikant Kudrimoti, often said. In the early 1960s, he was the first postgraduate physician and cardiologist to practice in the then backward district of Aurangabad.

My parents' dedication and the respect they had garnered became evident to me only after I started appreciating the world of medicine. However, even as a child, my keen eyes did not miss the gentleness in my father's hands as he touched the trembling shoulders of an anxious patient and explained the illness, ever so patiently, to the apprehensive relatives. I could see the fear disappear from the patient's face, as the stethoscope rested on his chest and the medicines were prescribed. I would be amazed to see men and women, much older than my father, touch his feet with tears of gratitude as they got better. I realised my father was not just a doctor, he was a healer, a friend and an integral part of their life. My doctor mother would invariably become a godmother to the patient and his/her family, irrespective of their age, and we as a family became a part of all the happy and sad occasions of their lives. We were invited for marriages and birthdays, farmhouse parties, shop inaugurations and every other important event. The adulation and respect my parents received at such functions only strengthened my resolve to become a doctor. Back then, the doctor-patient relationship extended beyond the confines of hospitals and illnesses.

Therefore, when I entered the world of medicine in the early 1990s, I was equipped not only with surgical skills but the ability to understand the suffering and anxiety of my patients. My parents had made sure that I became my patients' close confidante, friend and someone they could trust with their lives.

I assimilated the body language, voice modulation and the genuine compassion and empathy my parents and teachers at medical school showed when dealing with the sick. I learnt that becoming a doctor was not enough to treat an illness. One had to shoulder the huge responsibility of not just healing the mind and body but healing the family that had been uprooted by the disease. The poorest of poor patients I came across during my training, in return, taught me lessons that would last a lifetime.

During the course of many years of practice, I learnt that patients and diseases changed and so did the way we treated them. I had to look at the patient holistically, rather than just the problem he/she had come to me for. I had learnt to keep my face blank, hiding the pain I felt when I was about to disclose the fatal diagnosis of cancer to the patient and his/her relatives. I learnt to suppress my tears when tragedy struck families, who lost their loved ones to disease or accident. I learnt to think with crystal clear clarity when I was woken up at an ungodly hour by an emergency call and had to rush to save the helpless life. I learnt to leave family functions and happy occasions, as calls from the hospital inundated my pager. I learnt to hide the guilt I felt when I could not attend parent-teachers meetings in my children's school because we were operating on a patient with a perforated gastric ulcer. I learnt that I was blessed to be in a profession that was endowed with an exalted status, where personal sacrifices were a small price to pay for the sheer joy of bringing a smile on the face of a suffering human being.

My patients happened to be mostly poor and as time went by, most of them considered me a part of their family and consulted me on issues medical or otherwise. Sometimes they even asked my advice when it came to choosing a profession for their children. I became involved with their lives as a trusting friend would. On many occasions when I let go of part of the hospital bills which the patient was genuinely not able to pay, I was rewarded with bags of farm-fresh vegetables and grains and, on one occasion, a live giant crab! This patient was a fisherwoman and although I am a strict vegetarian, I could not say no to this gift from her.

Once I remember I had operated on an old man for an obstructed hernia. He had come to me in severe pain and a very poor general condition with his wife and son. No other relative came to see him in the post-operative period. The young man who claimed to be his son had left him in the hospital and disappeared after surgery. I looked after the old couple for the next eight days and would spend some time inquiring about their home and family. The old woman was a short, stout lady with a pleasant smile, a wrinkled face and forearms full of green bangles. She would speak to me at length, sharing the stories of her life. Her bangles would chinkle as she spoke and a gold bangle, in the centre of the green bunch, would shine prominently. I used to admire her ease with the two dozen bangles, knowing how I hated to wear even a single bangle. When her husband was ready to be discharged, the same young man appeared, paid the bill and when it was time for them to leave, I suddenly noticed that her gold bangles were missing. As she was leaving the consultation room, I asked her about it. She smiled warily and pointed towards the hospital bill, 'My son said he cannot pay the bill and we will have to take care of it'. She looked at her hands and smiled at me, 'Small price to pay for my husband's life'. To this day, her smile haunts me.

Several patients like these who came into my life left me with profound thoughts on the 'art' of medicine, the philosophy of accepting destiny and the ability to face suffering and death head-on. As their doctor, I had the responsibility to not break their hearts or their trust. It was not easy to shoulder this responsibility. I had to be extremely patient when confronted with agitation, gentle and soft-spoken in the face of anger and courageous during tragedies. It took a lot of blood and sweat to be all this, but I had chosen this and was determined to follow the path taught by my parents, teachers and the discipline of medicine. I managed to imbibe and follow the teachings that were given to me to lessen the pain and the suffering of the patient and his family.

As time went by, things changed. Newer advances, newer techniques, newer drugs made diseases amenable to diagnosis and treatment but the cost of treatment shot through the roof. The world had opened up and the ubiquitous internet cables made information on any illness available at the click of the mouse. People became equipped with an expanding armamentarium to question the methods of the treating doctor. Gradually, I could feel myself moving out of the inner world of my patients, restricted to their medical problems only. I could sense the isolation, as I found myself on their outer rim. The respect was there, but the love was missing. The outside circumstances defining the medical practice gradually created a rift in the emotional bond that we once had with our patients. Society had finally turned us into just 'clinicians'.

Despite a good reputation, some patients began questioning advice, opting for second and third opinions and cheaper or exclusive hospitals, depending upon their economic preferences. Corporatisation brought in all services under one roof, the newest and swanky medical equipment and highly trained specialists. But sadly, it took away the human touch, as doctors rushed from one hospital to another. Steep bills demanded steeper care, which fell short of patient's expectations and slowly but surely, trust, faith, respect and above all love started eroding, making the relationship fragile.

Over the years, I could see the doctor-patient relationship gradually heading towards a breakdown. Trust was replaced by evidence and proof and the human touch was replaced by machines. Compassion became a victim of greed from one side and unfulfillable demands of the other. A strange bitterness invaded the bond, weakening it and hurtling it towards doom. The struggle of survival, the weakening economic condition and the frustrations of daily life changed the psyche of the people and a strange phenomenon came into being. Violence against doctors took roots and hospitals across the country began experiencing this previously unheard and unpalatable truth. Deaths became unacceptable, as communication channels broke down and the healer and the healed got separated into two warring factions.

A few years ago, I had the misfortune of being on the other side of the table. A loved one was seriously ill and during his surgery, we, the relatives, were helpless bystanders. All we wanted was a word of comfort to help us face this immense tragedy. But in the mad rush that doctors have embarked upon, our doctor had no time for this smallest 'big' thing.

I found myself in a strange situation. As a healer, I was pushed out by the exorbitant demands of the patients, unable to comprehend where and why the bond had tattered. As a patient, I could feel the angst and sadness of losing the compassion expected of doctors. But I knew I had to repair the tattered fabric and restore the lost nobility.

I had always believed that the sapling has to be nurtured for the tree to be healthy and I found an opportunity to nurture in the form of a teaching job in a medical college.

The young and enthusiastic medical students came with a mind as malleable as clay and a heart full of feelings and ideals. It was imperative to make them realise that we are in a profession dealing with the human mind and body. It's not just a business, it's, in fact, an act of love honed by our skills to lessen the pain inflicted on other human beings. Our chosen path is special but we have to tread cautiously, with compassion and empathy, putting in backbreaking hours of hard work and, often, sacrificing our happiness and luxury. I made it a point to instil these values through bedside clinics, which brought my students face to face with the suffering human being. A word of sympathy, a gentle pat on the back and an appreciative and listening ear goes a long way in healing. Understanding the physical state of the patient comes easy with diagnostic tools, understanding and appreciating the psychological turmoil caused by the disease requires special efforts and is the only way to a patient's heart and health.

We often hear our patients say that half the illness disappears when the doctor talks to them. Imagine the responsibility and power of our words but with power comes responsibility, and the responsibility is of being the healer, not God.

I have faith in my teaching as my teachers and parents had faith in theirs. We inherit goodness from our former generations and it's this goodness that forms the foundation of trust. I believe that it's a matter of time and effort before we can once again restore the trust and faith and become true healers, not just clinicians in sterile environments. It's a matter of time before the suffering patient puts all his trust and his life in our hands, accepting fully well our dedication and ability to help him. The institution of medicine will always remain important as long as we have faith in our ability to reach out to the patient in a just and humane manner.

As I stand on the threshold of passing on this legacy, I am confident that the doctor-patient relationship will remain sacred.

***Dr Reina Khadilkar works as a professor in surgery at Dr DY Patil Medical College in Pune. A gold medallist in surgery, she is specialised in laparoscopic surgery, upper GI endoscopy and perianal surgery. She is passionate about teaching surgery and guiding postgraduate students in surgery. She is also a published author and blogger. She is the author of two books—*Oh! To Be a Lady Surgeon *and* At the End of the Day: Essays from Life.**

Did You Know?

The widespread use of the internet as a source of health information has caused a knowledge outcome towards attitudes and practices of people in general, as well as in the doctor-patient relationship. Thus, thousands of websites and millions of daily internet health-related information searches enable an enormous and rapid change in health behaviour. Along with the benefits of easily accessible information, there are concerns about the quality of the obtained content and its effects on the doctor-patient relationship. These concerns include unreliable information, which consequently may result in misguided self-treatment and wrong diagnosis; language barriers; commercial biases; longer clinic visits, resulting from disagreements on the patient's information presented to the healthcare professional; unnecessary tests and treatments resulting from the patient's internet search. Thus, the physician's insight, experience and encouragement are necessary to help the patient to accurately interpret and apply this information.

Source: Kim, J., & Kim, S. (2009). 'Physicians' perception of the effects of internet health information on the doctor-patient relationship'. Inform Health Soc Care, *34(3), 136–148.*

Dear People,

'As doctors, we may revel in accolades and awards, but it is smiles like these that make our professional lives worthwhile.'

Dr Rinky Kapoor and Dr Stuti Khare Shukla

Beauty Is Not Just Skin-Deep

Twenty-two-year-old Sunaina walked into our dermatology clinic in Mumbai, accompanied by her mother. True to her name, she had beautiful doe-like eyes and a lovely bronze skin tone that most Hollywood celebrities would die for. The moment she walked through the door, we were stunned by her striking looks and confident demeanour. Her skin was clear, healthy and glowing. It, therefore, broke our hearts, when, during the consultation, her mother asked us if we could do anything to make Sunaina look fairer. We pitied the elderly woman who failed to appreciate the beauty nature had bestowed upon her daughter.

We found out that Sunaina had used every home remedy and fairness cream in an attempt to lighten her skin. Finally, after everything had failed to make her fairer, she started seeking medical help. She was so pretty that we wondered why she wanted a lighter skin complexion. We explained to her that she had perfectly healthy skin with a beautiful skin tone and she must not try to change her natural colour.

Her mother, however, disagreed. 'Madam,' she said, 'she is 22 already, doing well in her studies and, hopefully, she will get a job soon. It is time she settles down in life. We have been looking for a suitable match for her for the past two years. We registered her on almost all the matrimonial sites. All they want is a fair, slim and tall girl. We have already lost some of the best matches due to her dark complexion. Please do something.'

We felt sorry that despite being a mother, she failed to encourage her daughter to be herself and allowed societal fault lines to affect their lives. Of course, she wasn't alone as an obsession with fairness has been deeply ingrained in our society for ages.

We started by explaining to Sunaina's mother that our children inherit the skin complexion from their parents. If parents themselves discriminate against children on the basis of their skin colour, imagine what they would be subjected to by the outside world. Alas, all our efforts were in vain. 'Madam, please, I am here for a solution. We are middle-class people, but we are willing to take a loan for her treatment,' the mother insisted. The lady had obviously done her research and knew it was possible to lighten one's skin tone. However, she was aghast that the dermatologists sitting in front of her were refusing to share that knowledge.

In the end, we told them about the so-called 'melanin-reduction surgery'. This therapy is something we only recommend to those patients whose skin has been discoloured or those who have an uneven skin tone. While talking about the treatment, we also explained to the mother that it would more likely harm the skin than help it if used without valid indications. At the same time, we continued to emphasise that it was a bad idea to get this procedure done just to become fair. We certainly didn't want a young girl to undergo such procedures—and all that just to bag a man.

The mother, however, was insistent on knowing more and we had to explain other skin-lightening options to her even though we didn't advocate their use. We told her about skin-lightening creams, which have to be used strictly under the supervision of a dermatologist, and about injectable glutathione—an antioxidant which acts in the melanin cycle and inhibits its production, thereby lightening the complexion.

In the end, however, we made our stance against such procedures very clear. We explained to her that we advised against a skin-lightening procedure for her daughter for both medical as well as ethical reasons. They had travelled all the way from Pune to Mumbai in the hope of getting this treatment. The mother was obviously not too pleased with our refusal to treat her daughter.

We, on the other hand, were glad that we stood our ground because this is a problem that needs an urgent solution.

The unfairness of the fairness obsession permeates very deep into our culture and it is no surprise that this unhealthy fascination has led to the creation of a multibillion-dollar fairness and skin-whitening industry. The sad reality though is that 99% of these fairness products do not work at all and instead lead to all sorts of skin ailments as side effects. We have seen thousands of patients develop side effects such as melasma, ochronosis or pigmentation disorders as a result of applying fairness creams. What's most unfortunate is that despite being aware of the facts, many of our beloved celebrities, who also serve as role models, endorse fairness products. However, exceptions do exist—and it has been heartening to see a leading actress refuse to endorse a popular fairness cream recently.

This doesn't mean numerous people don't conform to trending global beauty standards. All over the world, there is a breathless race to become size zero, have well-contoured jawlines, thigh gaps and, of course, to be fair. We've forgotten that beauty is not just skin-deep.

Last year, a couple of luxury French fashion giants banned ultra-thin, size-zero models from walking the ramp. As dermatologists, we wish something similar could be done to curb the overzealous craze for fair skin, which almost borders on the verge of being an eternal obsession in Asia. Fair skin is undoubtedly at the top of the wish lists of most Asian patients seeking dermatological intervention.

We have spent endless hours explaining to our patients that the dusky Indian skin contains the wonder molecule called melanin, which is actually a blessing, as it protects us from sunburns, skin damage and cancers—something far more common in low-melanin Caucasian skin tones. Melanin is also the reason why Indians age more gracefully. We have tried logic and reason, yet people remain persistent in their quest for a lighter skin tone. Relics of a colonial past, perhaps.

However, it'll be unfair to blame the women who desire fair skin as no matter how successful or inspiring she may become, she is always judged by her appearance. The reality is that whether it is marriage or getting a new job, women with dark and dusky skin tend to face more challenges in Asia.

At the end of the day, each one of us wishes to look like the best version of ourselves. The problem lies in equating beauty with fair skin alone. It is an unhealthy notion that needs to be shown the door with immediate effect.

This brings us to our next story. When Anuradha, a 28-year-old engineer from Chhattisgarh, walked into our clinic, we could see that she had battled with numerous skin ailments in her young life. Once she hit puberty, Anuradha had struggled with stubborn acne which left her face, back and neck severely scarred. The acne was so aggressive that it affected her shoulders and scalp as well. No conventional medicine was able to treat it. Conventionally, we do not think of acne as a disease, but only a person suffering from it knows how it can affect one's productivity and in worse cases, even take away one's identity.

Anuradha's case was similar. She had never discovered the girl hiding under all those painful acne scars because the affliction of her acne had practically taken over her life.

Everywhere she went, people commented on her skin and tried to offer unsolicited advice. So much so, that she would wake up worrying about how she would look that day and how bad the acne would be. Many people shunned her, as they thought her skin looked 'unhygienic'. She had consulted several dermatologists but, sadly, the effects of treatment were only temporary.

'Doc, it is my dream to wake up to clear, acne-free skin,' she told us during her first visit and we felt determined to make her dream come true. Not only is acne painful and bothersome, it slowly strips a person of their self-esteem and makes them withdraw from social situations. The impact of aggressive acne, therefore, is as much psychological as it is physical. It was similar in the case of Anuradha: her body language screamed self-consciousness and she avoided eye contact.

Anuradha confided that all her life she did everything in her capacity to avoid social gatherings, especially parties and weddings. She did not want people to see her because all they saw was the acne on her face and not the person to whom that face belonged. She was tired of the unending advice provided by well-meaning relatives and her colleagues. She hated the attention. Even at work, she shied away from presentations or networking with new people. She had her lunch in one corner, away from her colleagues although she missed being a part of all the fun during lunchtime. She said she was great at her job but had missed out on several opportunities for growth as she couldn't muster the confidence and courage to step forth and grab them.

We were keen on helping her and knew that we had to get to the root of the problem. We ran a battery of tests to ascertain the cause of the resistant acne and discovered that she had been living with gross hormonal imbalance all these years. The girl was shocked to know that an internal cause could affect her skin so much. With a combination of medications like isotretinoin and a procedure called carbon dioxide laser resurfacing, we were able to effectively cure her acne. This was followed by skin peels and over a period of time, her skin started looking normal again.

The delight on Anuradha's face when she came to meet us a few months after her treatment was unparalleled. She shared with us how amazing it felt to look at herself in the mirror every morning—a moment she dreaded all her life—and how she now felt more confident because she no longer needed to worry about how people perceived her. Her confidence shone through and we were truly happy for her.

As doctors, we may revel in accolades and awards, but it is smiles like these that make our professional lives worthwhile. As skin specialists, we come across varied demands from patients and clients. Some we are unable to fulfil, some we wouldn't or shouldn't fulfil for the sake of ethics, but for all, we give our 100% to bring a positive change in people's lives.

However, this is one thing we want all our patients to do themselves. We want them to realise, for themselves and others, that beauty is not just skin-deep. It lies not in fairness but in loving oneself and in being oneself.

Dr Rinky Kapoor is a renowned dermatologist and is the Director and Co-founder of The Esthetic Clinics, which have multiple centres all over India. A fellow from the Stanford Medical School, US, and National Skin Centre, Singapore, Dr Kapoor has won many awards from multiple agencies, in the field of dermatology. Dr Kapoor has many international research publications in the field of Cosmetic Dermatology and a US patent for the invention of the revolutionary QR 678 hair growth factor formulation. Besides academics,

Dr Kapoor dedicates a lot of time to philanthropic activities for the betterment of society through the Debabrata Auro Foundation.

Dr Stuti Khare Shukla is a dermatologist who has been involved in a number of campaigns against female foeticides and child abuse. She is also a fitness enthusiast and a trained Kathak dancer. Dr Stuti was a Fellow at The Esthetic Clinics, when she assisted her preceptor Dr Kapoor in writing this chapter.

Did You Know?

In 2017, the global skin-lightening industry was worth $4.8 billion, and it is projected to grow to $8.9 billion by 2027, fuelled by a growing middle class in the Asia-Pacific region. According to a Confederation of Indian Industries (CII) report, the Indian beauty and cosmetics market size stands at $950 million and is projected to grow between 15 and 20%. But now the union government, fired by the awareness of the damage that skin-lightening products like cream and lotion cause, is thinking of amending the Drugs and Cosmetics Rules, 1945, to put an end to their indiscriminate use.

Source:https://www.dnaindia.com/analysis/editorial-dna-edit-fairly-dark-the-indian-obsession-with-fairness-2673931

Dear People,

'Today, technology might be our greatest ally, but in the coming years, it will be the power of faith that would help make the world a happier place.'

Dr Rohit Shetty

Your Faith Shall Heal You

After a particularly relaxed weekend, it was a real drag to get to work on a Monday. The steering wheel in one hand and a sandwich in the other, my feet playing tango with the brakes, clutch and accelerator, I reluctantly drove to the hospital. I wasn't the only one as the traffic around told me that everyone was fighting their own battles to get to work as soon as possible. I managed to reach just in time and intuitively knew it was going to be a hectic and demanding day; the appointments in my OPD were full.

Meera, a 28-year-old lady, was the first on my list. She looked quite distressed as she walked into the OPD. She said that everything around her appeared smaller to her. Four years ago, I had performed a LASIK on her to correct her vision and the operation had been successful. This time, when I asked her to read the vision chart, she was able to read up to the last line. I meticulously checked her eyes from the cornea (the front transparent part of the eyes) to the retina (the layer of tissue at the back of the eye). Everything looked fine.

I tried to explain to her that there was no problem with her eyes but Meera seemed dissatisfied and unhappy. On the other hand, I felt that I couldn't do much to help her as I hadn't found a problem that I could treat. I escorted her out to the waiting area as I ushered the next patient in. No sooner had I left her than I heard the loud cry of a recently born baby. This was Meera's newborn, who was waiting with a nanny, excited to see her mother. I immediately realised that there was more to her problem with her vision than what, literally, met the eye. I asked Meera to use the adjoining room if she wanted to nurse the baby and decided to see her once again.

Meera came in again after I saw a couple of patients and I began asking her about her baby. She spoke about how she was adjusting to motherhood and how she spent sleepless nights because of the baby's erratic routine. 'The problem is only with my vision,' she said. 'The rest is perfect.' She talked about her uneventful delivery three months ago, as well as the happiness she felt on holding her baby for the first time. In the background, I could hear the baby cry louder and I had a strong feeling that there was a hidden pathosis there.

I asked her to get a visual field examination done. My suspicion was confirmed when the field test showed a defect in the sides of her vision—a classical bitemporal hemianopsia. Like a bolt of lightning it struck me—this was a case of Sheehan's Syndrome. A pituitary apoplexy is a rare complication of pregnancy. This syndrome occurs secondary to massive blood loss during childbirth. It leads to complete destruction of cells of the pituitary gland and, subsequently, a decrease in its function. Patients with this syndrome can experience a variety of symptoms. One of the common initial symptoms of this syndrome is decreased breast-milk production. A few patients can be asymptomatic and may remain undiagnosed for years until the symptoms of hypopituitarism (which leads to premature ageing in adults) are manifested. In this case, however, it was the baby's crying (most likely a result of hunger as the mother had decreased milk production) and not the ophthalmic examination that had led me to the diagnosis. I then referred her to a neurosurgeon for further care where she underwent surgery for pituitary apoplexy. When she visited me a few months later, her baby was smiling. It was almost as if he was telling me: 'See, I told you.'

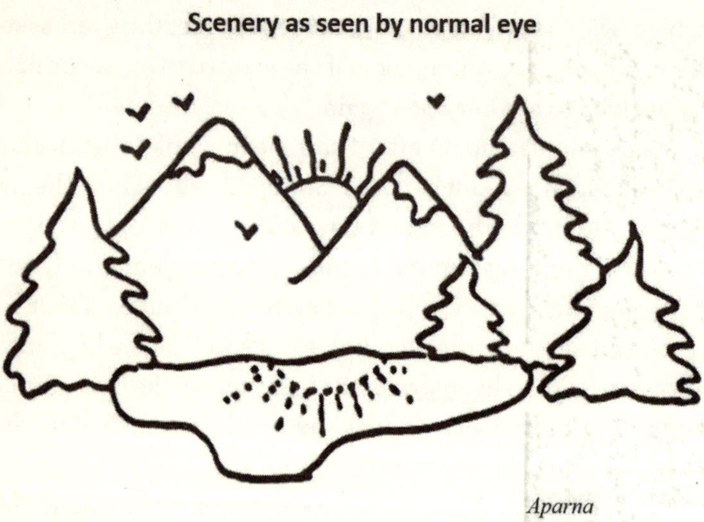

Figure 1: Scenery as seen by a normal eye

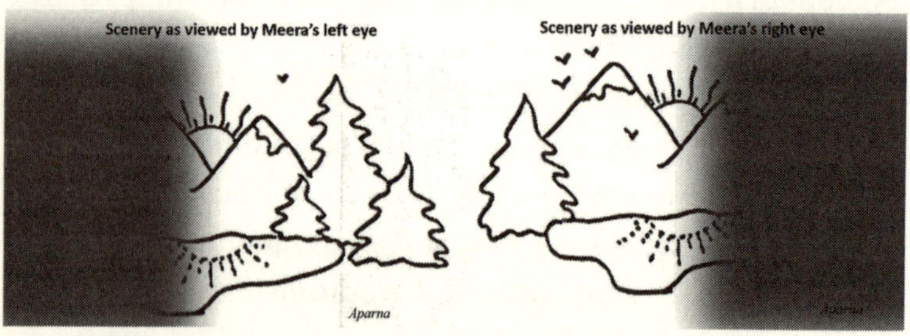

Figures 2 and 3: The same image as viewed from Meera's left and right eye respectively

Meera's case taught me that our current allopathic healthcare system aims for corrections at a macro level. Our treatments right what is easily quantifiable. This often means that the imbalances at a quantum level remain unaddressed and continue to trouble the patient and by extension, his doctor. Meera's case is one of the rare examples of how a disease manifested itself in a different way. If I hadn't paid attention to the crying baby, I would have turned Meera away and denied her the treatment she needed. Listening, therefore, is an art that every doctor needs to develop.

Good health requires homeostasis, a regulation of the immune system, clean external factors such as food and environment, a balanced flow of energy governed by the three *doshas—vata, pitta* and *kapha*—and finally, our thoughts and attitude. These factors are interlinked. An imbalance in one can trigger a domino effect, causing other systems to collapse. The reverse also holds true where regulated thoughts and energy can set right any defects in our body. Healing, therefore, must be holistic and the doctor-patient relationship plays a crucial role in helping the patient walk on the path to recovery.

Not too long after Meera, 22-year-old Dev visited my office. He complained of seeing white and black dots in his field of vision—almost like snow. He had visited many ophthalmologists before coming to me and had been told that there was nothing wrong with his eyes. He was, however, very distressed with the symptoms and hence had come to seek yet another opinion.

A software engineer by profession, he would spend long hours in front of the computer. He used to experience frequent symptoms of grittiness and dryness, for which all the doctors had advised him eye drops. The problem with his vision was also attributed to be a part of the dry eyes that he had. The drops did give him relief from the dryness but failed to ameliorate his visual symptoms. Eventually, the symptoms assumed such severity that he had to quit his job.

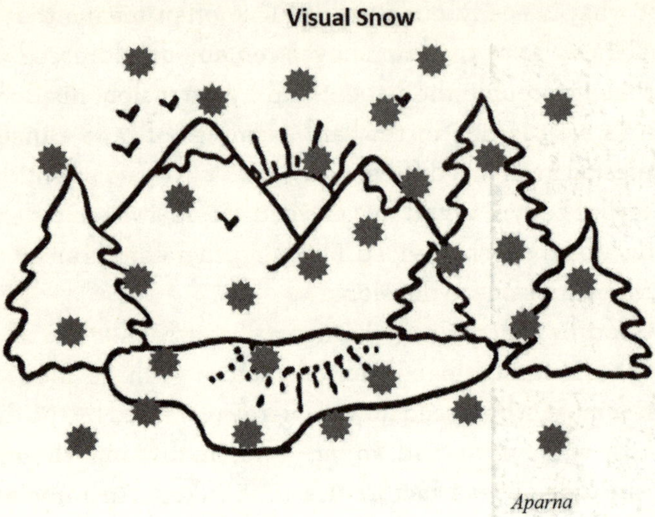

Figure 4: Visual snow causing snow-like opacities in the visual field

A frequent moviegoer, he used to catch the opening show of most movies. Over the last few months, however, the frequency of movies had dwindled as watching them had become troublesome. The screen would seem to be filled with haze which made the entire experience irksome for him.

I examined him thoroughly and found no apparent problem in his eyes. His refraction was perfect, pressures were normal, the lenses in both eyes were crystal clear, and the retinas were healthy, too. I found nothing that could explain his symptoms. I resisted the urge to tell him that there was nothing wrong with his eyes and that it was all in his head. He looked at me once I finished examining him and asked with a wry smile 'Didn't find anything, did you?' The smile soon faded into a glum expression of resignation. It was heart-breaking to see someone lose hope. That was when something in me decided that I wouldn't let him down. Suddenly, it struck me—maybe the problem was indeed somewhere in his head.

'I'm not done yet,' I told him. I assured him that I understood what he was going through and that we would get to the root of his problem. I told him that we would start with an MRI scan. He, in turn, seemed somewhat buoyed that finally someone took his complaints seriously.

The MRI scan revealed a small non-compressive pituitary adenoma (a tumour in the pituitary gland) and that's when I realised what his problem could be.

Dev was suffering from the visual snow syndrome which is a poorly understood phenomenon. Much like the noise we see in our TV sets or we hear on our radios, these dots in front of the eyes can be confused with floaters or after-images. The snow could be more in low-light conditions or may be exacerbated by the excessive use of computers. Some doctors believe that this happens due to an intrinsic noise in the brain which could be due to the increased excitability of the neurons. As of now, no established treatment exists for this condition.

However, when Dev came for his second consultation, he surprisingly seemed much happier and upbeat. He said that he had noticed a reduction in the snow since yesterday. He believed that the MRI scan was therapeutic and had relieved his symptoms. From what I had learnt in my medical training, an MRI scan only helped to diagnose a problem, not treat it. That's when I realised that maybe a different approach would work in his case. I went through his MRI in detail. It was essentially normal; however, I marked a few areas as abnormal. He felt that the areas marked on the MRI were the ones that were leading to 'noise' and subsequently to the snow-like effect in his vision. I then told him that there was a new vitamin in the market that would help him with his troubles. He seemed ecstatic and was excited about the new treatment. I asked him to come back for a visit after a month.

When Dev visited me a month later, he was a changed personality. It is known that placebos cure with a rate as high as 30%. Dev's case proved that this is because faith works in miraculous ways. Most scientific evidence claims that placebos mainly help in subjective symptoms, while hardly any change is seen objectively. However, there is a growing body of evidence that claims an improvement in the objective measurements in chronic illnesses like diabetes, hypertension or autoimmune disorders.

Dev's symptoms were the same, but he seemed far more positive. He had even resumed work. The movies were once again on his watchlist. I told him he was making great progress, to which he agreed. 'I always had faith in you and knew you would make me all right,' he said. Clearly, faith was the newest drug I had discovered and unlike many other treatments today, it came free.

Along with faith, I believe that it was the doctor-patient relationship which played an integral role. In the case of Dev, and also generally, it infuses positive thought, expectation and a commitment in the patient. It gives the patient a sense of companionship—a feeling that they are not alone in their journey towards recovery. This unquantifiable positive energy works by reducing anxiety and restoring normal physiology and indirectly controls blood pressure and immune mechanisms. The release of endorphins ameliorates the symptoms and offers immense subjective improvement.

My years in practice have taught me that it is imperative for us as caregivers to treat the patient with a holistic approach. Today, technology might be our greatest ally, but in the coming years, it will be the power of faith that would help make the world a happier place. Treatment outcomes are unpredictable even in the most skilled or experienced hands, but a strong doctor-patient relationship can be easily achieved, which, in turn, goes a long way in the overall recovery of the patient.

Dr Rohit Shetty is the Vice Chairman and corneal and refractive surgeon at Narayana Nethralaya Eye Institute, Bengaluru. He obtained an FRCS from Glasgow, Scotland in the UK in 2006. Dr Shetty has introduced cutting edge technology at the institute and is spearheading treatment for challenging eye disorders. He has close to 200 publications in peer-reviewed journals. He has presented his research work at numerous prestigious international conferences across the world. He defended his PhD from Maastricht University, Netherlands. He was awarded the prestigious Col. Rangachari award in 2015.

Did You Know?

Medicine's goal is to heal, which can include cure, control of disease and symptom relief or provision of comfort. When no cure is available—an inevitable occurrence at some points—medicine's ultimate mission is to relieve unnecessary suffering. Supportive and attentive healthcare (preferably with effective medications, but even without) legitimately creates a 'therapeutic bias' in patients toward hope and an experience of relief and reprieve. Research suggests that distinct neurobiological mechanisms are activated. Empathic healthcare creates a cognitive-affective sensory orientation, tapping into conscious and nonconscious mechanisms that can predispose patients toward reduced symptom severity and lessened reactivity to underlying pathophysiology.

Source: https://www.nejm.org/doi/full/10.1056/NEJMp1504023

Dear People,

'Medicine is a Pandora's box and every patient adds to our learning experience.'

Dr Samiran Nundy

The Power of Clinical Acumen

Many years ago, when I was an assistant professor of surgery at AIIMS, New Delhi, I had the duty to accompany my students every Friday to our satellite hospital in the small village of Ballabhgarh, Haryana. India lives in its villages but, sadly, most rural hospitals do not boast of high-end medical services. While in the olden days, most doctors derived clues from a detailed patient history and clinical examination, today, running a battery of investigations to arrive on a clinical diagnosis has become the norm. The aim of these visits to the satellite centres was to familiarise our medical students with the challenges and realities of practising medicine in small towns and villages. We believed that every doctor in the making must learn how to make the best use of available resources for the betterment of the patients.

One day, on the bus to Ballabhgarh, I was boasting to my students that they could present any patient to me and I would reach a diagnosis based only on the patient's medical history and clinical examination without the aid of any kind of investigations. When we arrived, my students presented the very first patient to me and challenged me to make a diagnosis. There were no pathology laboratories, ultrasound machines or CT scanners available for miles and I knew I had to stay true to my word.

The patient was a 12-year-old boy from a nearby village. He had a swollen abdomen and was in great agony. He was groaning with pain and was unable to say a word. His father sat with him on the floor and was extremely worried. I started asking his father about his medical history, the duration of the pain, whether it was sudden or gradual in onset, etc. The father did not know much about it but emphasised that he was the naughtiest of seven siblings and was always busy playing when he should've been going to school or doing his homework.

I turned to his mother to know what had happened. She told me that her son had always had a swelling on the left side of his abdomen. They had visited a doctor and were told that his spleen was enlarged due to fever and it would gradually regress with treatment. However, he had been given a cocktail of anti-malarial medication. Unfortunately, despite completing the entire course of medicines, the lump had not decreased in size. While hearing his story, I was thinking of all the possible differential diagnosis for a lump in the left side of the abdomen. I asked his mother a few more questions about whether he had ever vomited blood or passed black stools. I was particularly interested in the subject of extra-hepatic portal hypertension and wanted to rule it out. It is usually seen in younger patients like this young boy and can lead to enlargement of the spleen which occupies the left side of the abdomen. She informed me that he had never experienced such symptoms like blood in vomiting or stools, but he had always been a weak child.

The mother recalled that the day the boy got sick had begun ordinarily. He had gone out in the field to play with his friends but was gored in the abdomen by a cow. There were no external signs of injury but he complained of severe pain. Since that day, his abdomen had grown bigger and bigger. The mother was alarmed at the severity of the pain and the growing size of his abdomen and had asked her husband to bring him to the district hospital immediately.

Once we were done with history taking, I told the students that he suffered most likely from a traumatic rupture of the spleen, which was enlarged due to either malaria or extra-hepatic portal hypertension. Once we had made the differential diagnosis, the next step was to conduct appropriate investigations to confirm the diagnosis. This was a big challenge in Ballabhgarh as none of the advanced investigations could be performed in the area. I asked my students, in the absence of advanced facilities, which simple test could be done to confirm the diagnosis. After all, that was the purpose of the entire exercise—to make them think about how to make the most of the meagre facilities that are available in such places. They suggested that it would be best to transfer him to Delhi and get an ultrasound examination or a CT scan performed at the earliest.

Unfortunately, Delhi was an hour away and he was too sick to be moved. It was not a good idea to send him on a ramshackle bus on a bumpy journey. His systolic blood pressure was on the lower side and was hovering at about 90 mm Hg. He was in no condition to travel. We had no option but to manage him locally with the available facilities or the lack of them. My students then suggested doing a complete blood count, liver function tests, X-ray of his abdomen and a myriad other investigations. However, they were inexperienced and didn't know that these tests were of no use in the child's immediate management.

I decided that the easiest way to confirm the diagnosis, in this case, would be to inject a needle in the abdomen and aspirate (the act of removing liquid from the body). If the aspirate was bloody, it would suggest a ruptured spleen. If it showed intestinal contents, then it was likely that the bovine assault had led to a perforation of the gut. We decided to take it forward from there. I asked the child to take a deep breath and I put a needle inside his abdomen. The aspirate showed dark bloody fluid which looked a bit like blood-stained urine. That brought us to the next question—how to confirm the nature of the aspirate. My students suggested that I send the fluid to get its creatinine level measured. Though this would be confirmatory, it would need to be done in a laboratory in the town and would take at least four hours. With every passing minute, his condition was deteriorating and we did not have the luxury of time. I decided to do something simpler and poured the fluid in a kidney tray and smelled it. It was indeed urine. The diagnosis was confirmed. The child had congenital hydro-nephrosis of the left kidney. In this condition, the kidney gets enlarged and thinned out. This had ruptured into the peritoneal cavity after he had been hit in the abdomen by a cow.

Now, every passing minute was crucial as his condition was critical. His blood pressure was fluctuating and urine output had already started dropping. I had no option but to operate on him in Ballabhgarh itself. It irked me a little when I was told that there was no blood bank in the vicinity and we had to go ahead with the operation without it. Thankfully, my anaesthesia colleague was very competent and confident.

We took him into the OT and I opened the abdomen through a midline incision. I evacuated 1.5 litres of bloody urine, found a ruptured renal pelvis and, with great difficulty, managed to remove the left kidney. In the end, the child made an uneventful post-operative recovery.

I was pretty chuffed with my diagnosis and that I had managed to treat this critical patient in a place like Ballabhgarh.

I congratulated myself on this great feat and returned to my normal routine in Delhi. Over the years, I forgot all about it.

Three years later, a poor couple from a village came to see me with their adolescent son. The boy had had a high fever for a week and they insisted on seeing me. I told them that I was a surgeon and cases of fever were usually treated by physicians. I referred them to one of my physician colleagues in the department of medicine. It was then that they informed me that this was the same child who I had operated on in Ballabhgarh. I had saved his life and they only trusted me. I was rather quick and probably over-confident to freeze on the diagnosis that the child was probably suffering from infected hydronephrosis (excess fluid in a kidney due to a backup of urine) of his remaining right kidney. However, this time, I did not have the requisite experience or expertise to manage this condition. In all honesty, I informed the parents about this and referred them to a consultant in the department of urology. Two days later, I met the urologist on my rounds and asked him about the young boy. He was flummoxed and told me that no such child had come to see him.

I assumed that the parents took the child elsewhere for treatment. However, the next day, the parents returned to my OPD and pleaded that I help the child. They did not want to be treated by any other doctor in the world. They trusted me blindly and I was the only one they had faith in. They insisted that though this was not my speciality, I should do whatever I could and they would humbly accept the result. I finally admitted the child to the hospital under my care and with some trepidation, started asking my urology colleagues what procedure I should follow for a 15-year-old boy with infected hydronephrosis of a solitary kidney.

As soon as we did some preliminary tests, I realised how wrong I was. The right kidney was absolutely normal and the child was, in fact, suffering from malaria. He was administered the appropriate treatment, the fever settled, and he went home after a few days.

The whole episode was a humbling experience for me. I learnt that a major operation could be performed and a sick child could be saved even in a small place like Ballabhgarh with minimal facilities. The second time around, however, I learnt not to be overconfident of my diagnostic expertise based on just clinical history and examination. As doctors, it might be our intention to strive for success on all occasions but we have to accept our shortcomings. Medicine is a Pandora's box and every patient adds to our learning experience.

The most important realisation for me, however, and the one I'll carry with me throughout my life, was how gratifying it is to be a doctor in this country. The couple and their child from Ballabhgarh taught me how wonderful it was to be a doctor in India where simple people from a small village in Haryana could have so much faith in another person who was just doing his job. This is an everlasting lesson for all doctors: to not just honour people's trust but ensure that we invest in a strong doctor-patient relationship so that outcomes that aren't in our control don't weaken it.

Dr Samiran Nundy is a medical undergraduate from Cambridge and Guy's Hospital London and trained in medicine and later in surgery at Guy's, Addenbrooke's Cambridge, the Hammersmith and the Massachusetts General Hospital in Boston. He has taught at the Universities of Cambridge, London and Harvard and returned to the All India Institute of Medical Sciences in 1975 where he eventually became professor and Head of the Department of Gastrointestinal Surgery. He started the Surgical Gastroenterology and Liver Transplantation Department at Sir Ganga Ram Hospital, New Delhi, in 1996.

He then retired as the Dean of the Ganga Ram Institute for Postgraduate Medical Education and Research. A prolific writer, Dr Nundy has written 37 books and 236 research papers. He has been on the editorial board of 24 journals which include the British Medical Journal and the Bhutan Health Journal. He also helped in lobbying for and drafting the Transplantation of Human Organs Act 1995.

Did You Know?

It is observed that 70% of the population has no access to specialist care as 80% of specialists live in urban areas. Only 13% of the rural population has access to primary health centres, 33% to sub-centres and 9.6% to hospitals. Healthcare personnel are reluctant to work at block or below level areas, as they have to face two challenges: first, the absence of reasonable living conditions (such as proper housing, 24-hour electricity supply, good school for their children, social isolation, etc.) and second, the under-functioning of majority of healthcare facilities in such areas and, hence, the lack of opportunity to translate their technical skills.

Source: Panagariya, Ashok. (2014). 'The challenges and innovative solutions to rural health dilemma'. Ann Neurosci, *21(4): 125–127.*

Dear People,

'Learn to calm your mind, recalibrate your emotions and fill the blank page of your life with happiness.'

Shivendra Kapoor

The Doctor Who Cured Me

I banged my forehead against a wall of my bedroom and then without paying any attention to the impact, I quickly stepped backwards—exactly eight steps—and with full force hit the back of my head against another wall. My spine suffered a sinusoidal jerk as it hit the wall with a thud. By the time I realised that I had attempted this strange act to ease my pain, I could feel pulsating pain in various parts of my body. This was my second unsuccessful attempt at an impromptu solution to the constant frustration that was brewing inside me since February 2010.

In my first attempt in late 2009—to get rid of, what I like to call, my 'Shaking Body Illness'—I had locked myself in my bathroom for hours without any food or water. The intent was to shock the body into submitting, but the drilling pain continued. 'What a life I have,' I yelled in frustration. The horror of that terrible day is still fresh as ever in my head.

I was ready to do anything to get myself out of this illness but could not find a way out. I had exhausted myself visiting all kinds of doctors: general physicians, orthopaedic to chest physicians, neurologists and even psychiatrists. Nothing in the past 10 months had worked. The only outcome of the visits and multiple blood tests, X-rays and CT scans was a single sentence: *the patient doesn't seem to have any problems, clinically*. Deficiency of vitamins was identified but despite proper medication, there was not much improvement in my health.

A year passed by and I lost interest in doing anything meaningful. I was almost suicidal and often prayed to God to send his messenger of death but even He didn't respond. Around the end of May 2011, I was shopping at a small grocery shop near my house in Mulund, Mumbai, where I saw a customer standing ahead of me in the queue. I could feel an aura around him. He turned around, looked at me, and smiled, 'Excuse me,' he said. 'I need to move out.' There was something about him that made me curious about who he was.

I immediately questioned the shopkeeper, 'Who is this person? I have never seen him here before.'

The shopkeeper replied, 'He is Dr Manish, a renowned psychiatrist based in Powai. I admire the principles he follows in his life.' It is unexplainable but meeting him made me feel that he was that one person who could heal me and pull me away from the shores of insanity. My 'Shaking Body Illness' was getting worse and it seemed like my body couldn't bear it anymore. I had to take a day off from work on 16 June 2011 as my body was writhing in pain. By sheer luck, I managed to get an appointment on the same day. I reached the entrance of Dr Manish's clinic and the first thing I saw was the signboard which said: *Welcome to Dr Manish's Den. It's hard to believe that I am a Doctor. MBBS, MD-Psychiatry.*

Before I could say anything, the receptionist pleasantly said, 'You are requested to enter the doctor's cabin after the gentleman inside comes out.' I nodded and sat down. After a while, the door of the cabin opened and a patient walked out.

Once he left, I knocked on the doctor's door twice and then stepped in. The moment I entered, the doctor got up from his seat, approached me with a warm smile which made me feel very comfortable.

'So, I know that you are in the pink of your health and, hence you are here to meet me and check whether I am fine or not,' the doctor joked.

I smiled. 'Dear friend,' the doctor said, 'Tell me, what can I do for you?'

I began my painful story, one that I had narrated to many doctors before.

'Okay. So, how do you feel right now in front of me?'

'It's the same unhealthy feeling all the time.'

'Okay. Please correct me if you find what I am about to say to be incorrect. I need to be doubly sure before we move further. For the past two years, you have had this strange feeling of imbalance in your body and it starts from the tip of the back of your head, *Rahu ki choti*, and runs throughout the length of your spine. You have high blood pressure as well. This feeling of imbalance is there all the time—during sleeping, walking, sitting, standing—and you feel that your body has two separate disconnected halves, that is, the upper half that sways in one direction and the lower half that moves in the opposite direction. You feel that your own voice echoes inside your body when you speak. Sometimes, there is a tingling sensation on the left side of your face. Despite all this, you are able to control your body from falling down.'

'Absolutely right,' I confirmed. I was surprised. He had described it exactly how I felt it.

'Relax Shivendra. There is no need to be stunned. I charge my patients and I devote my time and attention to their problems and give them my best.'

'Your words are soothing to my ears. I have never seen a committed doctor like you but I did not understand why did you use a phrase like *Rahu ki choti*? That's how astrologers call it? Isn't it?'

'You are right, Shivendra. Let me tell you that I am an ardent believer of Vedic astrology and I have personally seen miracles happening when I time events using principles of astrology. Using a combination of medical science and astrology has been my unique strength and it really helps me identify the root cause of the problem; sometimes even the most hidden issues. *Rahu* is the planet that plays tricks, creates illusion and deception.'

I was listening to Dr Manish intently when he pumped his fists in the air and got up, pushing his chair aside. He arched his brows and asked, 'Tell me quickly are you experiencing any swaying or anything strange right now?'

I thought a little and said, 'Yes, your observation is partly correct. When you asked me the question a fraction of seconds ago, I was lost in my thoughts, thinking about your desire to heal me. I mean...you understand what I mean?'

'Perfect, Shivendra. I have caught your problem and it's going to leave you soon. The American gentleman, Ram, who was here just before you,' Dr Manish said, 'works in a big corporate and is on a business trip to India. He has had a strange problem for the past 18 years. Can you guess his problem?'

'No.'

'Often, he joins his palms together, like when saying "Namaste", and attempts to touch all the fingers. He wants to ensure that they are in perfect alignment and then once he is satisfied, he relaxes his fingers. He agrees that it is an eccentric habit, but he doesn't know why he does it so often. This habit like an obsessive compulsive disorder and hampered his communication with others. The crux of the problem was that he did not receive any attention from others despite being in their good books and always supporting them. Somehow, there would be disharmony and his relationship with others would become unstable.'

The doctor had told him that his name 'Ram' was the holiest name in India. Ram was shocked when he heard about the Ramayana. 'I tweaked the story a bit and told him that Lord Ram was born to teach people the path of righteousness and that there was not much difference between the Lord's style of blessing and his style of hand-folding,' recounted Dr Manish. 'I convinced him that he was probably some incarnation of the Lord, the only difference being their place of birth. These words filled him with positivity and had such an impact on him that his habit vanished within a month.'

'Wow, what a story!' I remarked. 'I am impressed, doctor. You have a magnificent and unique way of dealing with your patients.'

'Shivendra, can I says something?' Dr Manish's voice suddenly had an emotional edge. 'Sure,' I answered clearing my throat.

He paused for a moment, looked around and then gazed at me. 'Let's first solve your problem, Shivendra.'

'But you were trying to say something doctor,' I sensed that he was hesitating to tell me something.

'Yes, actually...I was touched by the way you praised me, and I am glad that you have such admiration for a doctor. Otherwise, in today's world, life has become a give-and-take business; very mechanical and ruthless. Thank you, Shivendra.'

Before I could respond, he said to me, 'Okay Shivendra, let's focus. Close your eyes and don't open them till I ask you to and just do as I say. Be sincere. Stand straight, hold my hands and walk along with me.'

We took a few steps together and then, suddenly, he left my hand and switched off the lights. I was totally confused about what was happening.

'Walk further, Shivendra,' his authoritative voice pressed again. 'Let's see...'

'What is this, doctor?' I was frightened and was I struggling to balance my body due to the sudden build-up of stress.

'This is it, Shivendra. Don't let the darkness of the moment spook you. Now in this current state, you are blind, you have lost your eyesight, but you're not able to perform the most basic task of moving.'

Dr Manish was demonstrating to me that there are many who are blind, but there was something stopping me from appreciating the various gifts life has bestowed upon me.

'Your case is very simple, Shivendra. *The problem is that you are not firmly grounded but want to fly like a rocket and earn fame and money. You badly need friends who listen to you. You need to start re-fuelling your desires. I assure you that if you progress methodically, with patience, keep yourself peaceful at heart and learn to "let go", then all your dreams will come true. But for that, learn to calm your mind, to recalibrate your emotions and fill the blank page of your life with happiness.*'

The session was coming to an end, but for the first time, I wasn't tired after visiting a doctor. Instead, there was a celebration in my heart. I felt relaxed and could make out the difference his thoughts and advice had on my overall thinking in just one meeting. I had numerous follow-up sessions with Dr Manish. Each session was an enriching experience loaded with deeper insights into self-healing.

If today I am free from medication and my debilitating illness, it's because of Dr Manish's dedication and his soothing words. He proved to me that some doctors have a healing touch that works wonders and transforms the lives of people like me.

Shivendra Kapoor is an instrumentation engineer by profession and a writer at heart. He has published many short stories, educational and technical articles in reputed publications in India and abroad. He has a deep interest in spirituality.

Did You Know?

For people using healthcare services, being treated as an individual is an essential component of their whole experience and in retaining their dignity during a stressful period. Each patient experiences healthcare in a unique and individual way. For many, healthcare forms a small, but important part of their larger life. Being recognised and treated as an individual remains important to a person when they become a patient. In many ways, the need is strengthened, particularly at a time when a person can feel vulnerable. In accordance with this, there is an important need for health services to recognise that individuals are living with their condition(s), experiencing it in a unique way, and that family and broader life need to be taken into account as well.

Source: National Clinical Guideline Centre (UK). Patient Experience in Adult NHS Services: Improving the Experience of Care for People Using Adult NHS Services: Patient Experience in Generic Terms. London: Royal College of Physicians (UK); 2012 Feb. (NICE Clinical Guidelines, No. 138.) 6, Knowing the patient as an individual. Available from: https://www.ncbi.nlm.nih.gov/books/NBK115223/

Dear People,

'India has entered the league of the few nations where hand transplantation is a reality. It's been made possible much like any other innovation—by doctors who care and who understand that adversity, disease or illness are not just clinical entities.'

Dr Subramania Iyer

The Story of India's First Hand Transplant

On board a train to Kochi, a gang was harassing women passengers when a 30-year-old man, Manu objected. The fight took an ugly turn and he was pushed out of the running train. That fateful night, for hours, Manu lay next to a nondescript railway track. He had sustained serious injuries and lost a lot of blood. A passer-by heard his cries and arranged for help so that he could be taken to the nearest hospital. By the time they reached the hospital, Manu had turned pale due to massive blood loss and was gasping for breath. He had a severe concussion and injuries all over. While the doctors succeeded in driving death away, Manu lost both his hands in the accident.

Few tragedies can be as devastating for a person as losing both hands. A split second had changed Manu's life completely. All he could think of was being dependent on someone else for his entire life. He thought about the loss of income, his independence and how much distress this would bring to his entire family. While prosthetic hands are available, Manu knew that they could never substitute 'real' human hands.

The only way a patient with an amputation of both hands can recover is through a hand transplant. The first successful hand transplant was performed in 1997 in the US and the patient is doing well till date. However, hand transplants are one of the most complex and challenging surgeries. It isn't merely about surgical precision. Hand transplant requires significant organisational effort to establish a centre that can accomplish this difficult yet rewarding task. A large multidisciplinary team of plastic and microvascular surgeons, orthopaedic surgeons, anaesthetists, immunologists, rehabilitation experts, transplant nurses and social workers are essential for executing successful hand transplants.

I have been practising plastic and reconstructive surgery for the past 30 years, but it was on 13 January 2015, almost 18 years after the US case, that I helped carry out India's first-hand transplant surgery. For the first time, an Indian patient received a double hand transplant at the Amrita Institute of Medical Sciences in Kochi, and the recipient was none other than Manu.

After that ill-fated night, Manu had turned into a recluse and had thought of ending his life on several occasions. When I saw him for the first time in the OPD, I was moved to tears by his plight. By that time, our preparation for setting up a hand-transplant unit was almost complete. I could not think of anyone more deserving and suitable than Manu as a candidate for a bilateral hand transplant.

Of all transplant surgeries, hand transplants are probably the most demanding and difficult in every way. 'Hands', being the organs in question here, can only be harvested from a brain-dead donor. This also means that a mutilating procedure must be performed on the donor who would have to be buried or cremated sans the hands. Although awareness about organ transplant has increased considerably over the years, culturally, body-mutilating organ donation is yet to receive acceptability in India. We had to wait for a consenting donor family who would be magnanimous enough to donate the hands of their brain-dead family member. It felt like a ceaseless, unending wait.

In our quest of finding a donor, we would show the pictures of prosthetic hands that would be fitted to the donor's body as well as a picture of Manu without his hands to every prospective donor family. We would beg them to donate the hands so that life could be improved. As family after family rejected our requests, the thought of whether we'll ever find a family that would allow such a mutilating organ donation haunted us. Our chief transplant coordinator, Prasad, left no stones stone unturned in sensitising his team, along with the other teams in the state, regarding the need for such a donation. Usually, once a potential organ donor is identified, the treating team counsels the immediate family about the possible option of organ donation. If the family shows some inclination towards organ donation, they undergo more rounds of counselling by the transplant coordinators. The donation of internal organs is widely known, so it is comparatively easier to explain. It is not an easy task for the counselling team to encourage the donor family for organ donation. What drives the team, though, is the thought that their efforts may save or improve the lives of four to six patients. Although they are a very dedicated lot, we did not want to leave the counselling for the hand donation to them. Prasad and I took this task upon ourselves, with the support of the team.

Four consecutive families consented for donation of other organs but refused the donation of hands. In fact, one of these families had initially considered donation but declined later. It is an extremely sensitive matter. The mother and brother of the donor could not bear the thought of hand donation and burying their family member without his hands. We couldn't press too hard as we feared that they may back out from donating the internal organs as well. At such times, emotions are usually running high and most families are not able to accept the idea of body mutilation of their loved ones.

We had almost given up when, after a few months and multiple refusals, the family of 24-year-old Binoy consented. A brilliantly talented glass painter, Binoy was declared brain-dead after a motorbike accident. He was the sole breadwinner of his family and the only support for his ailing father who had been paralysed from the waist down for the last 14 years.

Manu was indeed fortunate to receive a pair of such gifted hands.

When we started the process on the night of 12 January 2015, it felt like we had stepped into a different world. I spoke to Manu and his brother once again in detail, before we took him for surgery, to ensure that they understood the enormity of the procedure.

This was the most momentous time of my career. The stakes were extremely high. At that time, it did not matter to me that the outcomes of this procedure would be watched keenly by not just my team but professional colleagues and the general public from all over the world. Our main concern was the safe and successful execution of the surgical procedure. In all honesty, it was the unfamiliarity with the task ahead that made it seem even more enormous.

Our discussion with Manu and his brother helped a great deal at that time. Their positive affirmation and faith in our capability was encouraging and reassuring.

Finally, when we began the procedure, the atmosphere in the OT, as described by one of our residents, was 'electrifying'. The surgery would take at least 14 to 16 hours and for many of us, it would be without rest in-between. There were many crises during the surgery and split-second decisions had to be taken. Four teams worked on four different tables. As the leader of the team, I had the challenging task of maintaining seamless coordination between all four teams. We had a few worrisome moments too. Initially, due to an old trauma, there was no blood flow in the transplanted hands. It took hours of tireless efforts for Manu's blood to start flowing through Binoy's transplanted hands. A sigh of relief was heard all around the OT.

The next day, when Manu moved his fingers, I thought how—both professionally and personally—nothing could be more beautiful, touching and satisfying.

Four days later, we attended a function in Varapuzha, a suburb of Kochi. Binoy (our donor) belonged to this village. The function was held to publicly appreciate Binoy's family. Manu was still in the ICU. He was doing well and, luckily, there were no signs of immediate rejection. We spoke to him about the function and asked him what we should say on his behalf. He still could not speak much, but he requested a paper and pen. With great difficulty with his transplanted hands, he wrote three legible words, 'Binoy, thank you.'

During my talk, when I projected pictures of Manu moving his hands and finally his thank-you note, written using Binoy's hands, the entire audience was choked with emotions. It was, undoubtedly, one of the best thank-you slides I have prepared in my career.

Binoy's family's altruistic decision opened people to the idea of a hand transplant. It made big news and was published in every newspaper of the country as the 'divine gift' and an 'unparalleled organ donation'.

It became obvious that hand donation was no more a taboo as, our second donor, Joseph's family was already aware of hand donation. Their only question was, 'Is it similar to that what had been done for Manu?' Subsequently, with excellent physiotherapy support and his own hard work, Manu's hands become fully functional. Over the next few months, Manu got involved with helping others who were suffering similarly. The hospital administration was impressed and they gave him the position of a 'Transplant Technical Assistant' in our hospital.

A hand transplant is a complicated surgery. It requires a team of more than 40 medical personnel who work continuously for 15 to 16 hours, intricately joining more than 30 structures in each hand. It also needs a year-long post-operative supervision by a team of immunologists and rehabilitation experts to achieve these fabulous results. This was the first time a successful hand transplant had been performed in India and we were quite chuffed about it.

However, even more moving was the thought of the family who agreed for the donation. The families who lost their members had lost them forever, but these donations were their contribution to the world and a way of keeping a part of them alive.

If I go back in time and think about how we established the hand transplant programme, it is still a blur and I cannot believe how far we have come.

The second recipient, Abdul Rahim, was serving as a captain in the Afghan Border Security Force. He was leading a team that specialised in defusing unexploded mines. He was an expert and held the experience of defusing more than 1,000 mines. Unfortunately, one of the mines exploded before he could diffuse it and grievously injured both his hands. Sophisticated medical care was not available in war-torn Afghanistan and Abdul did the rounds of many countries for treatment. Finally, he came to India. He arrived in Kochi after hearing about the hospital's transplant programme. He was listed at the same time as Manu for the transplant but he had to wait for four months before another gracious family agreed for the donation. The donor was 53-year-old Joseph, who was admitted to the hospital after a road accident. The transplant took place on April 10, 2015. After intensive physiotherapy for one year, Abdul regained near-normal function of the transplanted hands. Soon after, he returned to Kabul to rejoin his army unit.

Manu, as I mentioned earlier, started working in our institution. The day he got his first salary, he came to my cabin. He hesitated for a minute and then told me, 'I have a request and need your permission. Can I go and visit Binoy's parents? I want to hand over my first month's salary to them. After all, I earned it by working with Binoy's hands.' This was one of those rare moments when my eyes welled up and emotions presided over my otherwise professional demeanour. No one had prompted Manu to do this. This beautiful thought had emerged out of the goodness in his own heart. Imagine how Binoy's bedridden father and mother would have felt when they received this token of love from Manu. By donating his organs and especially his hands, Binoy's parents had made him eternal. When Manu visited them, Binoy's father caressed his hands, a touch that transcended into unfathomable goodness.

We organised a small function to felicitate Joseph's family after the second transplant for Abdul was successful. Joseph's wife and young daughter attended this function. After the meeting got over, just before we were dispersing, Joseph's wife came up to me and asked, 'Can I touch those hands once?'

Watching her touch those hands which had caressed her several times over the years was an extremely touching moment. The fact that those hands were now doing the divine job of making someone else's life easier was a heartening reminder of human goodness that exists in our world.

The gift of life

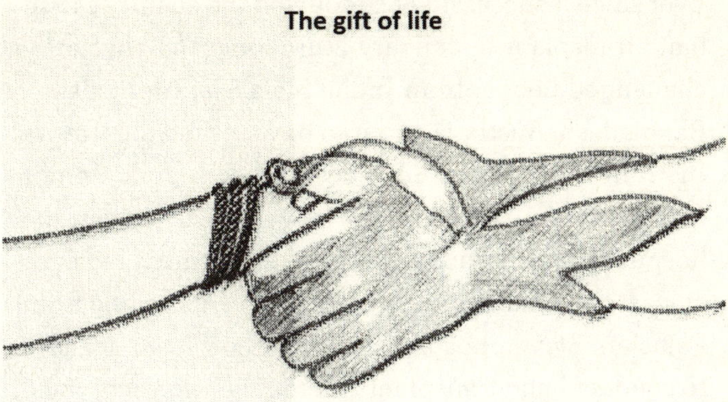

Aparna

I am proud that India has entered the league of the few nations where hand transplantation is a reality. It's been made possible much like any other innovation —by doctors who care and who understand that adversity, disease or illness and are not just clinical entities. In fact, they go far beyond it and demonstrate, to whoever is paying attention, the opportunity to do more for humankind.

Dr Subramania Iyer had higher surgical training in head and neck surgery and plastic surgery from the All India Institute of Medical Sciences, New Delhi, Medical College Calicut and various centres in the UK. He initiated the plastic surgery and head and neck surgery departments at the Amrita Institute of Medical Sciences (AIMS), Kochi. He has trained over 400 surgeons in microvascular head and neck reconstruction so far. He led the team that carried out the first two double hand transplants/double forearm/upper arm transplants in South Asia. His team has won the best surgical team of South Asia in 2015 awarded by the **BMJ.**

Did You Know?

Ever since it successfully conducted the country's first-hand transplant in January 2015, some 198 physically challenged people from India, Malaysia, Afghanistan, Bangladesh, Australia and Iraq have visited the Amrita Institute of Medical Sciences and Research Center (AIMS), seeking details of the procedure. Every day, the hospital's reconstructive surgery department receives at least five emails with similar queries, including from Pakistan. Eleven hospitals in India now have licences to conduct hand transplants. But in the two years since that first procedure, just two more hand transplants have been carried out, both of which conducted at AIMS.

Source: https://indianexpress.com/article/india/lend-me-a-hand-transplant-kochi4731270/

Dear People,

'Even 1% fear cannot coexist with faith.'

Dr Sundaram Natarajan

Faith with Fear Equals to Fraud

Prabha had lost vision in her left eye due to a childhood injury. Two decades later, in 1991, she suffered from a myopic retinal detachment in her remaining eye. She came to me, distraught and scared. The thought of losing complete vision at such a young age had caused her great agony and anxiety. I operated on her eye and, thankfully, the operation was successful. She was thrilled that normal vision had returned in the operated eye. A few years later, she got married and that was the last I heard of her.

In early 2017, however, she returned to me in an emergency situation with a sudden total loss of vision in the same eye that I had operated on 26 years ago. I was in a meeting when she arrived and asked the doctor on duty to prepare her for surgery. However, the moment I walked into the room, she sensed my presence and hugged me. 'You operate,' she said, 'I will be fine.' She then introduced me to her husband who also seemed confident in me.

I chatted with the couple before surgery and explained my 3F philosophy. 'If you have FAITH in your heart, you will not have

FEAR,' I said. When they asked me about the third 'F', I explained that many patients have FAITH only on their lips but deep down in their hearts, they have FEAR. I elaborated that if you have FAITH and FEAR together, it is FRAUD.

I often ask my patients how much FAITH they have. Most of them say 100%. Faith could be in God, a superpower, nature, themselves or their parents. I follow up with another question. I ask how much worry or FEAR do they have? Invariably, they come up with similar numbers. It's usually 70%. Next, I ask them what 100-70 is. They say it is 30. I immediately respond that in my dictionary 100-70 is equivalent to zero, and amounts to FRAUD. Even 1% fear cannot coexist with faith.

My 3F philosophy is inspired by my spiritual guru Swami Vivekananda, who had said, 'If faith in ourselves had been more extensively taught and practised, I am sure a very large portion of the evils and miseries that we have would have vanished.'

Thankfully, both Prabha and her husband were thoroughly convinced and had 100% faith. They were positive that if I operated on her, she would recover her vision. I performed vitrectomy with silicone oil tamponade to repair her retinal detachment.

The surgery was successful and Prabha recovered her vision. It was a sweet victory but what was sweeter was the knowledge how medicine changes the everyday life of the patient. Prabha, for example, liked to dance and I was glad to learn that she returned to dancing in the days that followed.

I believe that my interaction with her was especially rich because we had forged a strong doctor-patient relationship. A robust doctor-patient relationship is an intrinsic part of providing high-quality healthcare to a patient. A doctor should maintain a good rapport with the patient without compromising his/her dignity or privacy. For a good result, similarly, the patient must have confidence in the competence of his/her physician. In fact, even research shows that the doctor-patient relationship has a statistically significant impact on healthcare outcomes. It can increase the accuracy of the diagnosis, patient compliance to the therapeutic regimen, and overall success of the treatment.

On the contrary, if this relationship is poor, a comprehensive assessment of the patient may be compromised with reduced compliance, thereby affecting the entire outcome of the therapy. In extreme cases, it can be life-threatening, not due to medical negligence but poor communication, leading to improper diagnosis and incorrect treatment.

The benefits of developing a healthy relationship with the patients are immense. When a patient is in pain, a doctor's mannerisms can strongly affect the patient. When the doctor is kind and caring, the results more often than not reflect that.

As a retina surgeon with more than 33 years of experience, I have encountered numerous patients in my practice. Most of them regained their vision but a few, despite my best efforts, did not. Over the years, there were some patients like Prabha who I distinctly remember because they furthered my knowledge, not just about medicine but also human behaviour and how doctors and patients coexist.

My experiences have also encouraged me to believe in the law of attraction which says that you can attract whatever you wish for. There's another aspect to this law that's usually ignored: Gratitude. The law says the more you are grateful, the more you get. Recently, two young men accompanied their 65-year-old father to meet me. The father had diabetes and had lost vision in one of his eyes due to complications of diabetic retinopathy. The sons were sick with worry and pleaded with me to help their father. When I began to talk to the father, I learnt that he was a businessman who despite losing vision eight days ago, was still continuing with his business. The man clearly was blessed with a rare quality of optimism towards life. 'You operate,' he told me. 'I am sure I will get my vision back and will be able to continue with my business.' He was also immensely grateful for everything he had achieved and made it a point to exhibit his gratitude. It was, therefore, no surprise when the operation was successful and the man healed quickly.

Nowadays, however, there is a shift in patients' attitude toward their doctors. Previously, patients were largely unaware of their conditions and were fully dependent on us for the choice of treatment. They respected the medical fraternity much more and rarely questioned the decisions we took for them. Nowadays, information is available at our fingertips. At the click of a mouse, anyone can get loads of information about one's health condition. Therefore, the patients and their relatives who come to me are very over-informed about their condition. However, due to a plethora of opinions available on the internet, they are often confused.

They fail to realise that each patient is different. Some patients recover faster than expected whereas others take an indefinitely long time to recover. Those who recover faster are pleased with the doctors. Some patients may take longer time than usual to recover due to associated conditions such as diabetes or minor post-surgery complications. Sometimes such patients and relatives get irritated and vent their ire on the doctor. Doctors, then, should remain calm and communicate clearly with the patient about the reason for the delay. Timely discussion about the condition and a well-crafted revelation of poor prognosis can help dissipate their worries.

It is equally important to reiterate to patients that they need to be positive during the course of the treatment. In an effort to raise their morale, I often tell my patients about other inspiring patients whom I have treated. One such shining example is Sushmeetha Bubna. Sushmeetha was born with a congenital cataract in her right eye. At the age of seven, the cataract was successfully operated. However, a self-dissolving capsule which was placed in the eye after the operation caused complications and the eye had to be operated again. Unfortunately, after the second surgery, she had bleeding in the eye with retinal detachment. This led to a complete loss of vision in her right eye. Six years later, at the age of 13, she had a retinal detachment in the left eye as well which was operated upon at Sankara Nethralaya, Chennai. She regained vision in the left eye and continued with her studies. Unfortunately, when she was in the 10th standard, retinal detachment struck her left eye again. Her board exams were inching close but an operation had become essential. It was an extremely worrying time as it would take Sushmeetha two months after the operation to regain her vision. This would leave her with very little time to prepare for the exams. Sushmeetha, however, was determined and after the operation, she made sure she cleared her exams. With the help of a private tutor who recorded the lessons on an audiotape, she prepared for her exams and cleared them successfully. Over the years, Sushmeetha was left with very little vision in her left eye.

However, she continued with her education and graduated in commerce and went on to complete a diploma in Administrative Management from an acclaimed management institute. Later she enrolled into a rehabilitation course at the National Association for the Blind (NAB), Mumbai, where she learnt mobility, Braille, cooking and vocational trades such as broom making, cycle repairing and *agarbatti* making. Then she founded an organisation named Voice Vision, which works toward the empowerment, education and holistic development of visually challenged persons. She was given the Positive Health Award in 2010 for her extraordinary courage and inspirational attitude in combating severe disease and disability.

I've been lucky to treat Sushmeetha but I've also come across several other patients who don't exhibit her positivity or determination. They are, unfortunately, unable to get rid of their anger and worry. I don't blame them but I do believe that through the art of positivity, trust-building and effective communication, outcomes can be improved considerably. The doctor plays the most crucial role here and it was when Dr APJ Abdul Kalam gifted me *Medicine and Compassion*, a book about doctor-patient relationship, that I found an adequate description of what I've always felt. The book says, and I fully agree, that doctors should realise the fact that patients are acting in a particular way because they are not at ease. They are not insane but they simply can't handle what they are going through. Patients often find themselves dependent on others for help. In most cases, patients expect that the doctor can make them better. However, sometimes the doctor cannot do much due to the incurable nature of the disease. The doctors must try the best, with their physical actions, their words and their attitude. They must use their body, speech and mind to comfort the patient and seek help from other experts when needed.

I've imbibed this lesson in my practice and 33 years later, I pride myself on developing sound and long-lasting relationships with my patients.

Professor Dr Sundaram Natarajan is the CMD of Aditya Jyot Eye Hospital which is one of Mumbai's leading eye hospitals. A third-generation ophthalmologist, he has been elected as the president of All India Opthalmological Society (AIOS) in February 2019. He is considered an authority in Vitreo Retinal Surgery in the world and is keenly involved in academics and research for prevention of blindness. He was conferred with the Padma Shri for his achievements in the field of medicine.

Did You Know?

If you trust your doctor, you're actually more likely to do better when you're sick. Lower levels of trust in one's physician is associated with more distress over time in more anxiously attached individuals with cancer.

Source: Hinnen, C., Pool, G., Holwerda, N. et al. (2014). 'Lower levels of trust in one's physician is associated with more distress over time in more anxiously attached individuals with cancer'. Gen Hosp Psychiatry, *36(4): 382–387.*

Dear People,

'For every failing, guilty doctor, there are thousands who are honest and tirelessly treat countless patients and make their lives better.'

Dr Suresh K. Pandey and Dr Vidushi Sharma

Saving Sight with Courage and Compassion

In December 2012, we were conducting an eye check-up camp in Gadepan, a village 40 kilometres from Kota, when the village sarpanch requested us to accompany him to another village. He explained to me that there was a woman and her daughter in that village who were nearly blind and it was difficult to get them to the camp. We followed him to meet 28-year-old Banasi Devi and her four-year-old daughter Teena who was blinded because of congenital cataract.

Their hut was situated at the far end of the village as if its location represented the isolation of the people living inside it. When the sarpanch knocked on the door, a frail-looking woman opened it and ushered us inside. She seemed both surprised to see us and embarrassed because she could not host us properly. However, above all, she seemed distant, aloof and resigned to her circumstances. At about the same time, her daughter, slowly and diffidently, walked in from another corner. The young girl was as frail as her mother. She seemed almost scared to see the strangers in her house and promptly stood behind her mother, partly hiding from view.

I took out my torch and ophthalmoscope (an instrument, infrequently used in a hospital setting, that enables one to see the retina) to examine them. I could see that they both had dense cataracts, most likely congenital (that is present since birth). However, their eyes showed other signs as well: they both had irregular pupils, mostly caused due to previous inflammation in the eye, involuntary movements of the eyes (nystagmus) caused due to very poor vision since early childhood and sunken eyes, often caused due to eye rubbing in visually impaired children coupled with poor nutrition. To me, their eyes looked deep but also depressed, distant and despairing.

One of the toughest moments in any doctor's life is when he/she has to tell the patient that all their medical skills stop at making the diagnosis. That they really don't have much to offer beyond that. It is a hopeless situation, not only for the patient but also for the doctor. However, here that feeling was compounded. I was seeing not only the patients but also their life, which had been confined to this small hut and would probably remain so forever unless I could successfully treat them. I was also scared of giving them any false hope. Somehow, I would later introspect, seeing patients in the sterile environment of a clinic or hospital shields their plight. Here, the plight of these two was staring in my face.

I felt a grave burden of expectation but possibly, the patients expected nothing much out of me. By this time, it was obvious that they had accepted their life as it was and did not hope for miraculous changes in their life. I also found that eye doctors working in eye camps had told the mother-daughter that nothing could be done to regain their vision. As the sarpanch asked me for my verdict, I simply said that a detailed eye examination and further tests were needed to ascertain whether something could be done to help them. This way, I neither disappointed them completely nor gave them false hope. The mother and daughter were perhaps curious but their eyes could not express the curiousness and seemed blank, empty.

While numerous free eye camps for cataract surgery are conducted across India, congenital cataract, or any case that takes more surgical time and is associated with poor visual prognosis, is excluded from the surgical list of eye camp. Ophthalmologists are wary of dealing with congenital and other difficult cataracts in a camp setting as many of these eyes have other coexistent conditions and the surgery is technically challenging. A rigorous follow-up is required as well. Besides, the children need to be operated under general anaesthesia and the camps have no backup equipment or help to handle complications or surgical challenges due to comorbidities.

Banasi Devi and her daughter, therefore, had not received any kind of treatment for their cataract and were compelled to lead their lives with poor vision. It was appalling to see that despite medical advances, the mother and daughter had gradually lost their sight and were confined to their huts, miserable and dependent on others even for routine daily tasks. Often, challenges of treatment begin long before the patient reaches the hospital and in the case of Banasi Devi and her daughter, the challenges began as soon as we tried to examine their condition. The family's poverty and illiteracy made them sceptical of treatment. They were reluctant about coming to the hospital for the cataract surgery. While I told them that I wouldn't charge them anything, I was convinced that they were not going to make the effort of coming to the hospital. Instead, I told the sarpanch that if the villagers helped, we could drive the two of them back to Kota. The imposing sarpanch and a few others joined us and convinced the family.

Soon, I was driving back to Kota with my very unusual passengers.

We reached the hospital in the evening and after a detailed examination, I could confirm that they did have congenital cataracts. They also had posterior synechiae which means that the edge of the iris was stuck on the crystalline lens due to previous eye problems. This made it difficult to dilate the pupil for the cataract surgery. Now, in such long-standing congenital cataracts where there is evidence of previous episodes of eye inflammation, there can often be a retinal detachment. As the retina (the inner layer of the eye on which visual images are projected) is not working, any attempts to remove the cataract can be futile. As I was about to perform an ocular ultrasound examination (to ascertain the presence of retinal detachment), I wondered what if there really was a retinal detachment. Their apprehensions about the medical system would be confirmed and I would have to send them back to the same world of darkness.

The B-scan ocular ultrasound, however, was reported normal for Teena's eyes and Banasi's Devi's right eye. Sparingly, I gave them hope and planned the surgery. A detailed work-up was done to calculate the power of the intraocular lens (IOL) which would have to be implanted in their eyes. It's a fairly challenging task when it comes to children because (a) they are not cooperative during the examination and (b) their eyeballs might grow over the next few years (more common in children below two years of age) which would change the required IOL power.

I desperately wanted to explain to the patients how difficult the surgery was. I spoke evocatively but the mother and daughter stayed stoic. After receiving her informed consent, I proceeded with the surgery. I put dilating drops and hoped the pupil would dilate. In cataract surgeries, the dilation of the pupil is the most important because this stretching or dilation of the pupil gives a clear view of the lens surface behind and facilitates surgery. Then, a curvilinear opening (about 5 mm in size) is made in the centre of the lens capsule and the lens material is cracked and sucked open by means of ultrasonic emulsification. The capsule is a membranous layer covering the entire crystalline lens and the intraocular lens is placed through the central opening into this lens capsule (capsular bag).

We first operated on the daughter. I have done a fair number of paediatric cataract surgeries but it continues to wreck my nerves. I performed the surgery on Teena's right eye, removing the opaque lens with the utmost care and placing an intraocular lens. Ocular microsurgery is an art as eye surgeons need to work in 5–7 mm space in the eye without damaging the innermost corneal layer. The adhesions between the iris and lens were separated as much as possible and the iris was stretched using iris hooks. As the dense white cataract was removed, I could see a red glow (light reflected from the retina). I hoped that it was the warm red light of a new sunrise in Teena's life. There was another challenge: I had to make another opening in the posterior part of the lens capsule to prevent the thickening of the capsule over a period of time and ensure that it didn't block the visual axis. The surgery was successful but it still didn't mean much as children are amblyopic or have lazy eyes, and it takes a long time and some exercises for them to regain vision.

I then operated on Banasi Devi's left eye. During the surgery, I found that there was mild zonular dehiscence in her eye. Zonules are fine strands that support the lens capsule and are attached to the inner layers of the eye. In cases of long-standing congenital cataracts, the zonules become weak in some areas, causing mild displacement of the lens. This increases the risk of damaging the unsupported area of the lens capsule and can result in disastrous complications. Thankfully, the area of zonular weakness was not extensive. The leathery lens was removed and an intraocular lens was implanted along with the capsule tension ring which helps support and provides long-term stability to the intraocular lens. Normally, the eyes are not patched after modern-day cataract surgery but this time, I decided to patch the eyes because I did not want Teena to accidentally rub her eyes vigorously.

The next morning, I opened their patches with some trepidation. As I opened the patch, and the mother adjusted her eyes to the bright light, I thought I could slowly see a faint smile develop on her lips. She took a couple of minutes to adjust to the changed vision, and I noticed that she stretched out her hands to feel her daughter. She caressed Teena tenderly, as if she was doing it for the first time, and seemed overwhelmed at the first faint sight of her own daughter. Her vision was just about 6/20 but when she hugged her daughter and expressed her happiness at seeing her for the first time, my eyes moistened. Next, we dutifully opened Teena's eye patch. Teena's previously impassive mother was now anxious. This meant she was hopeful.

After opening the patch, we asked the daughter if she could see our hand and fingers. To our dismay, she did not seem to have any improvement in her vision. The happiness we felt moments ago disappeared and familiar gloom occupied us. When I examined her again, I saw that she had much more post-operative inflammation in her eye than is routinely seen. We reassured Banasi Devi (as well as ourselves) that this was just the first post-operative day and as the inflammation subsided, she would regain some vision. We gave them eye drops and medicines to use at home and asked them to come back in a week's time.

A week passed by and I thought I would have to bring them for a follow-up but the next day, the three of them—Banasi Devi, her husband and Teena—walked into my clinic. They seemed like new people as they were wearing bright colourful clothes and smiling. We learnt that while the mother was making some progress and that her vision was better than before, it was Teena who surprised us all. She could see the figures on the vision chart and her excitement at seeing toys for the first time was infectious. The mother and daughter, as well as the father, thanked us profusely for bringing this day in their lives. After all, for the first time in their lives, the mother and daughter could see each other.

One week later, I operated on Teena's left eye and she had a similar recovery. Soon after the operation, an overwhelmed Banasi Devi asked us if she and Teena could tie a rakhi to our wrists. Today, six years later, 10-year-old Teena goes to school and continues to visit our hospital every year with her mother to celebrate Raksha Bandhan.

Our experience with Teena and her mother showed that doctors might be able to perform highly complicated, challenging surgeries successfully but sometimes, it's the smaller surgeries which alter the course of people's lives. Few of us are lucky enough to be privy to such miracles and this is perhaps why we love our profession despite the long arduous training and other stresses.

Today, unfortunately, there is rising tension and an erosion of trust between doctors and patients. Sometimes, the looming doubts and patients' suspicions frustrate us. Sometimes, matters go too far and we end up in courtrooms or, worse, on hospital beds ourselves. However, for every failing, guilty doctor, there are thousands who are honest and tirelessly treat countless patients and make their lives better.

Medicine is a complex subject and patients' response to treatment varies because of many factors. At the same time, doctors must also remember that for every inconsiderate patient, there are thousands who are grateful—those who make the entire journey worthwhile. One such patient who came to us from Karachi, Pakistan, was Fahim Uddin. Fahim was near-sighted and had developed bilateral cataract at a relatively early age. At 42, his cataract had increased significantly and he was advised surgery. Fahim had looked up on the internet and had done extensive research on the best possible IOL for the implant. He had decided that he wanted a multifocal IOL so that he would be spectacle independent. It was during this research that he came across our hospital's website which demonstrated the implant of a particular IOL he desired. Fahim looked up our hospital's phone number and called us. Once the initial frenzy of receiving a call from Pakistan subsided, I spoke to him about the procedure and offered to get the IOL delivered to him, as it was not available in Pakistan at the time. However, he was more inclined to come all the way to Kota for the cataract surgery.

The distance between Karachi and Kota is only 500 miles but this 500-mile journey cannot be covered easily. There is a lot of hostility between the two nations and the paperwork (including visa verification from intelligence agencies and police and getting written permission from neighbours, etc.) and the fear involved in the travel can be worrisome and daunting. In the past, there have been few isolated instances of patients who travelled from Pakistan to India for difficult surgeries like paediatric heart surgery but most of them have been severely ill.

We had a few more conversations with Fahim to ensure that both of us were ready for the paperwork needed to undertake this formidable trip. Three months of extensive documentation followed and, finally, he landed in Kota on 8 July 2012. In a period of three days, he underwent cataract surgery for both eyes and was extremely satisfied with the visual results. However, what overwhelmed and surprised him the most was the warmth he received from the hospital staff.

Fahim's medical trip soon became the journey of a lifetime as he saw a Bollywood movie at a local theatre and was thrilled with his excellent vision. Before leaving, he also visited the grave of one of his ancestors in the nearby town of Chhabra, about 130 kilometres from Kota, to pay his respects.

People around Fahim were equally excited. The fact that he had come all the way from Pakistan for his eye surgery had made him a mini-celebrity and his visit was extensively covered by the local media. A programme called *Aman Ki Roshni* (Spreading Light Across the Border) was organised and was attended by the mayor of Kota city, the inspector general of police and other prominent personalities.

However, what was most heart-wrenching was our interaction with him. It reinforced our belief that when it comes to the common people, Indians have nothing but warmth and love for Pakistanis. We want to live as friends, leaving aside the hostility fanned by extremist groups. The same sentiment is true for Pakistanis as a few years later, in 2016, I had the opportunity to visit Karachi and Fahim ensured that he met me and treated me like family. The warmth and affection was visible in all his family members who were extremely grateful for the 'gift of sight' that he had received from India.

Dr Suresh K. Pandey is an internationally renowned ophthalmologist and director of SuVi Eye Institute and Lasik Laser Centre, Kota, Rajasthan. Dr Pandey completed ophthalmology training from PGIMER, Chandigarh, and worked in the US and Australia for seven years. He and his spouse, Dr Vidushi Sharma, returned to India in 2006 and established SuVi Eye Institute in Kota in 2006. Dr Pandey is the recipient of Achievement Award from the American Academy of Ophthalmology.

Did You Know?

According to a recent survey on the export of health services by the directorate general of Commercial Intelligence and Statistics, under the Commerce Ministry, the highest average earnings per patient through export of health services from India comes from Pakistan at $2,906. Pakistan is followed by Bangladesh ($2,084), CIS (Commonwealth of Independent States) countries ($1,950), Russia ($1,618) and Iraq ($1,530), according to the survey.

This means a patient from Pakistan visiting a hospital in India spends more than people from any other country, boosting India's foreign exchange reserves. But the number of medical visas issued to Pakistani patients in 2015–2016 stood at a measly 1,921 compared to 58,360 to patients from Bangladesh and 29,492 to patients from Afghanistan.

Source: https://www.livemint.com/Politics/qhkdfBzftgqH6eJC7HklJI/Sushma-swamped-by-requests so India-asks-Pakistan-to-endors.html

Dear People,

'Why are doctors put on a pedestal we possibly don't want or need?'

Dr Tejal Lathia

No Doctor Wants to Harm Their Patient by Omission or Commission

In 2001, I was assigned to work in a rural hospital in South Gujarat. This hospital had few full-time doctors and in case of emergencies, specialist doctors had to be called from the nearest town. I had just completed my internship and was mandated by college rules to do one year of rural service. Although I had been awarded a medical degree, my clinical skills and experience were still very limited. As an apprentice, I had spent most of the time during my medical internship collecting blood samples and monitoring blood pressure. Despite that, here I was treating patients with grave illnesses when, one day, a young man came in with a complaint of abdominal pain.

The general surgeon, a feisty grey-haired lady, had checked him and due to a lack of sophisticated interventions, she had performed an exploratory laparotomy which involves opening up the abdominal cavity to see what was causing the pain. She diagnosed pancreatitis. The pancreas is an organ which is situated behind the stomach, resting against our mid-spine. This organ, as I was to find out, is slow to anger but burns brightly once inflamed.

The next morning, I got an urgent call from the nursing staff. The patient was unresponsive. They could not find a pulse or capture his blood pressure. He was in shock. When the pancreas burns, it leaks large quantities of acidic fluid into the abdominal cavity, pushing the patient into shock. To be frank, I too was in shock. I had no idea what to do and once I reached the hospital, I stood paralysed by his bed as the staff and the patient's relatives looked on. After a minute or so, the ABC of medical training—airway, breathing and circulation—seeped into my brain and I began to act.

The patient was still breathing. Being a peripheral centre, we had no access to facilities and high-end investigations such as arterial blood-gas analysis. We did not even have a pulse oximeter to assess how much oxygen was saturating the blood. I immediately asked the staff to secure a robust IV line to start fluids. They, however, could not establish an IV line as all the blood vessels had collapsed and the patient was in shock. The next course of action would be to insert a line into a major blood vessel at the bottom of the neck or in the upper chest—a central line. But I didn't know how to do that.

I will never be able to forget, that as the young man lay dying, how utterly incompetent I felt. I rushed to and fro and it appeared as though I was doing a lot. But to be truthful, I was doing nothing. I felt useless. I had been a meritorious student throughout my MBBS but no amount of textbook reading and good grades can be a substitute for practical experience. In what felt like a lifetime, but was merely an hour, the patient passed away. I was horrified and deeply ashamed of my ineptitude and total uselessness. I now had the onerous task of explaining to the young man's elderly father that his son was no more.

I had tears in my eyes when I told him about his death. I cringed. I was waiting for the old man to call me out, to expose me—how useless I had been, how could I not save his son? How I had crushed his hopes and dreams. They were all the things that I knew I deserved to hear. But the old man sat me down, put his arm around me and gently said, 'I know you did your best. That is all I can ask for. The rest is up to destiny and God. Man must go when the call comes.' Such benevolence in the light of personal tragedy—what grace the man had! I will never forget his face, his calm demeanour and his gentle voice.

I don't remember anything that happened later but that moment has stayed with me forever. It taught me a profound lesson of acceptance. Death is inevitable, we can only do our best to postpone it. This patient's father restored my faith in humanity. Several times, a doctor is faultlessly blamed and at other times, a doctor is at fault. But even if the doctor is at fault, how should she/he be judged? Must we not keep into account the circumstances that led to the wrong decision? The possibility of mistakes and human errors are a reality in the world of doctors as they teeter under a heavy workload.

After a year-and-a-half of rural service, I started my post-graduation in internal medicine. One day, both the second- and third-year residents were on leave and I was all alone in the department for the 24-hour 'on call' duty. By 'on call', it means, that I would man the OPD of more than 200 patients, along with senior staff, from 8 am until 1 pm. After the OPD, I would need to rush back to the wards to treat new patients who were admitted from the OPD. At 3 pm, I would attend our weekly seminar for an hour and return to the wards to prepare for the consultant's evening rounds at 5 pm. On that day, we had an unprecedented 40 new admissions. I only had two junior interns to help me and they would mainly do the basic work—collecting urgent blood samples, taking blood pressure and attaching blood reports to patient files.

I had the job of assessing each of those 40 patients, recording their medical history, making a provisional diagnosis, ordering lab tests and imaging wherever required, starting preliminary treatment and documenting all of this in detail on their 40 files later in the night.

Once I finished the ward round, I proceeded to document the medical histories and details of examinations of the 40 patients. Any patient coming to the hospital for emergency medicine consultation, any time till 8 the next morning, would also be my responsibility. Thus, my documentation was constantly interrupted by a steady stream of walk-in patients who needed my attention.

By 9 pm, I was finally on top of things. I had a stack of 50 to 60 old patient case files which needed to be completed and countersigned by senior staff at next morning's mortality meet. As it was also my turn to present a case at the mortality meeting, I started preparing for it. In a mortality meeting, typically, a bunch of seniors would hear the course of events leading up to a patient's death and analyse where we went wrong. At this point, if I had told someone I needed help, the reply most probably would be, 'We have all worked harder than this. You just have to gear up and do it.' That's the way it was. Of course, as a new resident, it was also a matter of pride to be able to cope without help.

Finally, it was 11 pm. I was exhausted. I had just returned after dinner (a hastily gulped five-minute meal). My defences were at their lowest. I had been in perpetual motion from seven in the morning. It was then that my intern informed me that there was a walk-in emergency patient who needed to be seen. He was sitting on a bench and appeared to be breathing rapidly, but otherwise looked fine. He was an 18-year-old boy from the neighbouring engineering college. He said he felt out of breath. I asked him a few questions about his heart and lungs, as those are the common reasons for shortness of breath. I auscultated (examined) his lungs and heart with my stethoscope. All was as it should have been—clear breathing sounds, heart galloping away in its steady rhythm. I prescribed a few medicines and asked him to come back the next day if the symptoms worsened. I returned to the residents' room. My conscientious intern walked in. She had checked his blood pressure and had found that it was high. I can never forget the words I uttered when I heard this: 'Did I ask you to check his blood pressure? Just do what you are told'. Those words haunt me to this day.

The boy returned the next morning with the same complaints. Another less tired and less weary resident assessed him. They found a scar over his abdomen that elicited a history of a kidney operation. One of his kidneys had been removed and the remaining kidney had failed. The body was unable to get rid of the acids it made through this remaining defunct kidney, causing the patient to breathe faster, and hence, the shortness of breath. The high blood pressure was a clue I completely missed or, rather, willfully ignored. The next two days were torturous. Everyone knew what had happened, what I had missed. Here I had been congratulating myself on a call duty gone well when I had missed effectively assessing a critical patient.

Mistakes do happen, but are they justified at the cost of human life? Maybe if I had help, if I had someone to cover for me, I would have been less tired and would have taken the boy and my intern more seriously. Thankfully, the boy survived.

Ideally, things could have turned out differently. The patient could have told me about his surgery or I could have been more vigilant. But sometimes people genuinely don't realise the importance of sharing every bit of their medical history. Mistakes made at the end of a long day are not permissible but may, perhaps, be understandable. No doctor wants to harm their patient—by omission or commission.

It troubles me when we are quick to judge and the efforts expended on the 40-odd patients throughout the day are wiped out due to a single mistake. In 2016, the *British Medical Journal* published a study which said that medical errors were the third leading cause of death in the US. But my question is how do you judge a decision made in the best interest of a patient, but at a time when a doctor is short-staffed, utterly weary and hungry? Why are doctors put on a pedestal we possibly don't want or need?

This brings me to the story of a young Gujarati businessman, married with three little daughters, who was diagnosed with diabetes. I don't know what his symptoms were or how he was diagnosed but he was put on a tablet and asked to take it every day. However, caught in the whirlwind of financial and familial responsibilities, he didn't understand what the diagnosis meant.

He continued to live his usual life—eating what he liked, no exercise and occasionally missing his medicines. I wish someone had explained to the 35-year-old man the ramifications of diabetes, a chronic disease with no possibility of a cure. He was clueless that diabetes requires a progressive increase in medication and a rigorous lifestyle. He was also unaware of the silent, painless damage diabetes inflicts on the eyes, heart, kidney and nerves.

Had he known this, would he have been more compliant? Would he have made the necessary changes in his lifestyle? I don't know.

Fifteen years later, they found a lump in his neck. He was diagnosed with Hodgkin's lymphoma, a relatively easy-to-treat cancer of the blood and lymph glands. But the word 'cancer' had already knocked the family over. As he had just begun to enjoy his financial stability, the diagnosis made him very angry. At this time, if someone had taken the time to explain that this was a relatively benign disease with a complete cure, would it have lessened the anguish and pain he faced? I don't know. Did his doctor explain? Did our societal stigma associated with the word 'cancer' override all explanations by his doctor? Again, I don't know.

What I do know is that the stress ended his wife's life prematurely at the age of 42. She suffered a massive heart attack. It was a double whammy. On the one side, the family was gearing up for the possible loss of the father to cancer, and on the other, before they could wrap their mind around it, the mother was snatched away by a massive heart attack. The mother had high blood pressure. She, however, did not take her medicines because of what's popularly believed in Indian society: You will be addicted to the medicines, your kidneys will be damaged. The businessman was shattered. There ensued a long, lonely battle with depression and survivor's guilt. The irony is that in his case, the real danger was diabetes, not cancer. The cancer was cured by a small surgery but diabetes raged on silently. Ten years later, his three daughters had grown up to become a lawyer, a financial consultant and a doctor. With age, the businessman's everyday life, too, was changing: he could neither walk as fast as he used to nor climb stairs without stopping for breath. When he saw a doctor, he was told that his heart was failing. He was confused. There had never been any pain.

It was the diabetes—a silent but ruthless disease.

Medicines helped him limp on. But, after three years of relative stability, there was a sudden increase in the level of breathlessness and tiredness. He realised that the end was near. The cardiologist asked him to get admitted as soon as possible, but he delayed it. He wanted to postpone the day forever.

To the daughter who accompanied him for the visits, the cardiologist's conduct was dissatisfying. The cardiologist would keep bobbing his head and mutter inaudibly. Instead of empathy and understanding, they got a blunt order from the doctor—Get admitted or else!

The diabetes was now beautifully controlled but, sadly, it was too late. The damage was done. Over the next few weeks, he spent some of the most miserable days of his life in the hospital. However, the biggest cause of misery for this diehard foodie was that there was no salt in his food. Death is probably acceptable to a Gujarati but unpalatable food isn't.

His fate was sealed and very soon, it was the end. Thankfully, he passed away at his home, surrounded by his two elder daughters while watching cricket on television. It could have been a lot worse—blindness, kidney failure with endless rounds of dialysis or an amputated foot. But the question is, was this preventable? It probably didn't have to be this way. With good medication and some lifestyle changes, he would have possibly seen his grandchildren. They deserved to enjoy him too.

This is my own story. The businessman, battling diabetes and cancer, was my father and his wife who succumbed to a massive heart attack was my mother. This had a profound impact on me as a professional and a doctor. I now choose to be a non-judgemental endocrinologist. When patients tell me that they have gained weight, haven't taken medicines for a year, haven't exercised, I don't reprimand them. Before my father's death, I was a virago, giving well-meaning advice in a strident accusing voice—as if I alone could change the course of their life. How little I knew. Life has taught me the importance of being non-judgemental through the experience of my own father.

Today, to my patients I say, let's move on. Whatever you have not done is in the past; let's start afresh from today. The joy that shines through the patient's face at being accepted for who s/he is, is beyond words. I make an effort to listen to all their problems—especially the women, as so few of them have a voice in their own house. It's these problems that impact them far more than any physical ailment. At the same time, I try to explain their illness as simply as I can. You can fight a known enemy, not an unknown one.

Years later, when I was reading the Bhagavad Gita, a verse struck me, 'No man kills another. The soul is eternal and let no man feel that he or she is so powerful, that they can kill another.'

This helped me deal with my father's death and realise that doctors, too, are humans—we can extend our best possible effort at saving someone's life, but sometimes it's time for people to go and they do.

As a doctor, today I strive to ensure that each patient who leaves my office, does so with a smile. I ensure that they are not alone in their battle and there is someone by their side. No matter how grave the disease, we deal with it together.

Dr Tejal Lathia is a consultant endocrinologist trained at TN Medical College, Mumbai Central, Mumbai. She has worked as a senior registrar and then as an Assistant Professor at TN Medical College after completion of her residency. She has completed her MBBS and MD (Medicine) from MGIMS, Sewagram, Wardha. She is currently associated as a consultant with Apollo, Fortis and MGM hospitals in Navi Mumbai. She is a very good speaker and has multiple publications to her credit.

Did You Know?

Physician burnout is a dangerous mix of exhaustion and depersonalisation that contributes to physicians making mistakes while administering healthcare. A study found 45% of respondents experienced at least one major symptom of burnout, with those in urology, neurology, emergency medicine and general surgery at the highest risk. Regardless of speciality, high levels of anxiety and low levels of empathy reported during medical school were associated with burnout symptoms during residency.

Source: https://www.upi.com/Many-young-doctors-report-burnout-regret-career-choice/9181537318593/

Dear People,

'A close collaboration between modern medicine, modern science and ancient knowledge is the urgent need of the hour.'

Dr V. Mohan

The Power of Positive Thinking in Healing

The role of positive thinking in medical science is long debated. While studies like a recent one by Harvard T.H. Chan School of Public Health found that women who were optimistic had a significantly reduced risk of dying from several major causes of death—including cancer, heart disease, stroke, respiratory disease and infection—over an eight-year period, compared with women who were less optimistic, they could be taken with a pinch of salt.

Twenty-five years ago, when I had just begun my practice, a middle-aged gentleman came to me for the treatment of diabetes. He was a disciplined man who would regularly follow up at my clinic with his reports. In a few years, during a routine follow-up, he was detected with mild renal insufficiency due to diabetic kidney disease. Diabetes is a chronic progressive disease that silently and gradually affects the body from head to toe. Kidneys are the worst affected by long-standing diabetes.

Once kidney insufficiency sets in and the serum creatinine levels begin to rise, it takes about 5–10 years to develop an end-stage renal disease which may require either dialysis or transplantation.

At that time, this gentleman was around 50 years old. He was a businessman with tremendous willpower and even greater faith in God. When I broke the news to him—that his reports showed signs of mild renal insufficiency—he was aghast. He pleaded with me to help him. He was still young and didn't want to end up with kidney failure requiring dialysis or transplantation. 'Doctor, can you help me live at least another 25 years in good health?' he asked me. Twenty-five years of good health was a tall order by all standards for someone who had diabetic kidney disease and was already showing signs of renal insufficiency.

However, medicine is a field where the best results are achieved when both the doctor as well as the patient are equally invested. Hence, I explained to him that I would try my best, but then he would also have to regulate his lifestyle and take full responsibility for his health. He promised that he would follow my advice to the smallest detail and would be regular with his follow-ups.

Today, it has been a long journey of 25 years and he continues to maintain good control over his diabetes and blood pressure. He has been extremely meticulous about taking his drugs and very regular with his check-ups. For many years, after being diagnosed with borderline renal insufficiency, his serum creatinine levels remained constant. Thereafter, every few years when the creatinine would go up marginally, say from 2.5 to 3.0 mg/dl, he would tell me resolutely, 'Doctor, I will come back next month and bring my creatinine back to 2.5 mg/dl again.' I, of course, did not take him seriously initially, because there is no known drug that can reduce these creatinine levels and reverse kidney disease, let alone any kind of lifestyle modification that can help achieve that.

However, whenever he returned for his next visit, his creatinine would be down to the level that he had promised to bring it down to! I used to be struck with wonder and would ask him, what he was he doing to bring down the creatinine levels. He would simply say, 'Just prayer, doctor, and sheer willpower.'

In the initial days, I thought it was a mere coincidence, but every time, over the next couple of decades, he was consistent and would manage to bring down his creatinine levels again and again. Admittedly, after several years, the creatinine levels did go up, but the rate of increase was much slower than I have ever seen in any other patient. It should be noted that at the time of writing this, 30 years after he developed the kidney disease, the man has still not required dialysis or transplantation.

This gentleman's case study has had a lasting impression on me. It taught me that there is something beyond medicine and medication. There is a spiritual dimension and divine power which one can tap into. This may be difficult to define objectively, but it plays a pivotal role in healing. As healers, we need to be able to tap into this dimension of our patients, to help them get through the process of illness and recovery. The importance of the human dimension cannot be undermined and if you ask me, only a human being can connect with another at such a deep level.

Over the years I have become increasingly convinced about the power of mind in healing. As doctors trained in modern medicine, we are always taught about 'evidence-based medicine'. Anything which is not proved by so-called 'randomised clinical trials' is generally not accepted in the medical world as 'true' or 'scientific'. However, in real life, many things cannot be explained by randomised clinical trials. I have understood the value of 'practice-based evidence' which is sometimes as powerful as 'evidence-based practice'.

As doctors, we witness stories of success and failure on a daily basis. I still get perplexed when I see the most critical patients recovering while the health of a perfectly fine person deteriorates rapidly. It is therefore fair to ask if the opposite is also true? Can a disease worsen if one is pessimistic? I dare say 'yes', based on another experience that I've had.

Some years ago, a middle-aged gentleman came to me for consultation. He had recently lost his wife to diabetic kidney disease. She was a chronic diabetic patient for over 25 years and had developed a progressive renal failure. Eventually, she was put on regular dialysis and after a few years, she succumbed to the disease. The husband was diagnosed with diabetes just about two years ago. All his parameters, specifically his kidney function tests, were completely normal. He did not even have microalbuminuria—a marginal increase in urine albumin—which is the earliest sign of kidney disease.

During his first consultation with me, he told me, 'Doctor, soon I too will develop kidney failure.' I was appalled on hearing this and thought that he was overreacting because of his wife's recent demise. I tried my best to reassure him that the duration of diabetes in his case was very short and he would not develop kidney failure any time soon. However, nothing changed in his attitude and during subsequent visits, he would repeat the same statement each time, saying that he 'will' develop kidney failure soon. Within a year or so, his creatinine levels started increasing and by the end of two years, he had developed end-stage kidney failure that requires dialysis.

I was perplexed. I am not sure why his condition deteriorated so fast despite receiving the best possible medical treatment. I have no scientific explanation to offer. My humble submission is that the human mind is very powerful. While a positive attitude can do magic—and help people achieve the impossible—negative and self-deprecating attitude can weaken the strongest.

Somewhere, I felt that this patient did not want to recover. His deep conviction that he would develop renal failure was a form of prayer. It is possible that when the mind believes this so strongly, the body ultimately succumbs to it.

These two episodes have had a strong imprint on my mind. It has been incredible to learn that one's disease can both be slowed down as well as accelerated depending on the state of one's mind. Prayer, faith and devotion play a very important role in healing.

These two patients have made me think about the significance of positive thinking to achieve good results. Soon, I started experimenting—to see whether I could use the power of 'positive thinking' in addition to my medical management to induce a reversal of disease in my patients.

When my next patient with early kidney disease came along, I gave him a prescription for drugs and taught him a mantra in addition. It was just a simple statement, 'My kidney will become normal'. I asked him to stand in front of the mirror every day and repeat this mantra 20 times without fail with conviction. A couple of months later, the patient came for a follow-up and I was pleasantly surprised to see that the microalbuminuria had disappeared. It did not recur for years.

As a scientist and physician, I am in no way undermining the importance of proper treatment. I am conscious that we cannot rely solely on the power of the mind or spiritual healing without medication. It would be unethical to even think so. However, I do believe, that as doctors, it is important to add this spiritual dimension and the power of positive thinking to our daily lives to combat illnesses. Although this science is still in its infancy, studies are increasingly showing the benefits of positive thinking, yoga and meditation in decreasing inflammation, promoting healing and improving one's sense of well-being and quality of life. Hence, as doctors, we should not hesitate to add these alternative forms of healing to our practice. Our ancestors have used it for centuries and there's wisdom in it.

Unfortunately, in modern medicine, these are dismissed as being 'imaginary', 'anecdotal' or with 'no scientific evidence'. While I agree there is a need to 'scientifically' prove and measure everything, some of the best things in life do not require any validation. This spiritual dimension may be difficult to define but if we sit down and reflect, all of us can feel it in every aspect of our life. This not only helps our patients lead a better 'quality of life', but also helps to make the doctor-patient relationship more meaningful and fulfilling.

There is emerging evidence that positive thinking, through hitherto unknown mechanisms, hastens the healing process both for physical as well as mental illnesses. More research is needed to understand the power of the subconscious mind in healing. A close collaboration between modern medicine, modern science and ancient knowledge is the urgent need of the hour. India has the potential to contribute substantially in this field and the best part is that it really costs nothing. No costly investigations or medicines are needed—just a positive approach, both by the patient as well as the doctor and the healthcare team. My 25 years of practice have taught me that it's important to approach health with a positive focus, no matter what's going around us. It's those who stay positive and focused on the success they desire ultimately live a wholesome life. Therefore, the next time you take a pill, don't forget to self-prescribe some optimism.

Dr V. Mohan is the Chairman and Chief of Diabetology at Dr Mohan's Diabetes Specialities Centre, Chennai In South India which is a WHO Collaborating Centre for Noncommunicable Diseases Prevention and Control and IDF Centre of Excellence in Diabetes Care. He is also the

president and director of the Madras Diabetes Research Foundation which is an ICMR Centre for Advanced Research on Diabetes. He is deeply passionate about research and has published over 1,120 papers in peer-reviewed journals and received over 160 awards. He was awarded the Dr B.C. Roy National Award by the Medical Council of India and Dr B. R. Ambedkar Centenary Award from the ICMR. He is also the first Indian to be conferred with the prestigious Harold Rifkin Distinguished International Service in the Cause of Diabetes Award by the American Diabetes Association for his pioneering work in the field of diabetes. In 2012, the Government of India conferred the prestigious Padma Shri on him.

Did You Know?

There is no longer any doubt that what happens in the brain influences what happens in the body. When facing a health crisis, actively cultivating positive emotions can boost the immune system and counter depression. Studies have shown an indisputable link between having a positive outlook and health benefits like lower blood pressure, less heart disease, better weight control and healthier blood sugar levels.

Source: https://www.nytimes.com/2017/03/27/well/live/positive-thinking-may-improve-health-and-extend-life.html

Dear People,

'Medicine has the power to transform people and as doctors we are blessed to be able to practise it.'

Dr Vandana Jain

When Patients Leave an Indelible Mark

It had been a regular day at work. I did a few interesting surgeries and met some amazing patients during my consulting hours. I am a people's person and enjoy conversing with my patients. There is always so much to learn from everyone. Finally, at 6 pm, it was time to leave and I started packing my things to get into my car and drive back home. I had come to love these hour-long drives at the end of a hectic day. Soft soothing music and a good book are all one needs to get over the fatigue and stresses of a taxing ophthalmic practice. At that time, I was reading an extremely interesting book and was excited about getting back to where I had left it in the morning.

Just as I was about to get out of my clinic, my phone rang. As I picked up the receiver, I was informed that a young boy was insisting that his grandfather be seen by me despite being told that my consulting hours were over for that day. The receptionist also informed me that the patient was very poor and would not be able to pay the consulting fee. I asked her to send them in. I put my purse and other things back on the table and sat down once again. After a while, a young boy peeped in through the door of my consulting chamber. With a sheepish, guilt-ridden expression on his face, he asked if he could bring his grandfather in. An old man followed the young boy, walking in very slowly as if measuring each step. It was apparent that he could not see beyond a foot or so. I was worried that he might stumble and fall and hurriedly got up from my chair to assist. The young boy and I helped the old man sit comfortably on the chair. I asked them a few questions and examined his eyes. I realised that the old gentleman had only one functioning eye. The other eye was blinded in his childhood following an injury. His family had never bothered to get any treatment and he had lived his entire life with only one working eye. Being born in a poor family, they struggled for basic necessities; so getting good medical treatment was a luxury that was unheard of. He was more than 60 years old now and while he had managed beautifully with one eye in all these years, recently, he had begun to notice that the vision in the other functioning eye was also deteriorating. His grandson had taken him to a nearby eye doctor who told them that he had developed an infection in the cornea and it was completely damaged. He had callously declared that it was too late to intervene and nothing could be done to save his vision. The old man was devastated and appalled at the prospect of being completely blind for the rest of his life.

I examined the old man's functioning eye and found that the cornea was scarred from repeated viral infections over the years, infections that he had obviously ignored. He also had an active viral infection which was presently affecting his sight gravely. I decided that we first needed to treat the active infection and then address the scars depending on the visual recovery. I wrote the prescription and handed it over to the young boy. As I started to explain how to administer the medicines, I noticed that the boy, Gopi, was awfully quiet. It was what could be called a stony silence. I was a little annoyed at his lack of response and assumed that this grandson was not interested and did not want to take the responsibility of putting eye drops and ointments in his grandfather's eyes. A bit irritated, I asked him what the matter was and if he would be able to find the time to care for his grandfather. Gopi recognised the displeasure in my voice and began to apologise profusely. He said that he loved his grandfather and would do anything for him. He did not mind being at home all day to put the eye drops. This perplexed me and I asked him then what was the matter? Once again, he went quiet. This time, I asked him more gently. He looked up slowly and as his eyes welled up, he asked what the cost of the medicines would be.

I hated myself for being so naïve and for failing to see beyond the patient's eye condition. Immediately, I reached out to my purse and handed him a thousand-rupee note. He looked at it apologetically and refused to take it. I insisted that he take it then and return the money whenever he had it. I insisted that at that moment, it was more important for his grandfather to get the treatment. After some urging, he finally accepted the money. I felt better and finally left for home, feeling satisfied that I was able to help someone in need.

In the next few months, Gopi regularly brought his grandfather to my clinic for the scheduled reviews and neither of us mentioned anything about those thousand rupees. I was delighted that his grandfather was getting better and his vision was improving. A few months later, Gopi visited me. He grinned sheepishly and had the same look on his face he had when he first came in. I was glad to see him and asked him about his grandfather. He informed me that his grandfather was feeling much better. He had gone to his village and would be coming back for the review soon.

I was confused. I asked Gopi about the reason for his visit. He put his hands in his pocket and took out a neatly folded thousand-rupee note. My heart skipped a beat as he handed it to me. He had worked extra shifts to earn this money. I told him that I did not need the money back and he could keep it but he insisted that I take it. I understood that this was a matter of his self-respect and pride and I accepted the money. When I thanked him, he held my hand and touched his forehead to it. I was totally flummoxed and didn't know how to react. My eyes were brimming with tears as he left my room.

After Gopi left, my assistant came in and told me that he had brought sweets for the entire clinic. Gopi might not have been born with a silver spoon but he was blessed with a golden heart. Despite his meagre means, he was generous. He not only paid me back but also expressed his gratitude to everyone in the clinic. He must have probably missed a few meals to save that kind of money.

In recent years, medical science has advanced a lot and it continues to help doctors like me serve my patients better. However, nothing is as gratifying as meeting patients like Gopi who reinstate our faith in humanity. These rare cases exhibit profound doctor-patient relationship where doctors not only treat the patients but take back unforgettable memories that impact their personalities and learn more than any textbook could teach them. Each time I think of Gopi, I am reminded of what Ralph Waldo Emerson said, 'The purpose of life is not to be happy, it is to be useful, to be honourable, to be compassionate, to have it make some difference that you have lived and lived well.' This brings me to my next story.

Shripa was a very intelligent and accomplished girl. At a young age of 28, she had achieved a lot and I was very impressed when I learnt about her journey. When I congratulated her for her achievements, she confided in me that this was the only way for her to feel worthy; otherwise, her life had no meaning. I realised that there was something that was denting her self-esteem in a major way.

She had come to me to check if there was any new medical advancement that could help her to get rid of the thick spectacles. She had consulted many leading eye specialists in the past and they had not been very optimistic. She had an eye power of -30 D and her glasses were so thick that her eyes looked distorted through them. She had been pestered and ridiculed over the years due to her bespectacled look. Gradually, she stopped socialising and found solace in being a loner and had become extremely studious. Books had become her best friends. Even at work, she handled a very important profile but it was mainly a back-office job. She shied away from interacting actively with her colleagues. Other than her boss, most of her colleagues were probably not even aware of her existence. Her parents were also becoming increasingly worried about her as they could not find the right match for her due to the thick glasses.

Once I examined her, I realised that unfortunately, a single surgery could not help her. She would need multiple sittings and a series of procedures on both the eyes. After conducting multiple scans, I was relieved to know that apart from extremely high power, there was no other major problem with her eyes. She had a few weak areas on the retina, which we strengthened using a retinal laser. This was not a textbook case and I knew that I had to be creative to find the right solution for her. All this while, something inside me was telling me that this would be truly life-changing for her, which further motivated me to do everything I could to help her.

After a lot of thought, I planned to perform two procedures on each of her eyes spread across three different surgeries. First, we would need to do half a LASIK on each of her eyes, in order to just create the flaps and put them back in position without attempting to correct any power. After a month, we would perform the second surgery and insert the maximum powered implantable contact lens (IMC) in her eyes. This would correct two-thirds of her eye power. Over the next few months, we would need to wait for her eyes to stabilise, after which we would re-lift the old flaps and complete the LASIK laser procedure to correct the remaining thirds of her eye power.

When I discussed the plan with her, she was ecstatic to hear that finally there was a solution in sight. But after that initial euphoria settled, she panicked and asked me tearfully if she ran the risk of becoming blind after the procedure. After years of repeated disappointment, this solution sounded too good to be true! I reassured her and then discussed the pros and cons of both the surgeries. It was important for her to understand the risks and the possibility of different complications that could arise and the side effects of the surgeries. I encouraged her to do some research on her own too and think about the two procedures and then come back for a review after a week.

I had a gut feeling that she would return. She had a very strong urge to break free of the insecurities that were holding her back. As expected, she visited me after a week and wanted to go ahead with the treatment. Over the next four months, she underwent three surgeries on her eyes and, finally, we were able to give her the much-needed freedom from her bulky glasses.

For me, it was a cherished victory over a complicated problem and more than that, I was glad that I could help her. After three months, when she entered my room, I could not believe the transformation. She had a slick new haircut, had applied some make-up and was wearing a very smart dress. She looked no less than a model with her high cheekbones and her slender figure. Accompanying her was a very smart young man who she introduced as her colleague. The shy smile on her face made me realise that probably they were dating each other. She told me enthusiastically about all the new projects that she had taken up, her yoga routine and her upcoming trips and many other things! From a dull and depressed girl, she had evolved into this beautiful and confident young woman ready to take on the world.

It proved to me that medicine has the power to transform people and as doctors we are blessed to be able to practice it.

Dr Vandana Jain is a cornea, cataract and refractive surgeon and the Founder-Managing Director of the multi-speciality Advanced Eye Hospital and Institute in Navi Mumbai. She completed her post-graduation in ophthalmology from Maulana Azad Medical College, Delhi University, India and was awarded the University Gold Medal for the best student. She has specialized in Cornea and Anterior Segment at L. V. Prasad Eye Institute, Hyderabad where she won the Best Fellow award. Dr Jain also did a fellowship (FICO) from the MEEI, Harvard medical school, USA and completed her MBA from Stanford Business School, USA. She is the co-founder of a medical device business Clear Ear Inc running successfully in California and a Health tech start-up called Wondrx. She is the trustee of the NGO—One Vision Health and Research Foundation. She is the recipient of the Incredible Journey Award and Women Achievers Award. She is passionate about fitness and in her free time she travels and reads.

Did You Know?

A doctor's medical toolbox and supply of best-practice guidelines, ample as they are, do not address a patient's fears, grief over a diagnosis, practical issues of access to care, or reliability of their social support system. Overlooking these realities is perilous, both for the patient's well-being and for efficient delivery of care. Not only a clinician should share medical decision-making with the patient but also that it must occur in the context of an authentic relationship. Modern medicine's true healing potential depends on a resource that is being systematically depleted: the time and capacity to truly listen to patients, hear their stories and learn not only what's the matter *with* them but also what matters *to* them.

Source: https://hbr.org/2017/10/making-time-to-really-listen-to-your-patients

Dear People,

'Doctors can only perform their duty; they cannot control the outcome.'

Dr Vijay Agarwal

The Reversers of Immediate Mortality

I met eight-month-old Muthu a few years ago. He was just skin and bones and was struggling to survive. The moment I saw him, I knew that it was going to be one of the most difficult cases of my life.

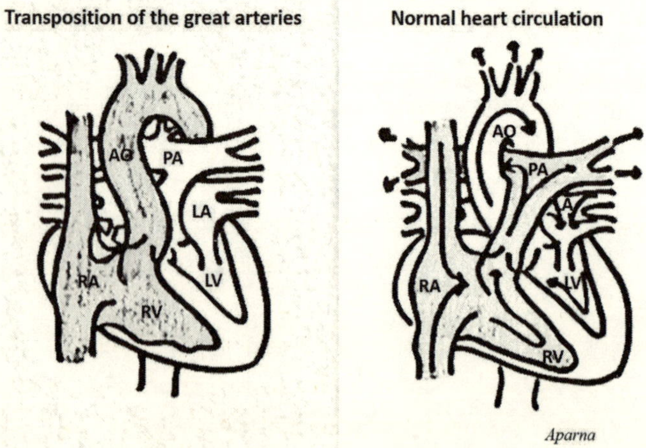

Figure 1: Transposition of great arteries

I am a paediatric heart surgeon and can confidently say that when compared to other medical disciplines, paediatric heart surgery is not only more emotionally challenging but also fraught with grave risks. When things go wrong, it requires immense grit and courage to look into a mother's eyes and deliver the bad news. It's as if I were stabbing into someone's heart. It doesn't matter how hard I tried, I am always guilty.

Muthu was suffering from a complex congenital heart disease called the Taussig-Bing anomaly. In this condition, there is an interchange in the position of the great arteries along with a ventricular septal defect (a hole in the wall between the heart's lower chambers) (Figure 1).

As the great vessels of the heart are swapped in this congenital heart defect, the aorta, which is the largest blood vessel in the human body that carries pure oxygenated blood, arises from the right ventricle instead of the left. The pulmonary artery that carries deoxygenated blood arises from the left ventricle instead of the right. This leads to a decrease in the amount of oxygen provided to the body and the malfunctioning heart can result in the blue baby syndrome—a condition where the baby's skin turns blue.

Like in most congenital heart diseases, the prognosis is always better when the infant is presented to us as early after birth as possible. The ideal time for the repair of transposition of great arteries is between one and two weeks after birth through a procedure called the arterial switch operation.

In Muthu's case, however, the treatment had already been delayed by eight long months and considering his low body weight, I anticipated it to be a complex and challenging surgery.

At first, the procedure involved surgically removing the left and right coronary buttons and placing them into the appropriate vessels (Figure 2). As always, there was no margin for error and no room for mistakes or excuses.

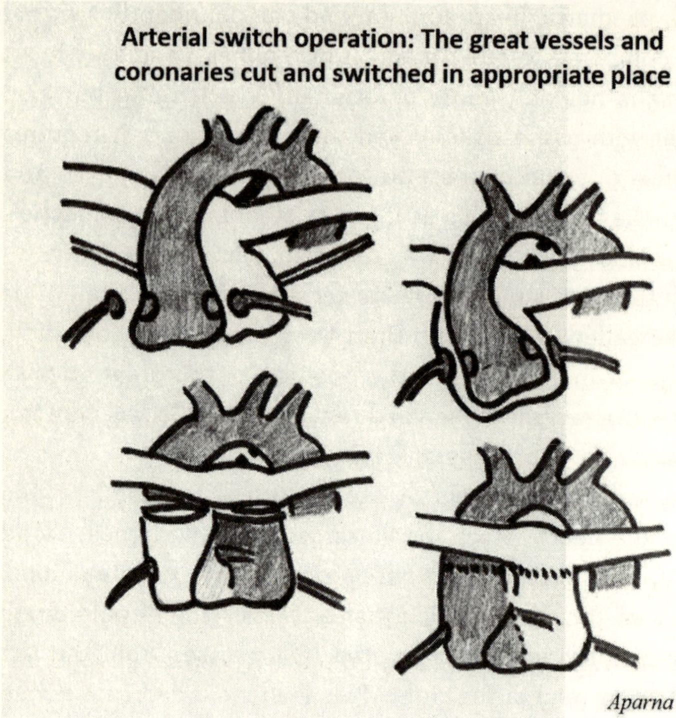

Figure 2: Arterial switch operation: The great vessels and coronaries cut and switched in appropriate place

My experience as a cardiac surgeon had taught me that the oxygen saturation starts improving soon after the swapped great vessels are put back into their normal positions. On that day, however, despite four gruelling hours into the surgery, the child's electrocardiography (ECG) continued to show abnormalities. His lungs were failing and his oxygen levels dropped below the critical level. Muthu's blood pressure was also low. These were worrying signs. Something was not right. Either the coronary button relocation was faulty or there was air in the coronary arteries. The senior anaesthetist, a towering personality in the institution, believed that the right coronary button was not fixed appropriately. Maybe that was creating the problem. He suggested that I should consider revising the right coronary button's insertion. In the meantime, I gave the heart some rest and tried to encourage the heart to beat without the support of the heart-lung machine but unfortunately that didn't work. With great reluctance, I again stopped the heart, put Muthu back on the heart-lung machine, and proceeded with the surgical revision of the right coronary button.

In paediatric heart surgery, the dictum is that the longer a child's operation takes, the lower are the chances of a successful outcome. That day, time was slipping away and as I was desperately thinking of solutions; an eerie numbness was creeping into me. It took another two hours to revise the right coronary button. We made one more attempt to take Muthu off the heart-lung machine. The heart held for two minutes and once again began to weaken and desaturate. Now, this spelt serious trouble. We were running out of time with no feasible solutions. With every passing minute, we were inching closer to the inevitable.

The same senior anaesthetist was now of the opinion that the left coronary button also perhaps needed to be revised. Revising the left button again would have been a technical exercise for another two hours and unfortunately, we didn't have the luxury of that kind of time. The surgery had begun at 10 am and it was already 5 pm. It was then that a younger albeit experienced anaesthetist entered and brought in a fresh perspective. He suggested that maybe the lungs also needed to be worked upon.

By then, we had been in surgery for more than six hours and I stepped out of the OT to speak with the parents. Much to my chagrin, they had to be informed that Muthu's chances were very weak, probably next to none. Before I saw them, my assistant had already spoken to them about their little baby's state and, therefore, on seeing me, they were aghast and inconsolable.

All this while, my mind was frantically searching for a plausible plan B that could save Muthu's life. I returned to the OT after speaking to the parents and decided to give it one last shot.

His heart was becoming weaker by the second. I needed to buy some time and embarked on an alternative option as a last resort. I was not sure if this would have any real benefits, but I didn't want to give up on Muthu. The younger anaesthetist, concomitantly, worked hard on the lungs and took out all the mucous plugs and blood from the endotracheal tube.

After a long, toilsome hour, we once again separated the heart from the heart-lung machine. The poor baby had been in surgery for 11 long hours by then. Although the blood pressure was still on the lower side, this time, the heart remained steady and held on for 5 minutes, then 10 minutes and then for a full 15 minutes. While this was happening, I was hardly breathing myself, anticipating that trouble would begin any second and the heart would start weakening once again. I asked the anaesthetist to start the stopwatch. Blood pressure was still borderline, but Muthu was holding on and there were no episodes of desaturation like the last time. Each passing second, we stared at the heart, the monitor and then at each other. We were scared to relax or even assume that everything was fine. After the 20 longest minutes of my life, we breathed easy; at 40 minutes we were strongly hopeful and at the end of the hour, we were totally amazed. This child was a born fighter and had made it. At last at 12.30 am, we shifted Muthu into the ICU. Usually, when an operation takes this long, there are high chances of post-operative complications but by God's grace, Muthu's post-operative recovery was uneventful and he was discharged within 10 days.

This was in Chennai.

Five years later, as I was stuck in Mumbai's traffic, my thoughts suddenly wandered to Muthu and I wondered how he was doing. I had his parents' number in my diary and I messaged his father. As I awaited his reply, somewhere deep inside my heart, I was dreading and expecting bad news. My phone pinged after a couple of minutes with a video of Muthu, now six years old, happily playing. His father replied with a beautiful thank-you note, revealing for the first time that Muthu had been conceived after almost 10 years of their marriage and was, to them, a treasure. Thank God for small mercies, I thought to myself. This piece of information before the operation would have needlessly stressed me out. I would have felt increasingly burdened knowing Muthu was a very precious baby and far more valuable to his parents than I had imagined.

Muthu recovered and went home a healthy child but soon after, two other children were wheeled in, needing my immediate attention.

Seven-year-old Madhurima and 12-year-old Raghav suffered from cardiomyopathy. A leading cause of heart transplant in children, it's a condition where the muscles of the heart become enlarged, thickened and stiff. The heart loses the ability to pump blood effectively and starts failing.

Raghav and Madhurima suffered from repeated episodes of arrhythmias and congestive heart failure and every few weeks, they would have to be admitted to the ICU. They would be sick with vomiting, breathlessness and massive swelling of their feet. Small triggers would push them into prolonged episodes of congestive heart failure. The parents had to be especially careful as in cases of cardiomyopathy, children's physical activity is severely hampered as it can lead to complications and, at times, even sudden death. Madhurima had long stopped going to school, as had Raghav. Both were confined to the four walls of their respective homes and desperately longed to lead normal lives like other children of their age.

Diseases don't discriminate between young or old, rich or poor, men or women. While Madhurima's parents were well off and could afford a transplant, Raghav's were poor farmers from drought-hit Latur. His father struggled to make ends meet and was never seen in the hospital. It was his mother who accompanied him on his frequent visits.

We had managed to raise enough money for Raghav but I was worried whether we would get the right match for his heart and if we would get it in time. Many children succumb while waiting for a donor of suitable size and match and I didn't want Raghav to meet that fate. In the past, both Madhurima and Raghav had got calls from our hospital to get admitted as a possible donor was in sight and on three consecutive occasions, the donor's family had either refused at the last moment or the heart was unsuitable.

Eventually, the day for transplant arrived for Madhurima when the parents of a seven-year-old boy decided to give her the gift of life by donating the heart of their brain-dead child. Madhurima's parents were hopeful and for the first time in many months, I saw a smile on their faces. Our team embarked on a transplant in the wee hours of the morning and the surgery turned to be a success. Madhurima sailed through and after the surgery got over, her mother showed me a small diary in which Madhurima had penned down some questions for me. One of the questions was, 'Did the surgeon see God inside my heart when he opened it?' Though I do not have an answer to such a profound question, it is this innocence of these beautiful children that keeps me going on tough days.

Two months after Madhurima's transplant, Raghav also received the heart of a young boxer who had died during a boxing match. An otherwise quiet and shy teen, Raghav had become quite aggressive during his stay in the ICU. The team joked that it was because he was to receive the heart from a boxer. In the end, our hard work paid off and Raghav made it. We were really proud that we had arranged the funds not only for his transplant but also for the medications he would need for the next two years. Raghav's story continues to give me hope that financial barriers can be overcome if the intent is right.

Without the transplant, these two children just had a few weeks to live. Even with the transplant, longevity is not guaranteed. Like other anxious parents, Madhurima and Raghav's parents had thousands of questions and one of them was the duration for which the new heart would last. We informed them about the 20-year survival period, as well as about the continued follow-ups of the patients who had undergone a transplant in the past.

It's a harsh truth but we have to remember that with a transplant, we have helped to extend the lifespan of these children but have not made them as healthy and normal as other children.

Despite that, we're happy that these families are able to spend a few more precious years and create beautiful memories with each other. One year later, my team informed me that Madhurima successfully ran a mini-marathon for children at a city event. For me, that was it. That's what we strive for—quality rather than just quantity—happy moments, living each day with laughter, mirth and happiness. In another part of the country, Raghav goes to school in Latur just like other kids. I'm told that he is back to being his quiet shy self.

Surgery teaches us big lessons in life and the biggest is that doctors can only perform their duty, they cannot control the outcome. We must continue to work bearing in mind an all-important fact—that we just stitch, it's He who heals. We administer, He cures.

Surgery may cure most patients, for some, it may bring relief from suffering and for others, it may improve the quality of life, but the surgeon must never feel that he/she can confer immortality on any patient. Lastly, when the doctor fails to save lives or even extend them, he must remember this verse from the Bhagavad Gita: 'Just when the caterpillar thought the world was over, it became a butterfly.'

Dr Vijay Agarwal is the Director and HOD of Paediatric Cardiac Surgery at Fortis Memorial Research Institute, Gurgaon. He operates almost 450–500 cases annually of which 30 to 40% are neonates. He has done pioneering work in the use of 3D printing in assisting planning of complex congenital surgery. Amongst other recognition, Dr Vijay Agarwal has been felicitated recently by the chief minister and the Government of Kerala during the National Heart Transplant Conference (2016) for his outstanding contribution in paediatric heart transplant.

Did You Know?

Physicians who display high levels of idealism and commitment are most apt to 'burn out,' as they often fail to live up to their own professional ideals. A study has indicated that the emotional pressures associated with patient interactions might play a larger role in producing stress in doctors than other more commonly reported factors (such as long working hours or sleep deprivation). Everyday experiences (for example, not being able to cure every disease, not being able to make everyone happy) can be regarded by some as crushing defeats, creating a vicious cycle of perceived failure and negative thinking.

Source: Larsson, E.W. & Stern, T.A. (2013). 'Helplessness in the helpers: etiology and management.' Prim Care Companion CNS Disord, *15(6).*

Dear People,

'A close collaboration between modern medicine, modern science and ancient knowledge is the urgent need of the hour.'

Dr Wolfgang Gubisch HC

Rhinoplasty Surgery Can Be Life-Changing

The daughter of a well-known surgeon had asked a famous ENT surgeon for a rhinoplasty (the plastic surgery of the nose). She wanted a profile correction as well as a better-contoured tip. However, displeased with the procedure and after repeated follow-ups, she came to me. When I saw her for the first time, I was shocked. She had a visible scar after transection of the columella (the bridge of tissue that separates the nostrils at the base of the nose), in an open approach rhinoplasty. The scar had healed poorly. She had a severe cosmetic deformity of the nose. The tip of her nose was wide and there was a lack of contour which was intensified by her thick skin. According to the patient, her profile had worsened over time. She was barely 17 years old and was already a nose cripple.

I felt sorry for this girl. Unlike normal teenagers of her age, she refrained from hanging out with friends. She felt ashamed of something she was not responsible for. The shape of her nose was affecting every aspect of her life and was pulling her down psychologically. I mulled over her case and decided to perform a revision surgery to set her nose right. During the revision rhinoplasty surgery, it became clear that much of the girl's internal cartilages had been removed, mistakenly with the probable thought that this would give the patient a very thin, small and chiselled nose.

I am an experienced rhinoplasty surgeon and I typically see very advanced issues in the nose. Most of my surgeries are revision surgeries of patients, who have undergone multiple surgeries. The internal cartilages of the nose give the nose structure. Some surgeons feel that in order to get a better-contoured tip, all cartilages (even those essential for the tip support) must be removed. Thus, in most cases the opposite happens: because of the loss of sufficient support, the nasal tip gets amorphous and loses its contour. Moreover, because of these kinds of rhinoplasty, the nose also loses the major function for which it was created by nature—breathing! The nose is an amazing organ in that it can withstand significant air pressure, when air rushes through the nostrils, during breathing, etc. This is possible because of the way the cartilages are aligned within the interior of the nose and the support thus provided to the nasal framework.

To better understand the process, the tip of the nose can be compared with a tent. If you lower the height of the bars of the tent, the triangular shape of the tent will become round. This is even worse if the patient has thick skin. Total removal of the cartilages in a thick-skinned patient is a catastrophe. In addition, this patient also had an obvious scar at the columella from the previous surgery. I thought that the girl probably had a severe septal deformity and breathing abnormality, which could have justified an open septorhinoplasty at the age of 14, but even this was not the case. The septum was totally intact and had been untouched.

While planning the revision surgery for the 17-year-old girl, I realised I had to reconstruct the lower cartilage framework completely, so as to support the nose better. The best material for such a complex reconstruction is cartilage grafts from the septum (central portion, dividing the nasal passage into equal halves) of the nose. Because this was intact, I was able to harvest a big piece from which I cut four stripes of cartilage measuring 5–30 mm. It is possible to remove the central septal cartilage, without compromising on nasal framework integrity and breathing in any way. In fact, this cartilage bit can be removed very often when it is crooked, in a surgery called septoplasty.

I placed a piece of septal cartilage at the columellar strut, to support the tip of the nose better. Then, I fixed a bent strip of cartilage to reconstruct the nasal domes on each side. These were then moulded by sutures. The fourth strip was split and then used as nasal spreader grafts, to support the central portion of the nose better. After placing the skin back, I realised that the thick and scarred skin was not able to shrink and re-drape the reconstructed cartilaginous framework. Think about this again in terms of a tent. If the cloth of the tent is too large compared to the height of the poles of the tent, the cloth would not drape well and hence the tent would not be held tightly! Similarly, in this girl, there was an imbalance between the size of the skin envelope over the nose and the size of the nasal cartilaginous framework within the nose. By increasing the size of the nasal cartilaginous framework, akin to increasing the height of the poles, I would have been able to get a good contour (tightly stretched cloth of the tent), but at the expense of a huge nose which no girl would like. The alternative option was a reduction of the skin envelope by excising and reducing the skin, but this was only possible by an elliptical incision in the supra-tip area (the area just above the tip of the nose). I had not done such a procedure before. I had only read about this technique and of course, I had no consent for a manoeuvre, which creates a scar at the dorsum (visible scar at the top of the nose) of the nose. What I did know, however, was that despite cutting across the relaxed skin tension lines, midline incisions at the nose mostly heal with an inconspicuous scar.

Therefore, I decided to cut out this extra, redundant skin, to get a better nose profile. It was an extremely difficult decision, but I knew that if I didn't use this technique, no acceptable result would be possible. This procedure seemed logical to me. Immediately after removing the skin, the wound edges collapsed, so that I only needed some subcutaneous sutures for adaptation, skin sutures were not even necessary.

The young girl was elated with the result and told me that she got a new lease of life. Nine years later she returned to see me but this time, she sought another procedure. At that time, she also told me something that shocked me. She said that if I had not been successful with my revision operation, she would have committed suicide.

The story of this patient impressively demonstrates that surgeons, especially those who perform aesthetic procedures, have a special responsibility and must ensure that they are able to get at least a reasonable result. In the case of rhinoplasty, a beautiful nose does not exist in isolation. The shape of the nose must match the other facial features. Rhinoplasty is not a life-saving procedure. Its goal is to improve the functionality of the nose and create a harmonious shape. I have met numerous children who are teased and ridiculed by their peers, due to their facial features and they end up carrying this stigma through their formative years and into their adulthood. When it comes to younger patients, I do not really think that patients under the age of 18 must be denied a corrective procedure, but as responsible doctors, we must discuss the consequences with the child and his parents. It is essential for me that young patients realise how every surgery comes with certain risks and not every surgery is a total success. There can never be 100% success in the field of surgery.

In my 40 years of performing rhinoplasties, there are some patients like the 17-year-old girl I will never forget. The other took place when I was guiding a workshop in a Mumbai hospital. After the lecture, a young man came up to me and presented me with a nice pen. He told me that he was extremely grateful that I had operated him. Now he looked good and could breathe perfectly. After meeting him, I continued with my operations and lectures. I stepped out at 5 pm, exhausted because of the long day. Suddenly, I noticed that somebody was running after me. It was the same young man from the morning who caught up with me and gave me a bouquet of roses. He wanted to give the bouquet to me in the morning along with the pen, but the guards did not let him in with the flowers. So, he waited the whole day outside of the clinic, missed a whole day of work as a fruit seller, just to show me his gratitude. I was really touched—I had never experienced such gratitude anywhere in the world.

Some years later, I met a young plastic surgeon who proudly told me that he was going into private practice. I found out that he had become an associate of a famous plastic surgeon but after working for the senior surgeon for a while, he had started his own practice. The cancellation of this contract disappointed the senior surgeon a lot.

This young colleague, however, came up to me and requested me to help him with a very difficult case. I agreed to see the patient and was shocked when the same young man who had gifted me flowers appeared. Originally, he had a minor hump nose and had asked this young surgeon for a surgical improvement, but the outcome was horrible and the young man's nose looked totally disfigured. He now had a severely shortened nose, a so-called piggy nose with an up-rotated tip, an inverted-V deformity and a saddling of the dorsum. This typically occurs when surgeons remove very large amounts of nasal cartilage, as was explained in the previous patient. Essentially, because of the removal of the structural support beneath, the nasal skin had completely shrunk!

The patient had trusted the doctor completely, but unfortunately the operating doctor may not have understood the specific responsibility when carrying out a rhinoplasty. The patient could not breathe anymore and he felt so insecure that he could not proceed with his work. He was unable to do his business and call his clients. He stayed home and his whole personality changed dramatically. His financial situation also became progressively worse. At first, I asked the patient to stretch his nose physically, by pulling on the skin, for at least half an hour daily, to loosen the skin and prepare it for lengthening as well as for nasal augmentation.

He felt so desperate that he strictly followed my suggestions and after three months the nasal skin had stretched enough, so much so that I was able to start the reconstruction. I used the cartilage from both ears (ear cartilage can be easily removed, without disfiguring the ears in any manner) as a double-layered L-shaped graft, to create a strong cartilaginous framework, which lengthened the nose. During the surgery, I found out that the septum had been almost completely resected so that there was no solid structure, which prevented the soft tissue from shrinking and shortening the nose. The saddle nose was built up with a temporal fascia tube, which was filled with finely diced residual conchal cartilage, a so-called Diced Cartilage in Fascia graft, which has revolutionised the principles for saddle nose reconstruction. This graft looks like a sausage and can recreate the entire dorsal part of the nose.

The primary result was just perfect and the patient gained confidence. Unfortunately, during the next few months, resorption of the diced cartilage graft downgraded the immediate result. It was still much better than preoperatively, but the patient became very depressed. He had lost his business and did not believe in a prosperous future as he did before.

I advised him to visit a psychiatrist and also assured him that we will do a revision surgery as soon as possible. This made him a little optimistic and overcome his desperate situation. The difficulty then was to define a goal for the surgery. He did not want a harmonious fitting nose, instead he wanted a large nose. Therefore, we spent a long time discussing his ideas. In the end, we were able to agree to a common goal. After nine months, I started my second attempt to enlarge his nose in all dimensions using a rib graft. Of course, this was an invasive procedure. In addition to that, it was not easy for him to accept a chest scar from harvesting a rib graft since he had exercised a lot for a perfect body.

It was the time when we had started using a lot of rib grafts in our rhinoplasty procedures. We had developed new concepts and techniques which allowed more reliable results. Again, a double-layered L-beam was built from rib cartilage and fixed to the forehead and the maxillary bone. The dorsum was once more built up with the above mentioned Diced Cartilage in Fascia technique, but now using the rib cartilage. Of course, a very strong and solid framework was the prerequisite for a long-term result.

The procedure was successful and once he was discharged, the patient phoned me, informing me that after coming home, he had cried for one hour. He was so relieved.

However, all was not well yet. Due to the extensive enlargement, the closure of the wound proved difficult and as a consequence, three months later, the patient developed a small defect in the nose which secreted pus. He lived far away and had no money to stay in the hospital. This made an optimal treatment of the infection difficult, but after three months the result was stable and most of the cartilage grafts had survived.

Some months later, the patient told me that the nose was perfect for him after the last surgery, but it had become smaller after the swelling had declined and the minor resorption caused by the infection became clear. Therefore, he asked me for further augmentation. I told him that we would have to wait for a while and he had to stop smoking. Smoking has an adverse effect on the survival of such cartilage transplants.

After three years, the patient explained that his whole life was focused on further enlargement of the nose. I was sceptical to operate this man again because his mental structure was really difficult and I had spent a lot of time talking to him. Then I decided to perform one more surgery as a final treatment and repeated another augmentation with rib cartilage. The surgery and the post-operative healing went without any complications.

After two years, the patient came back for a follow-up. He told me that I had changed his whole life. He was happy, he was back to his job, earned good money, he had a girlfriend and was back in the society.

My experiences with this patient showed me that an aesthetic surgeon has a very specific responsibility. Patients seeking an aesthetic improvement often have a specific mental structure which has to be respected. If the result is dissatisfying, subjectively or objectively, or even worse than before, the surgeon can cause severe problems for that patient, which might influence or even destroy his whole life. Therefore, patients must demonstrate their maturity before undergoing an 'aesthetic procedure'. It is also important for them to know that as in all aesthetic procedures, the result may sometimes be worse than the preoperative situation and it's important for them to be aware of and in agreement with the challenges of rhinoplasty. It is in these surgeries, that a good surgeon can really change the face and the lives of his patients!

Prof. Dr Wolfgang Gubisch HC started practising plastic surgery in 1974. He is double boarded in plastic surgery and ENT. From 2010 to 2012, he was the president of the German Association of Aesthetic Surgeons and board member of the German Society of Plastic, Reconstructive and Aesthetic Surgeons (DGPRÄC). He holds the gold medal of the All India Rhinology Society for special achievements in rhinosurgery. He has written more than 170 scientific publications and has produced several educational films. For the last 27 years he has been organising the 'Stuttgart advanced course for functional and aesthetic rhinoplatsy'. In 2011, he founded the Rhinoplasty Society of Europe. He is (the medical) senior director of the clinic of facial plastic surgery at Marien Hospital, Böheimstr, Stuttgart, Germany.

Did You Know?

According to Kurzweil and de Grey, in the near future, every 10 years or so we will march into a clinic and receive a makeover treatment that will not only cure illness but will also regenerate decaying tissues and upgrade hands, eyes and brains. Before the next treatment is due, doctors will have invented a plethora of new medicines, upgrades and gadgets. If Kurzweil and de Grey are right, there may already be some immortals walking next to you on the street—at least if you happen to be walking down Wall Street or Fifth Avenue.

Source: Yuval Noah Harari in his book Homo Deus- A Brief History of Tomorrow.

Dear People,

'There is a reason why people say we "practice" medicine.'

Dr Yusuf A. Matcheswalla

The Call of Duty Is Imminent

But What about a Call from Home?

A wise man once told me, 'Medicine is interesting but it also makes you feel helpless. It tears you down emotionally and day by day brings you closer to your life's biggest test: where your knowledge is up against your own emotions.' I understood the statement semantically but it would be a long time before I would fathom its true meaning.

It was only recently when an incident compelled me to look within. As the prescient man had suggested, not only was my knowledge challenged by my emotions, I was torn apart between my duty towards my patients and towards my family.

I am a psychiatrist and psychiatry is unlike any other profession. For us, merely treating an illness is never enough. We need to go beyond the illness to treat the person and their social networks. While families of patients can be their biggest supporters, at times, these very families prove to be the biggest hurdles in their progress. Therefore, one of the most difficult aspects of my practice as a psychiatrist is dealing with the parents of my young patients.

When adolescents are hit by an illness, the families are distraught. The parents and, often, the patients themselves are unable to cope with the illness. As a psychiatrist, I know that when treated in a timely manner, outcomes can change but because of the taboo associated with mental health issues, it is difficult to convince most parents to allow their children undergo treatment.

One such difficult case was of a 15-year-old girl who completely refused to eat any food. She had not been eating or drinking anything for over a week and had become extremely weak and fragile. She refused to talk to anyone and remained aloof and withdrawn. When I spoke to her, I found out that she was starving herself because her parents had refused to buy her a new phone. I also found that this was not the first time she had done this. At least on four different occasions she had behaved similarly and, each time, she had to be hospitalised. The parents were repeatedly asked to meet a psychiatrist but they were reluctant. Finally, as she did this for the fifth time, they decided to get help. The patient was resistant but the family readily admitted her and agreed to start the treatment. The treatment was going on as planned but within 24 hours, the parents changed their mind and decided to get her discharged from the hospital. We advised against it but they were adamant. They did not wish to continue the psychiatric treatment. For a long time, this particular case bothered me. I would worry about the well-being of the young girl. However, I realised that there are times when you cannot win. I have helped hundreds of patients but this has been a particularly disturbing moment as I knew what lay ahead for the girl. I was, however, helpless.

There is a reason why people say we 'practice' medicine. On some days we are just outnumbered and overwhelmed. We try and stand strong, keep pushing against all rational limits and not give up, but the truth is no matter how hard you try and fight to stay in control, sometimes you're just helpless. However, if we are able to break the walls and get through to our patients, the results are quite encouraging.

A young girl was brought to my clinic and her parents complained that she has been acting in a weird manner for the past week. She was scared, was refusing to eat, did not sleep, kept repeating words that had no meanings and sang and danced intermittently. The minute I saw her I knew that she needed to be hospitalised and was in dire need of immediate intervention. However, the moment I uttered the word 'admission', her parents lost their cool. They refused to agree to medication, let alone hospitalisation. It took me hours to explain and convince them to get her hospitalised and start the required treatment. She responded extremely well and was able to get her life back on track. It makes me immensely happy to say that today, she is doing well and is almost completing her graduation. However, for every successful case, there are numerous when I don't win the battle against the parents of some of my young patients. Sometimes they are extremely hostile towards us as psychiatrists. They are willing to accept everything except the reality and get treated by us. It's then that mediating between the family and the informants becomes a crucial aspect of the treatment. We need to maintain a professional distance while being open to their insults as well as their warmth. Neither can we be prejudiced, nor can we allow judgement to cloud our minds.

As a psychiatrist, I hear stories from my patients all the time. Some of these stories are routine, some are unique, and some are shocking. The stories have the potential to challenge the very fabric of our being and leave an everlasting impact but every story changes our lives bit by bit. I sometimes wonder, how my life would have unfolded if I weren't a psychiatrist. My wife often jokes that I have become devoid of emotions and I don't think she is wrong. I listen to stories of misery and grief almost every day. While I try to comfort and help my patients, I have to keep my own emotions away. At times, I even hide my sentiments against my wishes. For a long time, I had assumed that the years of training and practice in the field of psychiatry have toughened me up. That I had immense control over my emotions and nothing could break the armour I had created around me. It took one solitary incident to dissolve that belief. My mother was sick and that day, as she fought for her life, I introspected.

I remember the day vividly not just because how it turned out eventually, but also because how it had started—as routinely as any other day, with no clue of what lay ahead for me. I spent all day treating patients in the OPD and after a quick evening break, I left for my clinic. Numerous appointments were pouring in and even after we had exhausted the number of patients we could see in one evening, the requests kept growing. I arrived and commenced the appointments. Everything was normal until I got a call from home. My 80-year-old mother, who was otherwise perfectly healthy, had suddenly lost consciousness and had become unresponsive. My wife had panicked and promptly called me. At first, I thought it wasn't serious and tried to calm her down. I asked her to be patient and take her to the nearest hospital. I put my phone down and continued my work. I was oblivious to the storm that awaited me.

I continued to see my patients and an hour passed by. Soon, I got another call. This time it was the emergency department of the hospital where my wife had taken my mother. The doctor informed me that my mother needed to be admitted to the ICU. I had not expected this. While I was talking on the phone, a patient was sitting right in front of me. I was compelled to appear calm and maintain my poise. It took me a couple of seconds to grasp what I was told. I wondered what I should do. I wanted to spring up and run to the ICU instantly but then, I thought about all my patients who were waiting outside. They had taken appointments weeks ago; they had travelled across the city to see me and were already waiting for their turn. I decided to stay. However, each and every person, from the ICU doctors to my family, wanted me to drop everything at once and be with my mother. My phone kept ringing incessantly. Yet, the line of patients outside my consulting room kept me busy.

I felt helpless. I was torn between my duty towards my mother and my duty towards my patients. Ceaseless, unhelpful thoughts were constantly whirring through my mind when the ICU doctor informed me that my mother's condition was deteriorating and she needed to be transferred to a higher centre. She had suffered a massive stroke. At that moment, as soon as I heard what the doctor said, everything faded away. My whole world came crashing down. My years of experience told me that her prognosis was poor and the future seemed grim, yet my heart wanted to reject my knowledge. How I wished that just this one time I could be wrong.

My mother's life was in danger and I felt compelled to leave immediately. I got out of my chamber to rush to see her. But as soon as I came out, I saw the long queue of patients in the waiting area and I stopped. I retreated my steps, dialled my wife's number and spoke to her. I asked her to act as per the doctor's advice and shift her to another hospital. I informed her that I would join her as soon as I was done seeing my patients. That evening turned out to be the longest evening of my life. It was 1:30 am by the time I finished and could leave to see my mother. As I drove to the hospital where my mother was admitted, I recollected the wise man's words about the biggest test of duty against emotions. It was only now that I truly understood what he had meant.

This incident of my mother's illness shook me to the core. It brought back every emotion I had suppressed over the years. I thought about the moments I had missed, the times I could have spent with my family and how I almost lost my mother. It would not be unfair to ask if anything is really worth the sacrifice. I could have immediately got up and left the clinic. Most of my patients would have understood the reason, but then I wonder, would it have been fair? I do not know the answer. The thought that my waiting patients had pinned their hopes on me overpowered me and glued me to my seat. They were looking up to me for help whereas my mother had a team of specialists looking after her. This gave me solace and helped me keep my peace of mind. I was always taught to keep patients before myself and that day I practised it. I went through my test and stuck right by my patients. Patients who perhaps needed me equally: like the man who rushed to me after reading an article about cervical cancer. He was convinced that his neck ache was due to cancer. Or the numerous who were anxious because of demonetisation.

When you're a psychiatrist, you owe your patients solutions but the doctor-patient relationship doesn't end with just the patient becoming better. We have to continue to treat and be around them far beyond the illness. The doctor-patient relationship also extends to the families who look up to us for guidance and support from time to time. It's not easy being a doctor, but when one is a psychiatrist then it become even more difficult. It's equally rewarding to see the smiles on our patients' faces and watch them get back on their feet and become a part of the society they always wanted to be.

Dr Yusuf A. Matcheswalla is a Consultant Psychiatrist and an honorary Professor at Sir JJ Group Hospital and heads the Department of Psychiatry, Unit 2, at GT Hospital, Mumbai. He is also associated with Gleneagles Global Hospital, Mumbai. With an experience of more than 30 years, Dr Matcheswalla is an expert in forensic psychiatry, de-addiction psychiatry, general psychiatry and emergency

psychiatry. He has many awards to his name, including Lifetime Achievement Award by the Government of Maharashtra for his services at GT Hospital as well as the Dr CL Zhaveri Oration Award.

Did You Know?

Physicians find the role of physician-family member profoundly challenging. A study showed that through their training and position, they recognise the inherent contradictions of being both professional and personal caregivers, but still felt unprepared for the ethical dilemma that they encountered. The role conflict of physician-family members is a complex balance of internal and external influences that are either personal or professional in nature. Internally, physicians have an identity and responsibilities that are balanced between their familial and professional roles. Externally, the distinct familial expectations of the physician-family member's role contend with the expectations of other physicians and the health-care system.

Source: Chen, F.M., Feudtner, C., Rhodes, L.A., Green, L.A. (2001). 'Role conflicts of physicians and their family members: rules but no rulebook'. West J Med, *175(4): 236-239.*

Afterword: The Beautiful Bridge

Dr Rajas Deshpande

I want to become a doctor, save lives, and end suffering but will I be able to become a good doctor? Is it the right choice in today's legal scenario to become a doctor? I do not want to give up my comfort and pleasures, after all, I too have only one lifetime. I want to enjoy my youth, spend time with my family, read a lot, and explore the world like any other person. I don't want to be perpetually worried and stressed. A doctor always faces crying, suffering and dying people, their expectations and anger. Gratitude is rare. Will this profession allow me to live a happy life? When the newer generation asks these questions, I have observed my answers change over time.

About a decade ago, I was happy to welcome and treat poor patients free of cost, arranging free investigations and treatment for them. I thought it was my moral responsibility. Most of these patients respected the effort made for them and were extremely grateful. Those days, there wasn't a perpetual fear of legal punishment of western standards (read million-dollar compensations), or extreme mainstream media or social media defamation for simple mistakes in complicated medical scenarios.

Now, I am careful.

Times have changed and today there are unending expectations from healthcare. Legal action against doctors and their uncontrolled social defamation has become commonplace. Today, I feel the need to safeguard myself, because there still are those who genuinely need their doctor. Many lives depend upon me going to the hospital every day. Their care, too, is my moral responsibility.

There is a notion that, 'doctors are quite well to do' and that they can bribe their way out of callous mistakes or unfortunate outcomes. What's not known is that there actually exists in India small, politically-supported gangs who exploit doctors and hospitals for almost every death in the hospital. They create blocks during organ-transplant surgeries and vandalise hospitals to force them to waive off steep bills the patient's family promised to pay. Unfortunately, legal solutions are too time-taking and frustrating for any doctor or hospital to pursue.

The other side is not all bright either. The quality of good doctors is indeed lowering by the day. There is below-average staff, infrastructure and teachers, along with a relaxation of stringent clinical skill assessments to create 'student-pleasing' environments. This means that those graduating from medical school are not as prepared for the world of medicine as they used to be. The essential 'humanity and compassion training' seriously lacks in government and private setups alike, resulting in egoist, ill-behaved, arrogant and 'superficial' doctors who get upset when questioned by the patient. While teachers are equally responsible, the 'multiple choice' exam system has taken away the in-depth processing of medical wisdom that must form the core of a great doctor. Quick monosyllabic answers are now considered enough, and that also translates into poor communication with patients. Medical malpractices, referral-based practices are a reality. This is shameful and can never be justified, but one must also consider the reasons why these practices evolved in the first place.

Once a doctor begins practising, his/her objective self-analysis is replaced by whimsical conclusions from his/her own experiences. As one of my professors often said, 'The moment a doctor says "in my experience", he is being unscientific.' That's the origin of such wide difference in opinions: some strongly recommend surgery, while others denounce the very idea. The patient is thus confused. Doctors rampantly criticise other doctors in an attempt to impress patients which further creates a negative opinion about the whole profession in the society.

This shameful phenomenon that weakens the precious doctor-patient bond needs to be checked. Even if change is inevitable, every change is not good. In a world mostly governed by financial motives, we must repeatedly remind ourselves that money alone cannot be a reason for changes in the medical world. The core concept of 'best healthcare for all' must override all other pressures. At the same time, the concept that 'good quality healthcare comes at a higher cost' must be understood and accepted. It is time to evaluate 'who will pay for it' rather than forcing charity upon hard-working medical professionals.

The deliberate attempt to blame doctors alone for the rising healthcare costs serves only to further deteriorate the precious doctor-patient relationship. Medical practitioners have very little say in how the government plans healthcare policies. The perpetual inadequacy and failure of almost all state-run healthcare facilities might not be unique to India, yet there is no visible attempt to improve the situation. It is yet to dawn upon the state that good quality, well-educated and trained doctors are indispensable when it comes to the highest level of healthcare. With meagre salaries and sycophancy, only a few good doctors actually continue in state-run systems.

While my professors taught me to never turn down a patient who cannot pay, never to take less than the best decision for the patient, and to go out of the way to help them, the number of such 'good teachers' is plummeting day by day. To ensure their continued presence at teaching institutes, they must be respected and their expectations must be met. In the absence of adequate funding and provisions by the government, it is natural that corporates have entered the healthcare industry. This has drastically changed the healthcare scenario. To expect investors not to make profits and work as pure charities will destroy the purpose and distract potential investors in healthcare. Regulations to monitor and prevent 'excess profiteering' should be considered instead.

What's most disheartening is that doctors don't get their due in India. The government and politicians must acknowledge the contribution of private medical practitioners to the country's enormous healthcare requirements. Millions of poor people are treated by private doctors and hospitals without any propaganda or political benefit. Still, they are made to pay taxes like any other 'business'. Even a small reward like tax benefits to a doctor treating poor patient free will go a long way in encouraging them to see more patients who could not have afforded their service. It will also reduce the burden on the perpetually overworked government healthcare setups.

A doctor must make all effort to do the best for each of his patients. However, this applies to a doctor who is allowed a normal, healthy routine. Research has time and again proven that poor sleep and diet impairs normal performance and decision-making. Every judge in the world is provided with the best environment for optimal decision-making, with adequate rest and salary, but when it comes to doctors, who make life and death decisions many times a day, we discriminate. Inhuman working hours for doctors, nurses and other healthcare staff is the sad reality of today's healthcare. While private practitioners at least reap financial benefits for their overwork, those in government setups and especially resident doctors are exploited by brushing it all under 'duty towards humanity'. Inhuman exploitation of postgraduate students is rampant and is shamelessly labelled a 'prerequisite' for adequate medical experience. Anyone who has been a slave will never want the next generation to go through the same, but in medicine, we collectively encourage that.

An Indian doctor comes from the same cultural environment as his patient. He/she learns in the same primary and secondary schools. His/her parents and teachers teach her the same values like everyone else. And then, once he/she begins her training, the gruelling academic schedule and formative years of youth spent among the suffering, takes away the simplest pleasures from doctor's lives: dating, romance, togetherness, family life are all sacrificed to a great extent, only to learn the art and science of healing and saving lives. However, vilifying this entire community of hard-working intellectuals has become a favourite pastime for media and politicians alike. If a doctor commits a mistake, there must be a penalty, but only a medically-qualified judge should decide whether the doctor was wrong and what the penalty should be and not politicians who have barely completed their basic education or the attention-hungry media looking for sizzling headlines.

Every doctor in the world right now is under this fear of legal action and defamation. Therefore, all decisions made for the patients are medico-legal before being compassionate or courageous. Medical laws are grossly inadequate and unevolved, judges handling medico-legal cases seldom have had enough training to understand medical wisdom or logic in complicated cases. No judge ever ordered a *suo moto* enquiry into the inadequacies of healthcare provided by the government. It leads me to believe that 'law' is the worst thing that happened to medicine, because it did more harm than good to patients across the world, and that itself is against the very basic medical principle: do no harm. Medically trained judges, media restrictions and capping of compensations to be proportionate to the fee structure are essential logical solutions to this imbroglio.

This does not mean doctors don't need any learning. They do. Doctors, especially, must learn how to communicate. Communication skills among doctors need to be cultivated from the medical school days. The importance of explaining the diagnosis, investigations and treatment options to each patient, to understand their choices compassionately, and to make decisions in the best interest of the patient are all essential steps which cannot be bypassed. Allowing sufficient time for relevant questions that the patient or family may ask is as necessary as well. Informed consent must be obtained at all stages. All this will mean extra time, extra documentation and extra effort. If applied, fewer patients could be attended to per day which would mean an escalated consultation fee. It's then that society would have to understand and bear the cost for good service.

At the same time, compassion should be bilateral and not expected of the doctor alone. The patient must also be respectful and polite with the doctor. Arrogant, ill-behaved, threatening relatives and patients abuse the doctor very often, this must change too.

Every doctor in the world goes to work with an intention to cure, to treat and to heal. Every doctor wants to make the patient (and himself) happy with a good outcome. Healthcare could be improved to a greater extent only if the broken bridge of faith and trust is rebuilt from both ends: a combined effort by the patients and the doctors.

Dr Rajas Deshpande is the Director Neurology at Ruby Hall Clinic in Pune, India. He is a member of the international high IQ society and the author of the book,* The Doctor Gene: What Everyone Must Know about Doctors. *He is an acclaimed doctor and a prolific author.

Afterword: A Final Word—Doctors and Patients Are Teammates

Dr Jananee Muralidharan

I'm on my morning rounds when I pause uneasily. The senior consultant adjusts his tie nervously. The interns recheck their notes. Mrs X is the next patient we need to see. She is a tough patient. She has been in the hospital for the last two weeks, admitted with a fever that refuses to subside. We have done scores of tests, numerous scans and pumped her with multiple courses of antibiotics, and yet the fever is relentless. This is a rare challenge but we face it often enough to give it its own moniker—'pyrexia of unknown origin'.

This isn't the only thing that makes Mrs X a difficult patient. She has been poked and prodded since admission and remains ill after all these days in the hospital. She is understandably unhappy. As we enter the room, she voices her frustration with our treatment. Her son, visiting from the USA, has a list of complaints against us and the nursing staff. His father is less polite. 'What sort of hospital is this?' he roars. 'I have never seen such incompetent doctors. We have spent so much money here and it is of no use.'

As a group, we put up our defences. We list the tests done and the treatment planned. We tell them that occasionally these things take time and that we were waiting for some reports to plan our next course of action. And despite our genuine attempt to ease the tension, we walk out from the thick fog of negativity clouding the room with a heavy heart.

As we break for tea to let the frazzled unit calm down before continuing morning rounds, I pause to think:

DOES IT ALWAYS HAVE TO BE LIKE THIS?

In reality, doctors and patients are teammates with a common enemy—the disease. And yet for some reason, we have started to become suspicious of each other's intentions. Patients are losing trust in the current medical system and doctors have become the face of this distrust. On the other hand, it's not uncommon to see doctors barely investing their time to empathise with the patient at hand.

Every day since that realisation, I have been in a deep introspection of the things that need to be changed in order to make this relationship better. Doctors and patients are two sides of the same coin. While the medical fraternity has been under the scanner for a while now, I do believe that the other side also needs to introspect. Here is my set of suggestions for patients that may aid in re-establishing a healthy doctor-patient relationship with the hope that we can revive the genuine team spirit all over again.

Dear patients,

I invite you, with utmost respect and humility, to think about the following points before you visit a doctor the next time:

1. **Be patient**

   Nobody likes hospital food, the smelly hospital wards or the overall grim ambience. I know that you are missing your regular life and would like to go home at the earliest. However, reaching a diagnosis takes time. Response to treatment takes even more time. The wait may seem unbearable at times, but it has to be endured. You need to know that doctors have your best interest in their minds and a smile on your face may just make our day.

2. **Communicate effectively**
Being a hostile patient may not lead to better care. Doctors are humans too, and such behaviour usually puts them on the defensive. We understand that being ill is tiresome for you and your family but antagonistic behaviour may result in extra tests or extra drugs. Address your concerns and worries about the illness in a way that acknowledges that we are teammates. We are your well-wishers and would be the happiest to see you get better sooner.

3. **Take responsibility for health**
Your health is our shared responsibility. We do not judge you for having addictions, taking self-medication or not being compliant with what we ask you to do. However, do remember that probably that is what brought you to us in the first place. While we are under oath to take care of you, your health is not just our responsibility alone. We urge you to cooperate with us so that we can help you to become better.

4. **Understand limitations**
Medicine is no magic, it is an extremely complex, ever-evolving science. Even today, there are many diseases that modern medicine may fail to diagnose, let alone cure. As doctors, we are trained to look for a 'treatable cause' for a patient's illness. The multitude of tests we order is in search of this treatable cause. If one of those tests turns out to be positive, it will only help us alleviate your suffering. What we need to understand is that for each patient, the path to cure is different and for some, unfortunately, it may not exist at all.

5. **Take the right step**

   Most doctors are overworked, underpaid, and stressed about handling sick patients and anxious families. We are aware that our mistakes can cost you dearly, and that is what makes most of us conscientious workers. However, remember that doctors are humans too and just like everyone else, sometimes we may make mistakes. In the heat of the moment, you may not be the best judge of a doctor's actions. Instead of being impulsive, choose the legal route for redressal if you think that the doctor has been negligent. It may seem long-winded, but it is the only way to ensure that the innocent are not wrongly punished.

6. **Work as teammates**

   Most doctors have limited time to see the patient. In that limited time, an accurate history needs to be taken, a detailed examination is to be performed, the correct diagnosis is to be made, and the proper prescription is to be meted out.

   This Herculean task can be made easier by a few simple steps taken by you:

   - Be organised: File those old reports by date. Bring your latest prescription.
   - Focus on the problem: You have a worsening cough for the last few days. You also had back pain for two days, six months ago. Let your doctor know all your symptoms, but highlight what troubles you the most.
   - Be precise: Have a fever? Take a thermometer and write down the readings. Uncontrolled diabetes? Maintain a diary with all your blood sugar readings.
   - Be frank: Tell us about your addictions, or if you have not been regular with medication or any other medically relevant information. We are here to help.
   - No 'hand on the doorknob question': Doctors dread patients asking them a question just as they are leaving

the OPD. Take time to address all your concerns before ending the consultation.

- Google the right way: Don't spend the ten-minute OPD time on listing out your differential diagnosis from WebMD. Instead, be honest about your clinical history and let your doctor draw his own conclusions. In the end, let him know that you would like to read more about your disease and ask if he could suggest reading material.
- Avoid doctor shopping: If a patient comes back to me saying that he is not getting better, I spend more time on the patient looking for things I could have missed during the first visit. This opportunity is lost when you switch doctors endlessly and each doctor starts from scratch. You are entitled to a second opinion but please avoid endless doctor shopping as it leads to unnecessary confusion.
- Be time aware: Do not ask us if your niece who we have never seen, can take a certain medication. There are other sick patients waiting for their turn to be seen. Respect our time and theirs too.
- Be pleasant: We know you are sick and it has been a long wait. However, please do realise that we are here to make you smile and a hint of that beautiful smile on your face will cheer us up more than you can imagine.

7. Owning up to financial distress

Very often, families request the doctor to 'do everything possible'. When the bill is handed over, they struggle and end up blaming the doctor as they find it difficult to meet the expenses. Instead, we suggest that you confide in us about your financial difficulties. The upside is that it may result in cutting down on the tests ordered or using cheaper alternative medicines. However, sometimes, the downside is that it may lead to a missed diagnosis or suboptimal treatment. As your doctor, I will make the best effort to work around this limitation.

These are just a few of the many valuable steps we can take to recreate that magical doctor-patient relationship that often brings more relief than the treatment itself. *Now that I can expect the patients to be careful, I also hope that doctors will also revisit the Hippocratic Oath and stay true to every word they pledged at the beginning of their career.*

Dr Jananee Muralidharan is a consultant in internal medicine at St John's Medical College, Bengaluru. She loves her family, her job and her cats, in that order.

Manifesto of Doctor and Patient Rights

Dr Aparna Govil Bhasker and Dr Debraj Shome

With critical inputs from Dr Lalit Kapoor, Founder member of the Association of Medical Consultants (AMC) and the President of Federation of AMCs

A 'patient's rights' charter was adopted by the National Human Rights Commission in August 2018. This charter currently features on the website of the Ministry of Health and Family Welfare and is in the process of being finalised. While we welcome this charter whole-heartedly, as doctors, we believe that health is a two-way street. Doctors and patients are equal stakeholders when health is concerned. In a progressive society, rights and responsibilities of all stakeholders need to be defined clearly. This maintains an equilibrium and ensures smooth and effective functioning. The Doctor-patient relationship is built on mutual trust and protecting the rights of only one stakeholder and ignoring the other will eventually lead to discord and disharmony. Doctors are human too and have rights just like all other human beings. In fact, patients and doctors have rights and responsibilities that complement each other.

Given this situation, a *manifesto of 'patient and doctor rights'* has been jointly authored by Dr Aparna Govil Bhasker and Dr Debraj Shome, with critical inputs from Dr Lalit Kapoor.

This manifesto is a better elucidation of the 'patient rights charter' and will help to set the perimeter of this mutual relationship. Every right of patients is the responsibility of the doctors. Similarly, every right of doctors, in turn, is the responsibility of the patients.

Manifesto of Doctor and Patient Rights

	Rights of Patients	Rights of Doctors
Empathy	• To receive empathy from doctors and healthcare professionals.	• To be treated with respect by patients and their families.
Trust	• To be trusted by their doctors • To be treated without any prejudice.	• To be informed about all medical details and any other information in entirety.
Information and communication	• To receive complete information about the nature and cause of illness, diagnosis, proposed investigations, management and complications.	• To be informed about all the information pertaining to the patient's symptoms, past illnesses, medications, allergies and every fact relevant for proper diagnosis and management.

	Rights of Patients	Rights of Doctors
Cost of treatment	• To be informed regarding the expected cost of treatment and to receive an itemised bill. • To be informed duly about any additional costs that may be incurred due to any change in physical condition. • To change the doctor or the hospital if the cost of treatment is not agreeable.	• To be paid fairly and duly for their expertise and service. • To be duly informed by the patient and their family if they are unable to afford the cost of treatment at the time of commencement of treatment.
Identity and professional status	• To know the identity and professional status of the care-providers. • To know which doctor is primarily responsible for their care.	• To know the complete identity of their patient in the form of correct name, age, address and any other relevant information with due documentation.

	Rights of Patients	Rights of Doctors
Records and reports	• To receive copies of case papers, indoor patient records, investigation reports, discharge summary, death summary, etc., within 72 hours of discharge from the hospital and after paying appropriate fees.	• To retain copies of all past and present medical records, reports and any other relevant documents of the patient for their reference and further treatment.
Emergency medical care	• To basic emergency medical care in both government and private medical sector irrespective of their paying capacity. • To be informed about the limitations of the available services after emergency care is provided.	• To transfer the patient to another centre based on the patient's condition and the available medical infra-structure after basic emergency care has been provided.
Informed consent	• To provide informed consent only after understanding the limitations of the treatment in a language they fully comprehend.	• To not proceed with test/treatment if the informed consent is not provided by the patient.

	Rights of Patients	Rights of Doctors
Confidentiality	• To privacy and confidentiality about their illness and treatment. • To safe custody of all data pertaining to their illness	• To have an attendant inside the examination room/OPD/IPD while attending to any patient of any gender. • To follow due procedure in case patient confidentiality is to be weighed against a public health consideration.
Second opinion	• To receive second opinion from an appropriately qualified and competent medical practitioner of their choice.	• To be duly informed when patients are seeking a second opinion.

	Rights of Patients	Rights of Doctors
Non-discrimination	• To receive treatment without any discrimination based on their illness including HIV status or other such health condition, religion, caste, ethnicity, gender, age, sexual orientation, linguistic, geographical, social origins and others.	• To know about any illness that may have a bearing on public health consideration • To know about pre-existing infectious diseases.
Safety and quality care	• To safety and security in the hospital premises and to receive quality health care as per the currently accepted standards, norms and guidelines.	• To receive safe and secure working conditions in the hospital premises. • To withdraw their services, in case they are harmed intentionally, mentally or physically by patients or their family. • To pursue the lawful course in case of verbal or physical assault.

	Rights of Patients	Rights of Doctors
Deficiency in service	• To seek redressal in case of alleged medical negligence or damage caused to them due to deficiency in service delivery by a hospital or a doctor.	• To be considered 'innocent' until proven guilty by a court of law and to present their side in a fair manner without any prejudice. • To be protected from media trials.
Alternative treatment options	• To choose alternative treatment options.	• To be informed if the patient wants to change over to an alternative therapy or if an alternative therapy is being followed concomitantly. • To withdraw treatment after duly informing the patient if the doctor believes that the alternate therapy will interfere with existing line of treatment.

	Rights of Patients	Rights of Doctors
Source for obtaining drugs or tests	• To choose any registered pharmacy or laboratory to buy medicines or get their tests done respectively.	• To get the tests done inhouse or the nearest lab in case of an emergency to prevent delay in patient care. • To reorder the tests if they are not done from an approved/registered laboratory. • To not be held responsible for the quality of tests/medications from a laboratory or a pharmacy that the patient has chosen.
Discharge, Referral and transfer	• To timely discharge and to not be detained in the hospital on procedural grounds.	• To be duly paid for their services before the patient gets discharged from the hospital. • To have all dues cleared by relatives in case of death of the patient.

	Rights of Patients	Rights of Doctors
To be heard and seeking redressal	• To give honest feedback, make comments, lodge complaints about the care that they have received from the doctor or the hospital on the right portals.	• To counter the complaints made by the patients in a lawful manner and to provide apt justification. • To resort to a legal recourse if they believe that the complaint is frivolous and has been made for personal gains or to defame the doctor.

*This Manifesto of Doctor and Patient Rights was endorsed and released by Dr Vipin Checker, President, AMC, 2018–2019, on March 27 2019 at the Mumbai Press Club.

Dr Vipin Checker
President, AMC, 2018–2019

ASSOCIATION OF MEDICAL CONSULTANTS MUMBAI

About the Editors

Dr Debraj Shome is a surgeon, with specialisation in facial plastic surgery and facial cosmetic surgery. He is the co-founder and director at The Esthetic Clinics, which has multiple centres across India. Dr Shome has received many awards from numerous agencies and is known for his breakthrough innovations in facial plastic surgery. He has more than 55 research papers written in top peer-reviewed international publications along with a US patent to his credit for inventing the QR 678 hair growth formulation. He was the first recipient from Asia and the youngest globally to be awarded the prestigious Davies Foundation Grant Award by the Royal College of Surgeons, Glasgow, in 2010. Besides clinical work, Dr Shome is the Director of the Debabrata Auro Foundation.

Dr Shome can be contacted at debrajshome@gmail.com

Dr Aparna Govil Bhasker is a bariatric and laparoscopic general surgeon and practises in the city of Mumbai. She is associated with Global, Currae, Namaha, Suchak and Apollo group of hospitals. She has multiple publications and numerous book chapters to her credit. She is the managing committee member of many surgical societies and has a keen interest in clinical research. She is an avid reader and an artist. She is the co-founder of Debabrata Auro Foundation which was set up in 2016 to help the poor and needy. She is deeply involved in the activities of this foundation and through this she does her bit for the betterment of the society.

Dr Bhasker can be contacted at draparnagovil@gmail.com